Homelessness

Homelessness
A Critical Introduction

Cameron Parsell

polity

Copyright © Cameron Parsell 2023

The right of Cameron Parsell to be identified as Author of this Work has been asserted in accordance with the UK Copyright, Designs and Patents Act 1988.

First published in 2023 by Polity Press

Polity Press
65 Bridge Street
Cambridge CB2 1UR, UK

Polity Press
111 River Street
Hoboken, NJ 07030, USA

All rights reserved. Except for the quotation of short passages for the purpose of criticism and review, no part of this publication may be reproduced, stored in a retrieval system or transmitted, in any form or by any means, electronic, mechanical, photocopying, recording or otherwise, without the prior permission of the publisher.

ISBN-13: 978-1-5095-5449-2
ISBN-13: 978-1-5095-5450-8(pb)

A catalogue record for this book is available from the British Library.

Library of Congress Control Number: 2023931480

Typeset in 10.5 on 12.5pt Sabon
by Fakenham Prepress Solutions, Fakenham, Norfolk NR21 8NL
Printed and bound in Great Britain by TJ Books Ltd, Padstow, Cornwall

The publisher has used its best endeavours to ensure that the URLs for external websites referred to in this book are correct and active at the time of going to press. However, the publisher has no responsibility for the websites and can make no guarantee that a site will remain live or that the content is or will remain appropriate.

Every effort has been made to trace all copyright holders, but if any have been overlooked the publisher will be pleased to include any necessary credits in any subsequent reprint or edition.

For further information on Polity, visit our website:
politybooks.com

Contents

1	What is Homelessness?	1
2	Homelessness as a Societal Problem	23
3	Homelessness as the Experience of Violence	57
4	Being a Homeless Service User: Dependence and Autonomy	82
5	The Experience of Homelessness: Identity and Identification	109
6	What Can Societies Do about Homelessness?	136
7	Supportive Housing Models	159
8	What Should We Do about Homelessness?	177
	References	200
	Index	229

1

What is Homelessness?

The presence of homelessness constitutes evidence of societal failure. This is uncontroversial. People who are homeless in wealthy democratic societies with a welfare state powerfully demonstrate the numerous and interacting problems concerning how we organize society. At a straightforward and immediate level, homelessness is synonymous with a lack of the fundamental resource required to live as a participating citizen. The operation of society assumes that the population has access to housing.

It is not an exaggeration to say that housing is a precondition for being safe, for gaining an education and participating in the labor market, and of course for not only sustaining but also enriching relationships and family life. Housing is also necessary for maintaining good health. The absence of housing is so deleterious for health, it accelerates death. According to the OECD (2020: 3), people who are homeless die "up to 30 years earlier than the general population on average."

Housing is also central to accessing the opportunities to participate in democracy. Housing represents the resource that is necessary to "determine one's own life" (Roessler 2021: 171). The experience of homelessness throws life into an unpredictable chaos whereby one becomes reliant on the care, and subject to the control, of others: often on both. It directly subverts the aspects of basic human life and dignity that we take for granted, or at least that we hold as normative. Homelessness illustrates societal failings through the production of human suffering.

Both the impacts on people who are homeless and the societal dysfunction that homelessness represents animate public concern.

2   What is Homelessness?

Throughout Europe and the United States, with their varying cultural views on state intervention and citizen independence, the general public is concerned about homelessness. From what we know from recent surveys conducted in the United States (Tsai et al. 2017) and in Europe (Petit et al. 2019), the public want there to be more government spending on homelessness and, in the case of the United States, public perceptions about homelessness are becoming increasingly liberal. Homelessness is a problem that is widely acknowledged to threaten any notion we have of living together in a society characterized by fairness and mutual respect. In fact, similar to what we witnessed in the twentieth century with the eradication of polio and smallpox, governments of some countries even advocate radically reducing homelessness as a major social transformation to which their administrations commit. We saw this in 2007 when Australia's incoming prime minister and government pledged to halve the rate of homelessness. In Scotland, the government's 2020 formal strategy was to end homelessness. Albeit in a small and privileged subsection of the population, US values and rhetoric about less government occur alongside government plans and interventions to end homelessness.

Covid-19 brought these ambitions, or lack thereof, into sharp focus. Public commentators argue that the pandemic changed the world and challenged our taken-for-granted assumptions about how we live together, and homelessness, perhaps as much as anything, substantiates these claims. Both public and political concern about people who are homeless have been heightened since Covid-19. The virus has illustrated how homelessness constrains otherwise taken-for-granted ways of living, such as having a home to practice hygiene, complying with medical advice, and, of course, observing quarantining and physical distancing. A home is the fundamental resource we require to control our lives, and, as it turns out, to provide the best opportunity to protect ourselves and others from infectious diseases.

Covid-19 is a reminder that societies are interdependent, and the presence of homelessness is a health threat to us all (Parsell et al. 2023). The heightened concern has spurred on what is in some countries unprecedented state intervention to assist people in moving from homelessness to safe and secure accommodation. For at least a period of time during the pandemic in 2021, the widely held belief across the globe, that we are limited in what we can do to meet the needs of people who are homeless because of budgetary constraints,

What is Homelessness? 3

was thrown out of the window. It is worth noting here that government responses during the pandemic across many countries illustrate that deliberate state intervention into homelessness is both possible and successful at assisting people to achieve life changes. We will return to the opportunities for such government intervention in Chapter 8.

Of course, Covid-19 is a mere blip on the historical calendar, and public concern about homelessness in the wake of the pandemic is not generated by fear of virus transmission and the unequal impacts of the virus. Ordinarily, public concern for people who are homeless is most frequently directed toward its overt manifestation, known as unsheltered homelessness or rough sleeping. This concern is shaped by and embodied in representations in popular culture, such as sensational Hollywood movies including *The Soloist*, *The Pursuit of Happyness*, *The Lady in the Van*, and *The Fisher King*. Most people who are homeless, however, do not sleep in the open spaces of the urban realm. The overt forms of homelessness represent what might be metaphorically thought of as the tip of the iceberg. Countless more people who are homeless, a number we cannot even reliably estimate (Busch-Geertsema et al. 2016), are concealed from public view in formal homeless accommodation, doubled-up with others in shared and cramped housing, or living in makeshift structures and accommodation in both urban and rural areas.

In fact, homelessness in rural areas and small towns, in both its overt and concealed forms, is a concern for countries across the globe, albeit an all too unrecognized concern. Paul Milbourne and Paul Cloke (2006) argue that the focus among researchers, governments, and the media on homelessness in cities has downplayed rural homelessness. Homelessness is framed in the public imagination as an urban problem, representing both the decay of city life and city resources struggling to cope with the inflow of people from rural areas through migration. Rural homelessness certainly does exist, but it is hidden "within the physical, socio-cultural, and political fabric of rural space" (Milbourne and Cloke 2006: 2). To understand the state of homelessness in the modern world, we need to look beyond both the metropolis and its unsheltered form.

Most of us do not see, much less know about, the suffering that homelessness creates among the many. This book is largely interested in the hidden forms of homelessness in addition to the overt. This is not simply because of the mass of people whose homelessness

4 What is Homelessness?

is concealed. It is in the hidden forms of homelessness that we find disproportionate numbers of families and children who are out of view (Mayock et al. 2015). An insight into hidden forms of homelessness can, on the one hand, illuminate the dynamics of markets and, sometimes, government policy and inaction that perpetuate these forms of exclusion and suffering, and, on the other, shed light on the agency and survival capacities of people in dangerous and impoverished conditions.

The problematization of homelessness

The public are animated by homelessness because of the harms it causes to those impacted, but societal interest is also motivated by the myriad social problems that homelessness is symptomatic of. This book will take a keen interest in examining the divergent social processes – across numerous societies – that produce homelessness and represent latent opportunities for addressing it. As is illustrated in the next chapter, homelessness can be the culmination of societal problems that are both diverse and, on face value, may seem unrelated. Societal problems can be seen as the immediate trigger – for example, tenancy evictions and discharge from hospital – or they might be the result of underlying structural conditions, such as access to a livable wage and affordable housing. These two levels of problems cannot be neatly de-coupled, but rather should be understood as interactional. Moreover, societal problems do not produce homelessness randomly among the population (Bramley and Fitzpatrick 2018). The suffering that homelessness represents is disproportionately directed toward people whom society fails in multiple ways. The wide public concern about homelessness is a product of the wide sections of society that homelessness touches. We may all share a concern about homelessness because it represents societal failure, but the failures of society we are concerned about may diverge in material ways.

We care about homelessness because it can signify a problem concerning, for example, housing supply and affordability, income support and poverty, family dynamics, mental health, disability, addiction, domestic violence, veterans, incarceration and recidivism, migration, citizenship, systems of support, and collaboration across government and community organizations. These broad aspects of society have an equally broad set of interest and advocacy groups responsible for them, each with varying levels of power and influence. There are powerful lobby groups invested in veterans, for example, each one of which garners significant political support, support that has been used, in the United States specifically, to lead the federal government to plan to prevent and end homelessness among veterans. This is not just rhetoric. Massive federal government investment saw significant reductions in veterans' homelessness in the United States between 2007 and 2017 (Tsai et al. 2021). Meghan Henry et al. (2017) show that political will led to a reduction in veterans' homelessness by half.

The same political focus and downward trends in prevalence cannot be said to be the case for people exiting prisons, who are at great risk of ending up homeless, and in turn being reincarcerated. Social science knowledge, in accordance with intuition, illustrates that access to safe and affordable housing upon release from prison successfully prevents both homelessness and recidivism (Couloute 2018). This knowledge notwithstanding, in the United States as well as elsewhere, there are no bipartisan objectives to end homelessness among this cohort and only infrequent systematic examples of providing people with access to safe and affordable housing upon release from incarceration. Even though some of the same forces and societal structures place both veterans and people exiting prison at risk of homelessness, the former have wide public support and legislative access to resources, whereas the latter do not. These two brief examples illustrate core themes developed in this book. Homelessness, and the societal failures that produce it, evoke powerful emotive responses from the population. These emotive feelings are not, however, distributed evenly across the population of people who are homeless. Homelessness can be produced by societal processes that disproportionately impact some people, and we have at our disposal the political and policy tools to intervene to successfully disrupt homelessness among cohorts of the population.

Our willingness to alter social processes and to redistribute resources to address homelessness is shaped by what type of problem we understand homelessness to be, which in turn is shaped by which people in society end up homeless. The sections of the homeless population we focus on, or ignore, are significant because they are shaped by our beliefs about what constitutes a desirable society. In most countries, age is a critical determiner of how homelessness is understood as a problem, especially among children and older people. Gender too is a salient feature of the problematization of homelessness, particularly in many countries where older women's homelessness is a concern; older women's homelessness, in particular, represents the disturbing illustration of how patriarchal society disadvantages women in the labor market and penalizes them for child-rearing. The disadvantages that flow from a patriarchal society mean that older women may have fewer assets in later life to avoid homelessness.

Gender and age, along with military service and incarceration history, are just some of the ways that our problematization of homelessness – including what we should do about it – is mediated by how we make meaning of people's problems and how we interpret their homelessness as representing a particular type of societal failure. We can of course divide up the homeless population into other categories to determine the nature of the problem, including along lines of citizenship, race, indigeneity, disability, sexual orientation, and experiences with other forms of state intervention, particularly foster care and psychiatric systems.

The significant point being introduced here, a point that will be developed over the coming pages, is that our concern about homelessness can be either, or both, about the suffering that it produces and the way homelessness represents a challenge to our beliefs of what society should look like. When we focus our attention on some groups of the homeless population, such as veterans or older women, but gloss over others, such as prisoners, we are implicitly identifying what we believe society should look like in terms of those to whom we have a responsibility to provide care and resources and those for whom we believe society does not hold these responsibilities.

The problematization of homelessness has significant implications for what we do to respond to it. Driven by some scholarly research and public campaigns, people are invited to think about the issue through tropes such as "homelessness can happen to anyone" and "anyone is only two pay checks away from homelessness." These campaigns seek to destigmatize homelessness and help the population believe that they themselves are not immune to homelessness. These narratives have wide moral appeal. They serve as an impetus to appreciate our potential vulnerabilities, our shared need for safety and security, and they illustrate the risks that the commodification of housing produces. However, they obscure deep structural inequities within society that operate to put some groups at significant risk

What is Homelessness?

of homelessness, while protecting others (Bramley and Fitzpatrick 2018). In latter chapters, this book tackles head-on the challenges of reconciling the political and moral worth of destigmatizing homelessness with the empirical reality that some life experiences are strong predictors of homelessness in adulthood. The uneven distribution of homelessness represents a challenge to ensure that public debate and social policies are not framed as responses to a deviant at-risk population whose behaviors or demographics explain their homelessness. When we think critically about the sections of society that disproportionately end up homeless, we are forced to think about the unjust social processes that systematically produce these predictable forms of suffering. It is unlikely that homelessness can happen to anyone, and this is because society is organized in such a way that some benefit while others are systematically disadvantaged.

Some are drawn to identify with the homeless out of a romantic idea that homelessness constitutes a form of freedom or escape from the oppressive structures of mainstream society. This idea of homelessness has resonance in the history of many countries, where tramps, hobos, and frontier travelers are nostalgically remembered for their pioneering individualism (Cresswell 2001; Kusmer 2002). From this perspective, people are concerned about homelessness not because it's a problem, but rather because it is constructed as a solution to the oppressive forces of mainstream capitalist society. This form of homelessness constitutes a purposeful rejection of organized society, thereby creating moral heroes (Wilson 1956).

The idea that homelessness can be a solution builds on a long-held belief that homelessness can be the personal choice of *homeless people* (Parsell and Parsell 2012). This view is not only about blaming the victim; it is also put forward by those advocating a progressive politics. Often, as a way of rejecting punitive measures that force people who are homeless from public space (as we discuss in Chapter 6), some claim that people have a right to be homeless. This position, which foregrounds rights, evokes the higher-order normative stance that people ought to be free to live as they see fit, including the right to avoid traditional housing, consumerism, and dominant (Western) ways of living. The belief that homelessness is a chosen state is more frequently couched as a deviant choice. Here, homelessness is an indirect choice, a consequence of deviant behaviors such as addiction, not complying with norms of self-discipline, and selfishly relying on welfare. Be it as a romantic view or

What is Homelessness?

a means to blame the victim, the belief that homelessness is a choice is both pervasive in society and a significant constraint to altering social processes to address it.

Without any doubt, concern about homelessness is principally driven by the view that it represents a societal injustice by failing to provide basic resources to citizens. The provocation of citizenship is significant. On the one hand, it is unproblematic to assert that the experience of homelessness represents a failure of the state to provide people with their citizenry rights. On the other hand, the experience of homelessness subverts people's capacity to comply with citizenry obligations, and, indeed, it is an experience that can facilitate compounding disadvantage. The unpredictability and instability of homelessness make participating in employment, training, and education challenging, to say the least. Further, the experience of being homeless – including lacking a fixed mailing address or contact details – makes complying with government administrative systems and welfare rules difficult (Szeintuch 2022). Homelessness is thus a form of exclusion in and of itself, and a state that, moreover, reinforces exclusion.

Some see homelessness as evidence of neoliberalism and deliberate social processes to exacerbate the disadvantage of the poor (Beck and Twiss 2018). Concern about inadequate distribution of resources and the injustice that it represents drives advocacy for societal change. Across the social science literature, the framing of homelessness as a social injustice spurs advocacy for greater state intervention into the supply of affordable housing and increasing access to crucial resources, such as health care, education, training, and employment with livable wages (Fitzpatrick, Watts, et al. 2021; Lee et al. 2010; Pawson et al. 2020). The study of the social problem of homelessness fits hand in glove with advocacy for social change. The study of homelessness cannot be extracted from normative ideas of society. We engage with these in Chapter 8.

Others are similarly interested in homelessness out of a desire to bring about an ideal society, but rather than more state intervention into housing and the provision of public resources, they see the solution to homelessness to be charitable care. These charitable responses to homelessness are believed to be the hallmark of a community-based society, including subsidiarity and action from the ground up (Parsell et al. 2022). Homelessness can be a venue where people, including in faith-based organizations, can exercise care, compassion, and

What is Homelessness?

voluntary service. In the United Kingdom, responses to homelessness are part of wider ideological and political shifts about the organization of society, particularly the push toward more localized forms of governance and resource distribution (Fitzpatrick, Pawson, and Watts 2020). Some see the presence of homelessness to be an ideal venue where the new ethical citizen can demonstrate their commitment to society by providing the spontaneous ground up support that is indicative of a connected and solidary society (Parsell et al. 2022).

Homelessness captures society's imagination because it represents a bellwether for how society is traveling. Concern about homelessness is, at the same time, concern about what society should look like. Whatever our lens, we see homelessness either as an indicator that society is broken in some way, or that it represents a mechanism to achieve some type of ideal. Our proposed solutions to homelessness reflect and draw on our views about what we believe society should look like: freedom from capitalism, freedom to live off the grid, more state intervention to address poverty, more personal responsibility and family unity, or more community-based responses from engaged citizens to connect with their fellow humans in need. Homelessness is a problem that goes to the heart of ideas about how society should function and how we should live together. Our views about what we should do about homelessness, including nothing at all, speak volumes about what we believe our fellow citizens are entitled to, on the one hand, and what we the collective believe we should do for our fellow citizens, on the other.

Ultimately, we care about transforming society to address homelessness because of the way it meaningfully harms human life. It does so by excluding people from the resources they require to live healthily, in reciprocal and loving relationships, and by controlling their lives. According to Richard Wilkinson and Kate Pickett (2009), homelessness harms us all, including the lucky ones who are not homeless, because we live in demonstrably inequitable societies that are required to waste public money and observe the waste of human potential that homelessness represents.

This book

The way we make meaning of the problem of homelessness is thus far more than an academic exercise. Our construction of the problem of homelessness and, as noted, who is impacted, directly influences what society does about homelessness. The way we understand the problem is critical to how we might alter society to do better. This book has been written as a critical introduction to homelessness driven by analyses of debates, policies, and published research, including some of my own, to illustrate how the problem of homelessness has been produced, thought about, and debated internationally. These countries include the United States, Canada, the United Kingdom, countries across Europe, Australia, and New Zealand, as well as some countries in Asia, such as Japan, Singapore, and South Korea: a range of countries that we might as shorthand refer to as wealthy democracies with welfare states. These countries are diverse in countless ways, to be sure, but we will show that the experience of homelessness and the processes that produce them share many similarities. This examination includes a deep analysis of what countries do to respond to homelessness. Despite the profound diversity internationally in the generosity of state intervention for people who are homeless or the diverse forms of community or voluntary-based support services, all wealthy countries have formalized legislation, policy, and significant budgets to respond to people who are homeless. Each country has what Elizabeth Beck and Pamela Twiss (2018) refer to as their own homelessness industries. There are significant consistencies across these countries in terms of how they respond to homelessness. As wealthy democracies with welfare states, these countries share some similar opportunities for societal change to end homelessness.

This book analyzes these diverse homelessness responses for the primary purpose of articulating a way forward for what we should do differently. There is a vast international knowledge base that offers insights that may transcend national and cultural contexts to advance societal change to better deal with and ideally prevent homelessness. The examination of the multiple causes of homelessness in Chapter 2 can be read as an indicator of how we might act differently in order to prevent homelessness.

To advance an agenda to eradicate homelessness, we need more than a critical analysis of the societal problems that underpin homelessness and the limitations of what we do internationally. An empirically robust and morally compelling roadmap for what we can do differently, more productively, to address the issue must be informed by the reality of what it is to experience homelessness.

What is Homelessness? 11

This critical introduction tackles the experience of homelessness head-on. The empirical evidence presented in Chapters 3–6 demonstrates that the experience of homelessness is anything but a romantic or idealized life free from the pressures of mainstream society. Homelessness is dangerous, characterized by the absence of control, and is defined by what is lacking. In Chapter 4 we demonstrate, perversely, how many of the dominant modes of responding to homelessness replicate some of the negative experiences of being homeless. The experience of homelessness can include both the systematic exclusion from mainstream resources and being managed and controlled by homelessness services. We can do much better. In fact, there are examples from across the globe where societies, and movements within them, take radical and decisive action to address homelessness. We can only seriously grasp the issue by understanding the interacting structures within society that produce it among certain people at certain times. This is illustrated throughout Chapter 2. Chapters 7 and 8 then argue that sustainably addressing homelessness requires radical change to the organization of the society that generates the problems. We cannot address, much less prevent, homelessness, as Linda Gibbs and colleagues (2021) assume, by tweaking existing systems and leaving unjust institutional arrangements in place. We cannot, furthermore, address homelessness without meaningfully engaging with the experiences and insights of those who are homeless who can themselves contribute to driving an agenda of social change.

Prior to embarking upon this, we first need to engage with the question: what is homelessness?

What is homelessness?

The apparently simple question "what is homelessness?" turns out to be far more complicated than one may assume. To start with, this is because it is a concept that is characterized by the absence of something and a *something* that is in and of itself multidimensional and largely experiential: namely, home. To understand what homelessness means we have to first understand what *home* means. This is anything but self-evident; home is a contested concept (Easthope 2004). As opposed to housing, which can be defined in clear objective terms, such as building materials, size, color, design, etc., home is a concept that, as Shelley Mallett says, "functions as a repository for complex, interrelated and at times contradictory socio-cultural ideas about people's relationship with one another, especially family, and with places, spaces, and things" (2004: 84).

This engagement with what home means, especially emphasizing that the bricks and mortar of housing ought not to be conflated with home, offers a hint to the conceptual challenges defining homelessness. At its core, the scholarly literature on what home means stresses the importance of people's subjective meaning-making. Like community, home conjures up something positive about the human condition, but its precise meaning can be equally amorphous. For Sara Ahmed (1999), home transcends the spatial and, rather, encompasses a feeling of belonging. Peter Somerville (1997) makes an important addition to our understanding of the meaning of home in the context of homelessness, pointing out that home has cognitive and intellectual components whereby people have a sense of home even in the absence of experience or memory. People who are homeless may have aspirations about a future home that they have never experienced, but their aspirations meaningfully convey what they want that is different in life (Parsell 2012). Even for people who are homeless and have no access to one, the idea of home holds significance. It is this significance that we need to consider when thinking about how to define homelessness.

Yet an individual's subjective meaning-making of home is clearly a challenge to identifying an objective and cross-cutting definition of homelessness. We will return to this below. If we move beyond academic discussions about what home means, our next challenge is empirical: numerous countries have their own, country- and culturally specific, definition of homelessness. There is no such thing as an international definition: how we define homelessness depends on where we are in the world.

Kate Amore and colleagues (2011) pointed out that concerns expressed in the 1990s about the lack of an international definition, despite the need for one, were equally apparent in 2011. Writing two years later, Amore argued that "in sum, the field has seen a proliferation of definitions and classifications of homelessness, but a relative lack of engagement with ideas of conceptual validity or international standardisation" (2013: 224). It is difficult to conceive of the day when there is an internationally agreed definition of homelessness. It is always going to be a concept that says a lot about the norms

What is Homelessness? 13

and expectations of a given society. Leading scholars in the field conclude that it is undesirable to impose a one-size-fits-all definition of homelessness "uniformly across the globe" (Busch-Geertsema et al. 2016: 126).

Although there is no agreed-upon international definition, assertions from the 1980s that homelessness is undefinable and that the concept should be abandoned (Field 1988; Watson 1986) are no longer accepted. There is wide agreement among scholars and governments that each country does indeed require a definition of homelessness, for multiple reasons. Dominant among these is the need to have a count of the homeless population. Volker Busch-Geertsema and colleagues (2016: 127) conclude: "It is therefore vital that the definition employed is objective, operationalisable and measurable." Amore and colleagues agree, concluding that definitions of homelessness can shape policies and interventions to address it and that defining homelessness is critical to "monitor the effectiveness of such interventions" (Amore et al. 2011: 20). Here we can see that homelessness definitions can play a useful role in measurement by identifying successes and limitations of what we do to address the problem.

As well as the idea that definitions are important for assessing levels of homelessness, calls to establish objective and agreed-upon definitions are often driven by advocacy for homelessness to be recognized and put on the agenda as a prominent social issue, thus opening up conversations about social change. Articulating the significance of a homelessness definition vis-à-vis enumeration and social change, Graham Tipple and Suzanne Speak (2009: 103) conclude that "numbers tend to drive investment and can enable lobbyists or officials to direct funding to address the problem." From this perspective, defining homelessness is a means to ensure that it has the status and identifiable form to be a problem that can be addressed.

In addition to putting the problem on the political agenda through measurement and lobbying, a core reason to define homelessness is so that governments are able objectively to determine who is eligible – and, by implication, ineligible – for public assistance. Official government definitions of homelessness are therefore profoundly significant in the lives of people who meet the criteria. Even within one country, however, there can be multiple definitions or categories of homelessness used to allocate resources.

14 What is Homelessness?

The United States represents a noteworthy example of multiple official government definitions of homelessness, with many categories of the homeless population that receive resources based on their identified status. Different federal government departments, such as health, education, and housing, use different definitions, which are deemed necessary to appropriately identify and respond to their target populations. The most significant definition of homelessness in the United States is that of the Department of Housing and Urban Development (HUD). This is because it is used to determine eligibility for the Continuum of Care program (the primary homelessness response) funded by the federal government, as well as to inform point-in-time enumeration of the homeless population. This is considered the official count of homelessness (Henry et al. 2021).

The HUD definition is underpinned by the definition set out in the McKinney–Vento Homeless Assistance Act of 1987, which was amended in 2009 as The Homeless Emergency Assistance and Rapid Transition to Housing Act. Under this Act, an individual or family is homeless if they lack "fixed, regular, and adequate nighttime residence." In addition to lacking a residence, the McKinney–Vento Homeless Assistance Act defines as homeless an individual or family whose primary nighttime residence is a publicly or privately operated shelter, an institution that provides temporary residence, and public or private places not designed for humans to sleep in.

As well as formal definitions to allocate resources and enumerate the population, the United States has the category of chronic homelessness, pertaining to people who "have disabilities and have also: 1) been continuously homeless for at least a year; or 2) experienced homelessness at least four times in the last three years for a combined length of time of at least a year" (National Alliance to End Homelessness 2021). People who are chronically homeless in the United States are eligible to receive permanent supportive housing, an evidence-based and generous state resource (Rog et al. 2014). Individuals who meet the chronic homelessness definition are likewise identified as a priority for the state to "prevent and end" their homelessness (United States Interagency Council on Homelessness 2010).

Rather than an act of law, in Canada the most influential definition has been published by the Canadian Observatory of Homelessness. The Canadian definition is broad: it includes not only unsheltered people and those living in emergency shelters (as in the United States),

What is Homelessness?

but also people provisionally accommodated, meaning those whose "accommodation is temporary or lacks security of tenure" (Gaetz et al. 2012). The Canadian definition thus explicitly includes people whom we might think about as experiencing forms of hidden homelessness, and, as we discuss below, it draws on important ideas central to the meaning of home. The broad Canadian definition is very different from that used in Japan, where homelessness is narrowly defined. The official Japanese definition includes only those who are rough sleeping, and not people who are sheltered (Okamura et al. 2021).

The United Kingdom has a formal definition of homelessness which is referred to as "statutory homelessness." This is a broad definition. Statutory homelessness is defined as "unintentionally homeless and falls within a specified priority need group" (United Kingdom 2018). For people who meet the criteria of statutory homelessness, there are significant implications; they are referred to as "acceptances," and local government authorities have a "statutory duty to provide assistance." The UK government observes that people who meet the statutory homeless definition "are rarely homeless in the literal sense of being without a roof over their heads, but are more likely to be threatened with the loss of, or are unable to continue with, their current accommodation" (United Kingdom 2018).

There are multiple definitions adopted by different European countries, but most of them draw on the highly influential European Typology on Homelessness and Housing Exclusion (ETHOS) (O'Sullivan 2020). The New Zealand government draws on ETHOS to inform its official definition of homelessness. The ETHOS definition was developed to enable the collection of data to present a consistent picture of the incidence of homelessness across Europe. As Amore et al. (2011: 21) point out, "ETHOS is both a definition and a typology (or classification) of homelessness." ETHOS takes it that there are three core dimensions to home: the physical domain, the social domain, and the legal domain. Lacking access to these domains signifies homelessness or housing exclusion. Although there is an important debate about where the boundaries should be drawn between homelessness and housing exclusion and the conceptual basis for the boundaries (Amore et al. 2011; Amore 2013), the ETHOS definition is significant for specifying the important elements of home. It provides a framework for considering how the nature, quality, and social environment of a dwelling can shape how we live. It is attuned to how housing is not synonymous with home, but, at the same time, it considers how the built form and physical structure of housing influence whether people can experience the subjective, personal, and social dimensions of home.

In addition to academic debates about the meaning of home and contestation among scholars about validity and conceptual boundaries, definitions of homelessness are subject to vigorous debate (Fitzpatrick, Watts, et al. 2021) and challenges because of their political and human implications. Core to such debates is disagreement over a broad or narrow definition of homelessness, which at the same time is about who is included in homelessness definitions and who is excluded. The question of who is excluded from a definition that itself defines exclusion is an interesting paradox, but this is important for resource allocation and for what type of problem homelessness is accepted as being. A broad definition – for example, one that includes people residing in insecure and overcrowded housing – means that the size of the homeless population will be large. Where a statutory definition, such as exists in the United Kingdom and the United States, is too broad, the number of people for whom the state is responsible for providing services and resources is greater. Advocacy organizations will invariably favor a broad definition as it enables them to campaign for change on the basis that homelessness is a widespread problem (Busch-Geertsema 2010), as opposed to a narrow definition where *only* those who are unsheltered or in homeless accommodation are deemed to be homeless.

If the definition is too broad, it will include so many people and living situations that it can become meaningless and risk losing community support. If, for example, people who are at risk of homelessness are included in the definition, the conceptual clarity of homelessness – along with the additional ambiguities of identifying risk – becomes problematic. There is some agreement that definitions of homelessness need to be contained and not include those who are at risk of homelessness (Amore et al. 2011; Busch-Geertsema et al. 2016). This agreement notwithstanding, definitions are shaped by politics and prevailing attitudes, and raise difficult questions about subjectivity.

Politics, critique, and subjectivity

In the same way that the interests of advocacy groups lean toward a broad definition of homelessness, so governments responsible for

What is Homelessness? 17

homelessness favor narrow definitions that focus on unsheltered homelessness (Amore et al. 2011). Craig Willse (2015) argues that narrow definitions advocated by governments are used to demonstrate that the problem of homelessness is contained, and that it is a problem that concerns a distinct sector of the population rather than being about the organization of society. A narrow definition that ensures that only a small number of people are counted as homeless implies that the organization of society is sufficiently productive to adequately accommodate the vast majority of its citizens. In Singapore, for example, homelessness or homeless persons are not mentioned in government legislation, but rather the Singapore government deals with the issue through the Destitute Persons Act, the Miscellaneous Offences Act, and Vagrancy legislation (Tan and Forbes-Mewett 2018).

The way we define homelessness and the size and nature of the population it throws up, if one is defined and counted at all, thus says an awful lot about society. Homelessness definitions do not represent objective categorizations of social problems, but, as Keith Jacobs and colleagues (1999) observe, are structured by interest groups to have their agendas prioritized on the political landscape. Homelessness definitions are therefore not only about homelessness per se. They also give an insight into how advocacy groups can successfully have their interests recognized as a problem that deserves public and political attention. The way people live or ought to live is implicit in how we define homelessness and this constitutes a challenge to how we can objectively define a person as homeless.

A homelessness definition invariably takes a position on the cultural norms within a society pertaining to what citizens can expect housing to look like and how they should live in and use it (Chamberlain and Mackenzie 1992). These expectations are not universal. Cultural norms in society about what constitutes a home and adequate housing, moreover, change over time. What is considered as adequate housing and an appropriate way to live today in terms of size, privacy, and multigenerational families sharing one dwelling is materially different from what was seen as adequate at the turn of the twentieth century. In many wealthy countries, houses are far bigger now than they were 100 years ago (Viggers et al. 2017). This is associated with different cultural norms about access to independent bedrooms, bathrooms, and, thus, access to privacy. Privacy is recognized as a core domain of home, but what we consider adequate privacy in the home is anything but standard across societies and time.

In addition to our own ideas and expectations changing over time, broader ideas of home and adequate housing vary across cultural groups, both within any one society and across societies. The diversity in ways of living and in the use of housing puts pressure on definitions that assume adequacy means the same thing for all people. This challenge is highlighted profoundly when Indigenous people's homelessness is considered. As we demonstrate in the next chapter, in the United States, Canada, Australia, and New Zealand, Indigenous people experience disproportionately high rates of homelessness. Beyond the disturbing reality this represents and what it says about systematic racism, we must also ask whether our objective definitions of homelessness – which governments and scholars in the field agree that we need for a range of useful reasons – meaningfully reflect the experiences and realities of Indigenous people.

A significant issue to consider is whether definitions of homelessness are grounded in Eurocentric assumptions about the relationship between housing and home (Habibis 2011; Kearns 2006). The international field poses thorny questions about whether homelessness definitions constitute an imposition on Indigenous people by judging their housing and ways of living against standards that conflict with their own realities. Kelly Greenop and Paul Memmott (2016) argue that anglophone ideas about overcrowding and homelessness in Australia make little sense to the way Indigenous people live, particularly in terms of cultural responsibilities to share housing with extended kin. In Australia, severe overcrowding is officially defined as homelessness. For Indigenous people, however, welcoming extended kin into the household, even if it means severe overcrowding, is a source of pride and "key to their identity as an Indigenous person" (Greenop and Memmott 2016: 288). Rather than being seen as a problem and the antithesis of home, sharing housing with kin embodies the meaning of home.

Focusing on Indigenous people in Canada, but also making a broader point about Indigenous homelessness in settler societies, Julia Christensen (2016: 4) takes aim at objective homelessness definitions used by governments, as they "fall short of adequately describing and conceptualizing Indigenous homelessness." She goes on: "Not only are such definitions ill-fitting for Indigenous peoples' ideas of how to live properly, they also keep the focus squarely on occupation of a dwelling, with little to no regard for the socio-cultural dimensions of Indigenous homelessness" (2016: 4). Core to the debate about Indigenous homelessness and the limitations of objective homelessness definitions is the realization that dominant understandings of what home means fail to take account of Indigenous perspectives. Also writing in the Canadian context, Dominic Alaazi and collaborators found Indigenous people's sense of home and housing to be "qualitatively different from non-Indigenous people in similar circumstances" (2015: 31). Even though the physical structure of housing is an important element, the meaning of home for Indigenous people, and thus the definition of homelessness, must also be seen as a connection to land, identity, family, and culture (Alaazi et al. 2015; Christensen 2013). Robin Kearns (2006) engages in this debate in his work about Māori people, the Indigenous people of New Zealand. He illustrates the fact that Māori have a strong sense of feeling for home even when they are inadequately housed, or even sleeping rough, because they "regard themselves as *tangata whenua* (literally, people of the land), a status they acquired by living entirely off the land within their tribal territories for generations prior to European contact" (2006: 250). Analyses of home and homelessness for Indigenous people therefore represent a powerful challenge for objective definitions of homelessness used to enumerate populations and allocate resources.

The conceptualization of home for Indigenous people that focuses squarely on connection to land and identity provides an insight into how colonization and its legacy are experienced as homelessness. Scholars interpret this as spiritual homelessness (Christensen 2013; Memmott et al. 2003), an idea that not only puts pressure on objective definitions of homelessness anchored in the adequacy of a dwelling, but also, as Christensen says, represents a "profound irony of being homeless in one's homeland" (2013: 823). In a further reminder of the need to approach objective definitions of homelessness with some caution, Greenop and Memmott write that "housing measures become assimilationist when they continue to prescribe housing needs according to Anglo-Australian nuclear family norms" (2016: 294).

It is easy to conclude that Indigenous people in settler societies experiencing vastly higher rates of homelessness than non-Indigenous people represents an injustice and societal failings on many levels. In parts of Canada, for example, Indigenous people are anywhere

What is Homelessness?

between eight and eleven times more likely than non-Indigenous people to experience homelessness (Agrawal and Zoe 2021). The scholars noted above alert us to the additional burden and source of injustice when our objective definitions of homelessness serve to prescribe certain ways of Indigenous living as a problem. The stakes are high, especially given that our objective definitions of homelessness are used to say something about the *other*.

April Veness contributes to this debate with reference to non-Indigenous people in the United States. She clearly demonstrates the many problems with a relativist definition of home and homelessness, but her in-depth research among people experiencing objectively defined homelessness and entrenched poverty found that they "actively dismiss the broadly-based homeless label that threatens to envelop and invalidate their personal worlds. Instead they assert their own alternative to society's definition of home and hope that their homes are left alone, intact" (1993: 321). Veness does not romanticize the experiences of people for whom society has failed to provide adequate income or housing. In line with experiences of Indigenous people defined as homeless, her research forces us "to rethink what home means" (1993: 337). If we can accept that any definition of home must take account of people's subjective experiences and meaning-making (Easthope 2004), and that homelessness is the absence of home, we must be open to considering how our objective definitions of homelessness must be infused with the realities and subjectivities of the people *we* define.

Objective versus subjective definitions of homelessness

An objective definition is important for the many reasons articulated above, but also for the reasons engaged above there are important limitations when people's subjective experiences are discounted. However, a subjective definition of homelessness is problematic in many ways. People may not even perceive their situation as homeless when their life experiences show them that society is not going to provide anything better (Parsell and Phillips 2014). People come to accept as normal the deprivation, including demonstrably inadequate housing, to which society subjects them. We should not conflate people's acceptance (adaptive preferences) with adequacy. There are significant risks with a subjective definition of homelessness that does

What is Homelessness? 21

not take account how people's perceptions of adequacy are mediated by their experiences of societal failure.

It is also important to be cautious about a subjective definition of homelessness because it would almost certainly throw resource allocation into chaos. Without a clear objective definition, there would be no reliable or systematic way to provide public assistance to people who require it. A subjective definition would be equally problematic as it would very likely be used to discount the extent of societal failure that produces the consistent, and in many countries growing, numbers of the population experiencing homelessness. As Jacobs et al. (1999) note, dominant objective definitions have helped to put inadequate housing and our need to do something about it on the political agenda.

The limitations of a purely subjective definition mean that an objective definition of homelessness is required, but we need to consider how such a definition would be beneficial by taking account of the experiences of the people who are defined. The not-so-subtle emphasis here is on "the people defined." As Ruth Lister (2021) illustrates with reference to poverty, naming one's self is a right, whereas being defined by others is an exercise and illustration of power. Naming and constructing social problems not only shape what policies emerge as a result, but, by definition, they also work to restrict and exclude certain people (Bacchi 2009). Poor people face the challenge of having their own sense of identity recognized and socially validated. Definitions of homelessness are not benign categories that are merely used to enumerate and allocate resources; they are conceptualized in a way to prescribe a proper way of living and of judging people as lacking when they do not meet the criteria set out in the definition. The *other* people need to be at the table when definitions about *their* lives are constructed.

The definition put forward by Busch-Geertsema et al. (2016), which draws on both Amore (2013) and ETHOS, offers a promising start. They define homelessness as severe housing deprivation that is the state of "living in severely inadequate housing due to a lack of access to minimally adequate housing" (2016: 125). This definition emphasizes homelessness as a form of deprivation that is forced upon people, highlighting how living conditions can be imposed upon people and is beyond their control.

Given that homelessness is a state of forced deprivation, we must ensure that rigid definitions of homelessness are not also enforced on people. As we examine in some depth in the next chapter, we can only meaningfully grasp an individual's experience of homelessness by examining the resources that are made available or withheld through the deliberate structuring of society. Conceptualizing homelessness as forced deprivation and exclusion from adequate housing, and creating the conditions for people to determine whether these conceptualizations make sense of their experiences, serve as a start to ensuring that definitions of homelessness can be both broadly applicable and individually meaningful.

The priority given to people experiencing housing deprivation to have the opportunity to describe what home and homelessness means to them speaks to a broader point about labels and the language we use to refer to people. It is critical to not use language that assumes a person's experience of homelessness encapsulates their identity. In this book, we use the terms "people who are homeless," or "people experiencing homelessness." These terms are used to distinguish the state of homelessness from the people experiencing it. The book thus avoids the term "homeless person," a term that, as we examine in Chapter 5, can give rise to a misunderstanding that homelessness says something salient about the identities of the people defined in such a way.

2
Homelessness as a Societal Problem

In 1990, Elliott Sclar lamented the New York Times *and the liberal view that it pushed. The view presented homelessness as a mental health issue; more specifically, a problem of* homeless people *not being in mental health institutions. Still widely held years later, many link the deinstitutionalization of people in mental health facilities with the growth of homelessness. Yet, Sclar's comments from more than 30 years ago are as relevant today as they were then: homelessness is the decision to defund affordable housing, which culminates in too many people who are poor trying to access too few affordable housing units.*

If defining homelessness was not tricky enough, determining the nature of the problem provokes even more interest, angst, and debate. In its simplest terms, determining what type of problem homelessness is has revolved around debates about whether homelessness is a structural or an individual problem. The structure versus individual disagreement is characterized by contradictory questions about the extent to which we explain homelessness as resulting from the behavior of the individual who is homeless, including how they could (ought to) behave differently, or the extent to which a person's homelessness is a product of social forces outside their control. The general thrust of these debates is not of course unique to homelessness. They pervaded the social sciences throughout the twentieth century and are critical to contestations over other domains of human and social life, including unemployment (Sharone 2013), poverty (Lister 2021), and health (Marmot 2005).

The interpretation that homelessness is a problem caused by individual failings has two dimensions. On the one hand, this analysis assumes that homelessness is a result of individual problems such as mental illness or disability for which the person cannot be held responsible because they have care and support needs (Pleace and Quilgars 2003). According to this view, homelessness is caused by individual characteristics, but characteristics for which people are not held morally accountable. On the other hand, the individual is blamed for their homelessness because they have made deviant choices, for instance to use illicit substances, to deliberately avoid employment, or to refuse to pay rent (Parsell and Parsell 2012). This view of individual failing is not about characteristics so much as it is about behaviors, and thus it is associated with moral views of culpability. Teresa Gowan (2010) refers to these dominant narratives as "sick-talk" and "sin-talk."

I would like to be able to say that these ideas about homelessness being caused by problematic or sick individuals have been consigned to history. It would be pleasing to be able to report that no one seriously, certainly no one in a position of power to influence the extent of homelessness in society, any longer holds such views. Unfortunately, we do not have to look too far or hard to see evidence of the endurance of the belief that homelessness is a problem of deficient people. Whether it be to justify new legislation to forcibly remove homeless people from public spaces in Sydney city because they are constructed as illegitimate protestors (New South Wales Government 2017), to cite low levels of education, antisocial behavior, or selling one's home to explain to the public the presence of older people who are homeless in Singapore (Tan and Forbes-Mewett 2018), or to measure sobriety as an outcome of success (United States Interagency Council on Homelessness 2020), our political leaders frame homelessness as an individual problem that either calls for their need for intervention or highlights immoral behaviors.

The individual explanations for homelessness still hold some resonance among a relatively significant proportion of the population. Survey research from the United States, Europe, and Australia shows that people hold a mixture of views on the causes of homelessness, but many still believe that it can be attributed to poor decision-making and the inadequacies of people who are homeless themselves (Batterham 2020; Petit et al. 2019; Tsai et al. 2019). A representative sample from the United States, for example, believed that homelessness could be attributed to irresponsible behavior (62 percent), laziness (42 percent), or drug and alcohol abuse (88 percent) (Tsai et al. 2019). This individualization of the problem is not peculiar to the United States. Nearly half of a representative European sample (48 percent) agreed that people remain homeless by choice (Petit et al. 2019). It is methodologically difficult, with available data, to know whether the politics that cast homelessness as a problem of homeless individuals themselves drive public perceptions, or vice versa.

We can assume, however, that the sight of despair, including people sleeping in public spaces, people living in encampments, and people who are homeless (or assumed to be) displaying the effects of addiction, mental illness, or poor hygiene, perpetuates the public perception that homelessness is an individual problem. As we will argue in later chapters, many of the charitable responses inadvertently give credibility to the accounts that homelessness is a problem specific to incapable and dependent individuals. The sight of homeless people using, for example, soup kitchens, mobile laundries, or carparks confirms to the public that those who rely on these resources are in fact different from the housed population. If such people display problems, even if these are a result of their homelessness – such as lacking a space to clean themselves – it is not surprising that some in the public link them to their understanding of what type of problem homelessness is. It is easy to cognitively move from seeing someone who is homeless in a public space with an overt addiction to assuming that addiction says something about their homelessness.

Of course, the media play a role too. The media do not simply report the news, much less disseminate objective facts. The media also shape our understanding of society by selecting which social problems to focus on and how the social problems are portrayed (Neuman and Guggenheim 2011). Internationally, the media have represented the problem of homelessness with a dominant narrative that emphasizes the differences and at times inadequacies of homeless people (Hodgetts et al. 2005; Hrast 2008; Zufferey 2014). Elizabeth Bowen and Nicole Cappozziello (2022) illustrate this powerfully; they analyzed photographic media representations of homelessness in the United States. The media photographed people without eye contact, without presenting their names, and often depicting them by images of tents and shopping carts rather than affordable housing. Bowen and Cappozziello argued that these photographs were used

26 Homelessness as a Societal Problem

by the media to dehumanize people who were homeless. On the other hand, when the media represent charity toward people who are homeless, the virtues of the volunteers are highlighted and the need for affordable housing overlooked (Simpson Reeves et al. 2022).

As briefly noted, and elaborated in subsequent chapters, the view that homelessness is a problem caused by deviant and sick individuals making poor choices has a range of practical consequences. From a straightforward perspective, it feeds into punitive and paternalistic responses that seek to move on, control, and change people who are homeless. In Chapter 6, we examine this in some depth, including the ethics of such responses (Johnsen et al. 2018). The belief that homelessness is a problem of the sick, or people with care and support needs, drives an agenda that is more positive than punitive measures. This view leads to a range of objectives, policies, and practices that seek to prioritize housing allocation and ongoing support to end homelessness. The definition of chronic homelessness in the United States centers not only on length of homelessness but also on the presence of a disability, and individuals who meet the criteria of this definition may be eligible for permanent supportive housing. In Chapter 7, we take a closer look at how this idea of homelessness as a problem of the deserving sick feeds into some interventions that are demonstrably beneficial for the *lucky* ones whose homelessness is viewed as a problem of sickness decoupled from personal responsibility.

Structure and agency: a complex interaction

If we can say that it is unfortunate that many in society – including our political leaders, the public, and the media – still understand homelessness as a problem explained by individual failings, then we might equally conclude that it is pleasing that the literature on homelessness, social science and health literature alike, has moved well beyond simplistic interpretations. As we will demonstrate in this chapter and develop throughout the book, the volume of evidence that unaffordable housing and poverty cause homelessness has profoundly discredited the individual explanation of homelessness. Some sections of the population are at disproportionate risk of experiencing homelessness, but rather than anything specific about them as individuals, the evidence shows that it is societal structures, in particular the availability, or not, of affordable housing, that determine which individual groups are likely to become homeless.

The sheer weight of evidence showing the extent of homelessness across societies has sunk individual arguments that the causes of homelessness can be meaningfully found in the behaviors of those excluded from housing. Although there are complex interacting forces that produce homelessness – we discuss these below – we echo Gregg Colburn and Clayton Aldern's (2022) recent analysis from the United States arguing that homelessness is a housing problem. As C. Wright Mills (2000) showed, when a problem affects only a few people, it is easy to explain it away as a personal trouble of the individual concerned. When the problem affects large numbers of people, however, we are confronted with the reality that they are experiencing a social problem that is caused by how we organize society. The problem of homelessness is so vast in society that it can no longer been seen as anything other than caused by societal institutions. Identifying these causes, of course, is far from straightforward.

Leading scholar in the field Suzanne Fitzpatrick observes that "it is an extremely complex matter, in both theoretical and empirical terms, to analyse the causes of homelessness" (2012: 15). This complexity has been proposed as structural forces generate a population that is poor and thus at risk of homelessness, and individual explanations consider how some people at risk of homelessness because of structural conditions, including a lack of housing, become and stay homeless (Lee et al. 2010). Writing about the situation in the United Kingdom, Nicholas Pleace (2000) refers to this as the new orthodoxy: structural forces create conditions where people with individual problems – both characteristics and behaviors – are susceptible to becoming and staying homeless. The new orthodoxy is essentially an integration of the individual and structural explanations of homelessness. From the United States, Steve Metraux and Dennis Culhane (1999) refer to this understanding of homelessness as a moderate position, whereby individual characteristics that are a risk of resulting from homelessness are produced under certain structural conditions.

Fitzpatrick (2012) says that the new orthodoxy, or the approach of integrating structure and agency, is unambiguously an advancement on binary individual or structural explanations, particularly at the descriptive level. She argues that this understanding of the nature of homelessness, including how it is caused, is lacking on important conceptual grounds. Fitzpatrick refined and extended the new orthodoxy to encourage deeper thinking about the interacting causes of homelessness. Her work encourages us to think about how structure is often prioritized over agency and how the agency of people who are and stay homeless can be overlooked, and she proposed that ideas about structure and agency are based on inaccurate distinctions that characterize some forces specific to certain individuals when they can equally be thought about as structural. Child abuse, addiction, and relationship dissolution are examples that cannot neatly be categorized as either individual or structural. Drawing on a realist ontology, which she proposes is consistent with Anthony Giddens's structuration theory (1984), Fitzpatrick (2005) proposes a framework for analyzing the causes of homelessness.

For Fitzpatrick, the causes of homelessness should be thought about with reference to layered social reality. This takes into account multidirectional relationships and feedback loops between individual and structural forces. The critical realist model advocated by Fitzpatrick (2005) tackles agency head on, where personal factors can cause homelessness, and family relationships and social networks can prevent homelessness. At the same time, poverty and access to housing markets can also result in homelessness, including by undermining protective social relationships and creating conditions for individual risky behaviors. The presence of structural and individual problems does not inevitability lead to homelessness. In other words, something that may cause homelessness in some situations (e.g., a structural condition, event, or behavior) will not necessarily cause homelessness in all instances (Bramley and Fitzpatrick 2018).

The realist framework is a useful model for understanding the nature and causes of homelessness. Two important insights in particular are worth highlighting. First, the model emphasizes the importance of examining whether people actually have control over actions that are assumed to cause their homelessness. The second important contribution is to demonstrate that the causes of homelessness need to be substantiated empirically, rather than it being assumed that either structural or individual conditions are preeminent. The model put forward by Fitzpatrick pushes us to move beyond ideological assumptions about what we believe produces homelessness, and engage in complex empirical research to try and understand the causal mechanisms. Harry Tan and

Homelessness as a Societal Problem

Helen Forbes-Mewett's qualitative study from Singapore represents an excellent example that makes concrete these interacting causal mechanisms unfolding in a person's life. Using ethnographic research to engage closely with older people who were homeless, they found that many of them lost housing when they could no longer afford the costs due to unemployment. Unemployment was often associated with economic downturns or with alcohol misuse. Nearly all the people interviewed by Tan and Forbes-Mewett had strained relationships with family, and many had been divorced. Families were either unwilling to provide help, or older people who were homeless were unwilling to ask for help. Tan and Forbes-Mewett concluded:

> [Older people did not] speak of a specific external circumstance or personal issue that made them homeless. Rather, they spoke about different episodes in their lives, different issues they faced, and the decisions they made voluntarily or, at other times, felt compelled to make. The many influences and diminishing supports that contributed to the homelessness of the interview participants meant not one singular episode could be considered as the reason for their circumstances. (2018: 3591)

These firsthand accounts from older people in Singapore support the findings of Barrett Lee and colleagues who concluded that homelessness is "the product of several intertwined antecedents" (2021: 13). Tan and Forbes-Mewett highlighted the agency of older people, but older people exerted agency in order to respond to resources that they could neither control nor alter to prevent their homelessness under the prevailing structural conditions.

There is a developed body of work, often with robust quantitative research designs, that empirically examines the interacting conditions that unfold in a person's life and culminate in homelessness in the way identified by Tan and Forbes-Mewett. This work is vast and, collectively, it provides a strong evidence base to illustrate both the causes of homelessness and the closely related structural conditions that can make it so difficult to exit homelessness. The research shows that homelessness is produced by social forces that are largely within the hands of governments and societies to address. This key theme is articulated throughout this book, and it provides optimism and a framework for what we should do about homelessness, as outlined in Chapter 8. As Fitzpatrick has argued, the agency of people who are homeless must be empirically examined, but this examination must also include scrutiny of the environment and the way in which this can exacerbate the individual problems so often experienced by people who are homeless (which both underpin their homelessness and represent a barrier to exiting: see Piat et al. 2015). Thus, what we might otherwise see as individual attributes or even triggers leading to homelessness, such as addiction, mental illness, and domestic violence, must be conceptualized and empirically examined as layered among other forces, including structural conditions. We need to examine whether these individual features would actually lead to homelessness were affordable housing to be readily available (see Johnson et al. 2019).

For the remainder of this chapter, we will look at some of the extensive literature that has examined the multiple layers that act to cause homelessness. Emphasis will be on the interaction of layers and feedback loops. The international literature provides two fundamental lessons. First, and as Fitzpatrick observed, determining what causes homelessness is complex because the causes involve so many interacting aspects of people's lives and society. The vast majority of people who experience homelessness exit after a short period of time (O'Flaherty 2010), but this chapter takes into account people entering and staying in homelessness; this is critical for a more comprehensive understanding of what contributes to prolonging and reducing its prevalence. I use the terms "causes homelessness" and "produces homelessness" interchangeably. Second, although without any doubt complex, the state of homelessness is largely predictable. There exists an important knowledge base about how our organization of society produces homelessness for people with particular life experiences. There is nothing more critical than the availability of affordable housing.

Housing

The self-evident centrality of housing in the problem of homelessness, given that homelessness is the state of residing in no or inadequate housing, has generated a growing body of research on the relationship between the two. An important early example of this type of empirical analysis comes from John Quigley and Steven Raphael. They predicted that a 1 percent increase in the private rental vacancy rate, in addition to a reduction in "average monthly median rent-to-income ratios from 17.5 to 16.8 percent," could reduce the rate of homelessness by 25 percent. They concluded:

> We find that rather straightforward conditions in US housing markets – not complex social pathologies, drug usage, or deficiencies in mental health treatments – are largely responsible for variations in rates of homelessness. We find that rather modest changes in housing markets, in vacancy rates and rents for example, have substantial effects upon the incidence of homelessness. (2001: 324–5)

These conclusions are intended not only to highlight the role that housing markets play in causing homelessness, but also to explicitly challenge the belief that homelessness is caused by individual attributes and behaviors. Quigley and Raphael's findings are broadly consistent with other significant studies from the United States conducted around the end of the twentieth century. The research found that unaffordable and affordable housing, both with and without government subsidies, played a far greater role in predicting homelessness or promoting stable housing trajectories than personal characteristics (Metraux and Culhane 1999; O'Flaherty 2004; Shinn et al. 1998).

The combined contributions of these early empirical studies from the United States, consistent with the advocacy of a wave of scholars, not-for-profit-organizations, and community groups ever since, locate the problem of homelessness in the insufficient supply of affordable housing. With a conclusion that is both simple and powerful, the research shows that this is the main reason why people become, and remain, homeless. This is a compelling argument for those motivated to address homelessness through intervention into housing markets. Although the problem has been exacerbated in many countries since the Covid-19 pandemic, in the years prior to 2020 there was growing recognition across the OECD that an insufficient supply of affordable housing was a growing societal concern affecting a larger section of society than simply "the poor" (OECD 2021a).

As a problem that started to impact large sections of society in addition to people living in poverty or with so-called care and support needs, growing rates of housing unaffordability are easily perceived by the general population as a structural problem rather than a problem of people who lack adequate income and wealth. To again draw on Mills, housing unaffordability has increasingly been seen as the result of the "economic and political institutions of the society," not "the personal situation and character" of those trying to access housing (2000: 9). The empirical evidence that homelessness is caused by a lack of affordable housing is intuitively appealing and resonates with the experiences of what many people in society see.

Important work from the United States has been significantly developed since the early 2000s, with robust data and complex analyses. With the benefit of a large sample from the US Department of Housing and Urban Development (HUD) department, scholars extended the evidence on the role that housing can play as a structural determiner of homelessness. Jamison Fargo and colleagues (2013) were unable to make causal claims, but their analysis demonstrated that housing costs and income were key predictors of homelessness among families and single people. Also using HUD data, Thomas Byrne and colleagues (2013) found housing markets, and unaffordable housing in particular, to be the core structural determiner of homelessness. Specifically, in non-metropolitan areas, their model predicted that homelessness would increase by 32 percent, with an increase in median rents of $100 per month (Byrne et al. 2013).

Colburn and Aldern (2022) add to this analysis. Referring to the diverse rates of homelessness across US cities, they conclude that they vary in line with the cost and availability of housing. Housing markets, and in particular whether housing is affordable to people who are poor or unemployed, explain the rate of homelessness. Drawing on US regional housing market and homelessness data, Colburn and Aldern found that regions (cities and counties) with high absolute rent costs have the highest rates of homelessness. They argue that low rates of homelessness are observed in Detroit or St. Louis because median rents are between $600 and $700 per month. Conversely, high rates of homelessness are observed in San Francisco or Santa Clara Country because median rents are three to four times higher (Colburn and Aldern 2022). They argue that, because they have extremely high housing costs, particularly rents, New York, Los Angeles, Washington, DC, San Francisco, and Boston between them account for 29 percent of homelessness in the United States, even though they only account for approximately 7 percent of the national population.

Broadly similar findings have been identified outside the United States. James O'Donnell (2021) conducted important empirical work

Homelessness as a Societal Problem

in Australia which examined how different types of housing are associated with differences in incidences and duration of homelessness. Informed by insights from longitudinal data, he concludes:

> A key finding and contribution of this study in this respect is that social housing is associated with greater stability in housing trajectories for disadvantaged populations. People who enter social housing are more likely to maintain their tenancy and less likely to experience homelessness or other forms of disadvantage than people living in privately rented housing. (2021: 1722)

In an analysis involving longitudinal data from Australia, Guy Johnson and colleagues concluded that public housing is "a very strong protective factor reducing risks of homelessness. Public housing is particularly effective because it is affordable" (2019: 1106). Their analytical model predicted that, among their sample, 2.4 percent would become homeless where affordable housing was plentiful, whereas this rose to 17 percent in locations where rents were very high (Johnson et al. 2019). Similar findings were reported by Tim Aubry and colleagues (2021) in a study from Canada. They found that the critical determiner of whether people exited homelessness, and did not return, was not primarily individual characteristics, but the availability of subsidized housing. Zachary Glendening and Marybeth Shinn (2017) observe a similar finding in that the provision of subsidized housing for families exiting homelessness is associated with long-term housing stability.

There are many ways that housing conditions can be regulated by the state to prevent and reduce homelessness, including through a provision of public housing and government assistance in renting in the private market. In the United States, housing vouchers are a prominent means through which the state subsidizes housing costs. Tyler Haupert (2021) conducted a study of a representative sample from New York City and concluded, "rent control's association with lower rates of homelessness suggests policies promoting long-term stability in rental costs might be effective in stemming homelessness – especially in high-cost areas."

The state's role in intervening in or subsidizing housing costs varies, and the variations reflect different cultural ideas about the role of the state in society, such as whether the state should own housing (such as public housing, which is common in parts of Europe and the

United Kingdom) or whether the state should leverage the market (which is frequently done in the United States). Subsidized housing can assume other forms, with the state playing a more distant or different role. In Japan, for instance, large-scale homelessness is prevented as affordable housing is provided by companies to employees. Reflecting on the low rates of homelessness in Japan (and taking into account definitional variations), which the OECD (2021b) says are the lowest among member countries, Hideo Aoki (2006) and Matthew Marr (2012) observe that the state provides limited social services and subsidized housing; instead, it facilitates labor market policy that works to prevent and address homelessness by reducing unemployment and ensuring that employees are securely housed by their employers.

As with research from elsewhere in the world, Marr (2012) observes in Japan that individual vulnerabilities that are assumed to produce homelessness are irrelevant under conditions of labor market partici-pation, affordable housing, and social ties. But in accepting secure and affordable housing provided by their companies, employees will always face the risk of homelessness when they lose their jobs (Okamoto 2007).

Singapore represents another interesting example of intervention into the housing market that functions to dissipate the causes of homelessness. Although there is some homelessness in Singapore, as we have already seen (Tan and Forbes-Mewett 2018), and notwith-standing definitional differences that make international comparisons limited, the proportion of the population who are homeless in Singapore, according to the Singapore government (Ministry of Social and Family Development 2019), is extremely low relative to the United States, the United Kingdom, and most of Europe. This low rate of homelessness is attributed to heavy government intervention into, and subsidizing of, the entire housing sector. The vast majority of Singaporeans, about 90 percent, own their own home. Such a high level of home ownership is attributed to housing being built on state-owned land, and then sold to the population on a 99-year lease basis (Teo and Chiu 2016). Even those on very low incomes can rent housing built by the state at heavily subsidized rates. Home-ownership in Singapore was originally conceived of as a means to ensure that citizens had a stake in the country (Teo and Chiu 2016).

State intervention also assumes the form of determining who is eligible for subsidized housing. Deborah Cobb-Clark and colleagues

Homelessness as a Societal Problem 35

(2016) found that parents with dependent children are more likely to exit homelessness and move into secure public housing. This is not necessarily state intervention in order to create additional affordable housing stock, but rather to legislate and determine who in the population should be prioritized over and above others such as those without dependent children. State intervention can shape the availability of both affordable housing and its accessibility.

The research is unequivocal. Unaffordable, inaccessible, and insecure housing are the core drivers of homelessness, while myriad forms of intervention into the housing market to promote affordability are associated with lower rates of homelessness. Typically, the intervention is through the state, but the private sector also plays a role in some contexts, such as providing company housing in Japan and publicly facilitated individual ownership in Singapore. In 2017, to give another example, the incoming Mayor of London, Sadiq Khan, initiated a policy that enabled developers to fast-track through the planning process, a process that could take many years, if they committed to building additional affordable properties in new developments. On private land, at least 35 percent of the housing would have to be affordable in order to receive fast-track planning approval; the threshold on public land was set at 50 percent. This is another way in which the state can intervene in the housing market to put downward pressure on homelessness even in the absence of direct state involvement in house building or in subsidizing the private market. Scholarship has demonstrated countless times that, through numerous means, intervention alleviates the causes of homelessness. We will return to these ideas in Chapter 8.

Although housing is the fundamental problem underpinning homelessness, an extensive body of research illustrates that we need to think about homelessness as dynamic, and consider the way that housing markets work in concert with other forces to produce homelessness. Housing matters, but it matters in relation to other things. Housing markets can both produce and prevent homelessness, but we can never think about housing, particularly whether it is affordable or unaffordable, as separate from other institutions in society.

Housing and poverty

Poverty is a core determiner that explains whether intertwined events culminate in homelessness. Housing markets, and the unaffordability of housing in particular, interact with poverty in important ways to produce homelessness. In many countries, people who are unemployed, either with or without disabilities, live below the poverty line and affordable housing is often out of their reach (Parsell et al. 2021). Maria Hanratty's study from the United States found that high rates of poverty impact housing stability. Her analysis presented compelling evidence demonstrating that "communities with high rents and high poverty rates have higher risks of homelessness" (Hanratty 2017: 653).

The lack of affordable housing as a cause of homelessness must be considered in concert with poverty. In an influential study from the United Kingdom, Glen Bramley and Suzanne Fitzpatrick (2018) found that, although housing markets do indeed drive homelessness, poverty is in fact the key driver. In an insight that will be critical in our examination of prevention in Chapter 8, they found that childhood poverty is a key predictor of homelessness in later life. Other research found that, alongside poverty, income inequality contributes to homelessness indirectly by denying low-income households access to the housing market (Byrne et al. 2021).

These examples help us think about the links between housing unaffordability and other forces. Rather than focusing on housing markets in isolation, we need also to consider the ways in which poverty leads to homelessness. Apart from the obvious fact that low earnings will not pay the rent, poverty can also contribute to homelessness in less explicit but equally dynamic ways. The day-to-day realities of poverty induce stress and conflict, and can undermine protective family and extended supportive relationships (Lee et al. 2021). Matthew Desmond's (2012) ethnographic work from the United States shows how living in poverty forces people to be reliant on their social networks for resources and support. However, the realities of living in poverty make those networks of reliance fragile. In these ways, the personal and social consequences of poverty can cause homelessness (Bramley and Fitzpatrick 2018).

Implicit in the evidence about either, or both, housing markets and poverty as causes of homelessness is state intervention, which can create the conditions to prevent homelessness; at the same time, state inaction can lead to homelessness. The power of state intervention or inaction to determine a person's homelessness, including whether it exists at all and, if so, its duration, helps us think about homelessness as a political problem. Unaffordable housing and poverty certainly do cause homelessness, but the extent to which they exist in society is determined by policy decisions.

Through income support to people outside the labor market, including because of job loss, age, parenting support, and sickness and disability, the state has a significant influence on poverty rates, and thereby the extent of homelessness, in society. Both the coverage and generosity of state support and welfare measures are critical. In an analysis from the United States, Zachary Parolin (2021) found that government income support, by means of the Temporary Assistance to Needy Families (TANF) program, reduces homelessness among families. Here we are presented with some of the complexity and multiple layers that Fitzpatrick theorized. Homelessness is produced through unaffordable housing markets that impact people in poverty. There are additional layers to consider, however. The affordability or unaffordability of the housing market is shaped by governments directly through subsidized housing and indirectly through income support, welfare measures, and labor market policy that can shape the extent of poverty in society. Thus, multiple structural forces produce homelessness and these can be, and often are, mitigated by deliberate intervention through public policy. It is meaningless to think about the rates of poverty or affordable housing, and thus homelessness, without also thinking about state intervention.

Trigger events

Housing affordability and poverty are far from being the full extent of the picture. They interact with countless other forces to produce homelessness, such as domestic violence, family conflict and dissolution, eviction, and discharge from institutional care. Lee and collaborators (2021) refer to these as trigger events that, under certain structural arrangements and social conditions such as a lack of family support, can tip people into homelessness. Consistent with our comments above about state intervention and opportunities to influence the supply of affordable housing and the rate of poverty, the power of these events to push people into homelessness is to a large extent within the hands of governments.

The international evidence presents a clear yet frightening finding: the experience of domestic and family violence (DFV), also referred as intimate partner violence (IPV), is one of the most common factors that pushes people into homelessness. Notwithstanding definitional differences across countries that create an undercount because some women who leave DFV situations and enter safe shelters are not included in official homelessness statistics (Bretherton 2017; Busch-Geertsema and Fitzpatrick 2008), DFV is reported as the primary, or one of the primary, triggers for homelessness internationally (Baker et al. 2010). Of US cities surveyed, 50 percent reported that domestic violence is the primary cause of homelessness (American Civil Liberties Union 2008). A study from Minnesota found that 32 percent of women who became homeless did so after escaping an abusive relationship (Wilder Research 2007). The Australian government reports that the main reason given by people seeking homelessness service support is domestic violence, which was the case for 42 percent of all those requesting assistance in 2020 (Australian Institute of Health and Welfare 2021). Paula Mayock and colleagues (2016) note that data limitations prevent firm conclusions from being made about domestic violence as the major cause of homelessness in Europe. Nevertheless, qualitative research from Europe and the United Kingdom does indeed show that many women report moving into homelessness after fleeing DFV (Mayock et al. 2016).

This straightforward link resonates closely with many women's firsthand experiences (Jasinski et al. 2010). For example, Megan Ravenhill reported the experience of a 27-year-old woman who was homeless in England:

> I'll tell you why women become homeless, it's because of violent men. They live with men that become violent and then they have to leave, but they've nowhere to go so they end up on the streets. Take me: I had four good men but the relationships were trashed because of drink. Drink turns the man bad, he goes violent. (2008: 132)

At face value, the massive number of women who first become homeless after escaping DFV suggests that, even if there were no more affordable housing and governments did nothing to address poverty, the rate of homelessness would plummet if incidences of DFV were reduced. We have to think about DFV as a trigger for homelessness alongside other factors, such as unaffordable and inadequate housing, broader rates of poverty, and other forms of exclusion. On the one hand, poverty and the unavailability of affordable housing place people (particularly women and children) in environments where they are at risk of DFV because they are likely to be dependent on a violent or controlling partner (Menard 2001). On the other hand, the experience of poverty and inadequate housing can induce stress, dysfunction, and alcoholism, and thus foster conditions where DFV is more likely (Fahmy et al. 2016).

Thus, although the link between DFV and homelessness is unambiguous, it is not, as Charlene Baker and colleagues explain (2010), "necessarily a direct one." Reflecting the complex and layered causes of homelessness, they show that DFV can produce homelessness through multiple mechanisms, including the link between past experiences of DFV and difficulties finding and maintaining employment. Furthermore, DFV can be the trigger event for homelessness through "insufficient income to live independently, limited availability of affordable housing, potential housing discrimination against them as domestic violence survivors, histories of credit or rental problems, a criminal history, or ongoing harassment and assaults by the ex-intimate partner" (Baker et al. 2010: 431). As we illustrate in the next chapter, escaping DFV and becoming homeless can place women and children in dangerous and coercive situations. The deeply disturbing irony is that for many women and children, the violence that characterizes their homelessness reflects the violent event that pushed them there in the first place. The challenges inherent in distinguishing between the causes and consequences of homelessness, along with the multiple causal layers, are illustrated in the fictionalized case study that follows, which nonetheless reflects realities experienced by many women across the world.

Far less frequently reported than DFV as a trigger for homelessness is family dissolution (Narayan et al. 2017). Reporting on the international evidence, Fitzpatrick (2012: 16) observes that a relationship breakdown between spouses or partners, even in the absence of violence, "is a very prominent cause of homelessness." In a study of adults in Finland who were homeless, Eeva Kostiainen (2015: 72) found that "the principal reason for homelessness is divorce or separation," which was reported by 21 percent of people. Although we often do not know if the relationship is causal, in some ways similar to the mechanisms through which domestic violence triggers homelessness, family dissolution may result in homelessness because of an unexpected shock, limited income of a single person or single-headed household, or as a product of conflict that may have led to separation. Julie Moschion and Jan van Ours (2019) add to this

Elizabeth's partner violently assaulted her. After being discharged from the emergency department with minor wounds, she took her 2-month old daughter and 15-year old son to the municipal homeless shelter to escape the violence of her now ex-partner. Caring for her children, especially with a desire to continue breast-feeding her 2-month old, Elizabeth could find neither employment nor affordable childcare. With the support of shelter workers, she applied for state-subsidized housing, and was advised that she was eligible; she would be required to wait approximately 24 months for a housing allocation. After two months in the shelter, her son started to display aggressive behaviors, leaving other women and children in the shelter intimidated. The shelter operators advised Elizabeth that she would be required to move her son into residential youth accommodation on his forthcoming 16th birthday. Refusing to leave her son, Elizabeth returned to her ex-partner after he promised to no longer use violence. The violence soon continued, however, and Elizabeth and her partner both consumed alcohol on a daily basis. Elizabeth found that this dulled her fear and helped her deal with the daily abuse. Her partner lost his job and the household was evicted. With her son now 16, the municipal shelters would not accommodate Elizabeth and her two children, so they lived temporarily in her car. The child protection authorities intervened and removed the children. Elizabeth experienced significant trauma at the loss of her children and her drinking spiraled out of her control. When she entered a shelter for single women, the intake officer met with her to take details. First, the intake worker asked Elizabeth what led her to her to turn up at the shelter. Elizabeth's story is all too common. For our purposes, this example illustrates the complexity of even knowing what caused someone's homelessness. Does Elizabeth tell the intake worker that what brought her to the homelessness shelter was her drinking? Or the trauma of having her children taken from her care? Was it because of the violence she endured? Or because of the shelter policy that restricts adolescent males aged over 16 from residing with their mothers? Or the job loss and eviction of her ex-partner? Or is the cause of her homelessness the

Homelessness as a Societal Problem 41

> approximately 24-month wait for subsidized housing? It is all of these, of course. If we dig deeper, we can also identify the cause of homelessness to be Elizabeth's experience of having been in the state child protection system, and the limited support she received when she exited care at age 18, and the disrupted family relationships that meant these were not a resource she could draw on. Elizabeth's example is a case study on the challenges of identifying what causes homelessness. Needless to say, if Elizabeth had had immediate access to subsidized housing when she left her violent partner, her homelessness may have come to an end.

literature by analyzing longitudinal data from Australia. They found that if disadvantaged parents divorce or separate prior to their children reaching the age of 12, the children are at a significantly heightened risk of becoming homeless.

In addition to divorce and separation, there is an important recognition in the literature that dynamics and conflict within the family unit or household can constitute a trigger point. In an Australian study drawing on service provider administrative data, Maree Petersen and I identified conflict in multigenerational families as triggers for homelessness among older people. We saw that disputes about housing assets could lead to older people turning to homelessness services, which they interpreted as elder abuse (Petersen and Parsell 2020).

Family conflict is likewise a significant trigger event for young people. In an important early study from Scotland, Gill Jones (1997) found that young people who became homeless after family conflict disproportionately experienced poor education. She argued that family conflict and breakdown were products of unemployment and exacerbated by poor housing. Family dysfunction and separation were thus triggers for homelessness, yet wider structural inequities produced the conditions that were ripe for family dysfunction to culminate in homelessness.

A more recent body of research examines connections between family breakdown and homelessness among young people, but instead of focusing on limited resources within society and the stressors faced by households that are poor, it highlights stigmatized ideas about gender and sexuality. Referring to the disturbing incongruence between the estimated 5–8 percent of young people in the United States who identify as LGBTQ and who also constitute approximately 40 percent of youth homelessness, Brandon Robinson (2018) highlights research that shows how abuse, conflict, and disagreement about sexuality and gender pushes people out of the family home and into homelessness. In this way we can see societal stigma as a force that triggers homelessness for people who do not conform to heteronormativity. However, and as Robinson points out, family rejection that triggers homelessness for LGBTQ youth is disproportionately produced under conditions where poverty exacerbated conflict.

Eviction is another trigger for homelessness. Research from across the globe, including the United Kingdom (Crane and Warnes 2000), the Netherlands (van Laere et al. 2009), Finland (Kostiainen 2015), and the United States (Garcia and Kim 2021) shows how eviction often immediately precedes homelessness. Eviction might be a result of rental arrears, or the myriad individual and neighborhood problems that culminate in a person breaching their tenancy obligations. It may also be associated with enduring harms that not only push people into homelessness, but also prolong and make exiting homelessness more difficult (Rutan and Desmond 2021).

Discharge from institutional care is the final trigger event for homelessness that we want briefly to highlight. This includes exiting foster care (Dworsky et al. 2013), hospitals, and other health facilities (Olfson et al. 1999; Forchuk et al. 2008), as well as exiting incarceration (Metraux et al. 2007). Perhaps unsurprisingly, people who, on leaving hospital or prison, are homeless are at a heightened risk of returning to hospital or prison (Herbert et al. 2015; Laliberte et al. 2020). This is referred to as the "revolving door" (Doran et al. 2013).

There are many reasons why discharge from institutional care is a trigger for homelessness. These include the practice of housing providers, public and private alike, to screen for criminal histories of applicants (Schneider 2018). A criminal record that is serious enough to lead to imprisonment is a stain that makes secure housing hard to come by (Evans and Porter 2015). The severing of protective family ties as a result of time spent incarcerated, alongside limited welfare support and resources, further creates conditions where homelessness is a likely experience upon release from prison (Herbert et al. 2015).

The lack of discharge planning by health facilities and child protection systems is another way in which exiting institutions can trigger homelessness (Backer et al. 2007). In terms of the latter, young people exiting the child protection system will likely not have the resources from family to draw on that many other young people use to access and sustain housing. This includes the option of staying in and returning to the family home through late adolescence and into their early twenties. Wojtek Tomaszewski and colleagues' (2017) longitudinal research illustrates that, even when young people leave their parental home, they continue to draw on parental support to access independent housing. In addition, young adults routinely return to the family home throughout their twenties, particularly at times of transition, such as a relationship breakdown, ending education, or the loss of a job. This ongoing parental support is far less accessible to young adults who exit the foster care system.

Suppressing trigger events

The conditions discussed above constitute trigger events for homelessness, but they need not do so. Under different circumstances, they will not necessarily lead to homelessness. This is not simply a theoretical proposition. By comparing the policy and practice arrangements of one county with another, or even looking at change in one country over time (such as changes brought about in response to Covid-19), we can see strong evidence for how these triggers can be suppressed. Strategies adopted to mitigate the risk of these events pushing people into homelessness occur at the macro structural and program or intervention levels. In terms of the former, societies reduce the likelihood of these events triggering homelessness by providing affordable housing and through general welfare measures that, for example, mean youth or individuals (especially women) can afford to live independently of parents or a spouse.

These macro interventions are not explicitly framed as reducing the risks of entering homelessness, but they work to do so by minimizing poverty and hardship in the population by making resources available. A society where there is an adequate supply of affordable housing and universal income protection will mean that escaping domestic violence, experiencing family dissolution, being evicted, or even being discharged from an institution are not likely to trigger homelessness.

44 Homelessness as a Societal Problem

Gregory Preston and Vincent Reina's (2021) analysis from the United States shows that subsidized housing reduces (but does not eliminate) the risk of eviction simply because of the reduced rent burden. In a comprehensive study from a national data set in Denmark, Lars Benjaminsen (2016) found that homelessness is heavily concentrated among a very small cohort of society that is characterized by active illicit substance addiction. Benjaminsen refers to Denmark and the Scandinavian countries broadly as "representing some of the world's most advanced welfare systems" (2016: 2041). With low rates of poverty and universal resources provided to the population, the conditions that trigger homelessness outlined above are not dominant factors in Denmark. Suzanne Fitzpatrick and Mark Stephens's (2014) six-country comparison in Europe found that different welfare models and different cultural norms influence the conditions that trigger homelessness. They note, for instance, that the feminist movement in Germany has a "relatively strong, and discrete, network of provision for abused women" (2014: 229), thus minimizing the extent to which DFV occurs and, when it does occur, reducing the likelihood that women then experience homelessness. Similarly, the individualist norms in the United Kingdom, as opposed to familial approaches in other parts of Europe, provide stronger protection for young people ejected from the family home.

This comparative research is important for foregrounding the centrality of how cultural ideas within societies influence the potential forces that can produce homelessness. The extent to which the state provides resources, and who precisely benefits from them, is influenced by beliefs about the role of the family, the role of parents, and attitudes about women's independence from or dependence on men. These cultural ideas, as well as ideas about sexuality, shape what resources societies provide and in turn influence whether or not certain events trigger homelessness.

Where universal and comprehensive resources are available, homelessness is experienced less frequently by long-term disadvantaged people than by people pushed into homelessness as a result of a trigger event (Benjaminsen and Andrade 2015). Macro structures within society, as illustrated through the comprehensiveness of the welfare state or availability of affordable housing (Colburn and Aldern 2022), are thus critical in determining whether an event is likely to trigger homelessness.

Homelessness as a Societal Problem   45

The role of DFV as one of the primary triggers for homelessness has inspired a groundswell of legislative and practice initiatives to address the link. This includes supporting victims of domestic violence to stay in their home by enhancing security (Netto et al. 2009), providing access to new housing (Kuskoff et al. 2022), or by housing the perpetrator (Clarke and Wydall 2013). Some of these are referred to as "safe at home" programs, which were developed in England in the early 2000s and have since been adopted in New Zealand and Australia. Safe at home programs seek to keep women and children safe and remove the perpetrator of violence so that victims of DFV do not experience homelessness. These initiatives are generally closely integrated with the criminal justice system, whereby the perpetrator leaving the home is mandated to do so by a court (Breckenridge et al. 2015). Safe at home initiatives work on the premise that the victims of DFV should not be penalized with homelessness for escaping violence; such initiatives are, however, only appropriate under particular circumstances where the risk of ongoing violence is low (Diemer et al. 2017).

Jurisdictions across the globe have also intervened to reduce the likelihood of family conflict triggering homelessness. Reflecting the problems associated with adolescents entering homelessness after family conflict – either by leaving to avoid conflict or being forced out of the home – there exists a range of specialist mediation and reconciliation strategies to both prevent young people from leaving the family home and enabling their return (Gaetz 2014). The recognition that family rejection because of a young person's gender or sexuality triggers homelessness has led to new approaches. Robinson (2018) provides an important analysis and argues that strategies to support LGBTQ youth to avoid entering homelessness should take account of how poverty in the household represents a meaningful barrier to families participating in therapy and education. Further, strategies that work to assist families understand that a young person's gender or sexual identity must not frame parents as the enemy, but rather recognize how family rejection sits within "larger social, political, and economic contexts" (Robinson 2018: 393).

To prevent stigma about gender and sexuality from triggering homelessness, we must intervene at both the family and societal level. More acceptance of LGBTQ identities at the societal level can prevent homelessness indirectly by reducing discrimination that itself causes poor mental health and barriers to seeking mainstream healthcare (Perales and Todd 2018). We might think that reducing stigma about LGBTQ and promoting acceptance at the societal level are difficult to achieve at the basic policy level, but examples from countries that legislate same-sex marriage and reduce social stigma and discrimination show how it can be achieved (Hooghe and Meeusen 2013). Government policy can change the population's views on stigma and discriminatory behavior toward LGBTQ people, and these changes have myriad benefits, including reducing family rejection that can trigger homelessness.

Societies likewise approved macro policy changes that directly and effectively almost put an end to eviction. As a response to the uncertainty and the health risks that the Covid-19 pandemic represented, especially the fear of mass job loss and people's inability to afford housing costs, countries such as the United Kingdom, Ireland, Australia, and the United States instigated temporary widespread moratoriums on eviction. The United States classified these as public health measures similar to those on quarantining and social distancing (Centers for Disease Control and Prevention 2021). Evidence from the United States suggests that preventing evictions "may help avert illness and deaths due to Covid-19" (Leifheit et al. 2021). Further, moratoriums on eviction were highly successful in averting homelessness. Fitzpatrick, Watts, et al. (2021: xxi) report that 87 percent of councils in England "considered the evictions moratorium to have been 'very important' in preventing or minimising homelessness in their area." Referring to official English government statistics between April and June 2020, Fitzpatrick, Watts, et al. (2021) observe that the number of people assisted because of eviction "plummeted." When the moratorium in England ended in May 2021, eviction numbers increased significantly (Watts et al. 2022: xix). In the United States, Peter Hepburn et al. (2021) likewise found that evictions increased rapidly after the moratorium was lifted.

Policy responses to Covid-19, even if only for a short time, illustrate that evictions can be reduced, and result in significant benefits, including a reduction in homelessness. Elsewhere, governments have used policy tools to prevent eviction. The French government has a winter break policy, or *trève hivernale*, which prevents housing providers, including private owners, from evicting a tenant between the months of November and March. In French territories, this includes a ban on evictions during the hurricane season (French Republic 2021). Even in the absence of formal bans on eviction, homelessness scholars recognize that strong tenancy legislation that broadly protects tenants is an effective means to prevent eviction and, in turn, homelessness (Dej et al. 2020). Targeted interventions work too. Finland introduced housing advisors to work with people at risk of eviction, and reports that 2,871 evictions were prevented in 2017 (Allen et al. 2020).

Maureen Crane and Anthony Warnes (2000) present an important reframing of the connection between evictions and homelessness. Reflecting on the experiences of older people who were evicted and became homeless, they draw attention to the lack of support provided in the period prior to eviction, a time when their support needs were already apparent. They argue that "an alternative representation of the causes of homelessness can therefore be as a failure of the welfare state and, specially, its safety-nets" (2000: 769). This point is critical to understanding the non-inevitable link between evictions and homelessness, and to minimizing the occurrence of the former so as to prevent the latter. Evictions are often systematic of other problems, and if a formal court process is pursued to evict a tenant, the underlying problems are recognized to exist well before the final eviction event. Without radical changes to property law, it is not possible to simply prevent a property owner from evicting a tenant who, for example, has not paid rent. Changes can occur, however, so that people at risk of eviction are offered support interventions to assist them in addressing the issues that culminate in tenancy problems. The state has significant capacity to intervene and offer support when someone is at risk of eviction, and if it does not do so, it will almost certainly be involved once a person ends up homeless.

Similar and equally compelling arguments have been presented about conditions and practices that can disrupt discharge from institutions, thereby triggering homelessness. Rather than focusing on exiting institutional care as the event that tips people into homelessness, we can instead see the problem stemming from societal failure to engage in appropriate discharge planning. There is an important evidence base about the role that discharge planning can play in preventing homelessness for people leaving the mental health system (Forchuk et al. 2008). Amy Dworsky and Mark Courtney (2009) found that closeness to a family member was associated

48 Homelessness as a Societal Problem

with avoiding homelessness after exiting foster care. Based on their analysis of longitudinal data from the United States, they recommend strengthening children's connection to family members during their time in statutory care, for numerous reasons, including that this would likely reduce their risk of homelessness after exiting. This points to the importance of including discharge planning in broader measure to enhance entire service systems (Backer et al. 2007) so as to ensure that the resources, professional care, and informal support do actually exist.

Discharge planning to prevent homelessness among people exiting prison is challenging, perhaps in part because this cohort does not receive the same concern that the population holds for young people exiting foster care. Nevertheless, there are mechanisms that can work to reduce the likelihood that exiting prison means entering homelessness. Schneider (2018), for example, shows that the US federal government sought to remove the mechanism that required HUD to check for criminal history among applicants, a legislative change that can greatly enhance the capacity of people exiting prison to gain access to housing.

The international literature on the strategies that can reduce the likelihood of certain, predictable events triggering homelessness provides three important lessons. First, alongside the data on what events trigger homelessness, such as DFV, family dissolution and conflict, eviction, and discharge from institutions, there is a developed body of knowledge about how these risks can be minimized. This includes both macro societal features and specific interventions. Second, as with the dominant finding presented throughout this chapter, the availability or otherwise of affordable housing is critical to whether the events trigger homelessness. At a general level, a person who is evicted in a society where there is accessible affordable housing is less likely to experience homelessness than a person who is evicted in a society where there is limited affordable housing. A tight housing market with limited affordable housing and many people trying to access housing may create the conditions where landlords are more likely to evict. We can thus reframe the problem as being not one of an event that triggers homelessness, but rather as certain types of societal failures that culminate in people's predictable needs for housing not being met. Third, many of the things that we can do to lessen the risk of events triggering homelessness have multiple benefits that extend far beyond preventing homelessness. These

Homelessness as a Societal Problem

include enhancing family relationships for people in foster care or reducing stigmas in society about sexuality.

Race

The proposition that it is beneficial to the broader functioning of society to intervene to mitigate the risks of events that trigger homelessness helps us further grasp how homelessness is a problem that is symptomatic of societal failure. We saw this above in relation to stigmas about gender and sexuality, to young people in foster care being disconnected from family, and to the mind-blowing statistic of the many women and children who are homeless because a significant male in their lives perpetrated or threatened violence toward them. When we prevent homelessness, we are at the same time intervening in society to address other higher-order problems. The evidence in this chapter is clear that homelessness is principally produced under conditions of unaffordable housing, yet these structural conditions interact with and are significant for people who experience other societal harms. It is the combination of these harms, for some people at certain times in their life, that culminates in homelessness. Our discussion on the nature of the problem of homelessness and the conditions under which it is produced requires close, critical, and challenging discussions of race. Race and racism are often central to the circumstances that produce homelessness for many people.

We cannot understand homelessness as a societal problem without also understanding race. Marian Jones (2016) shows that historic stereotypes that homelessness was an issue for white, alcoholic men were shattered when empirical evidence showed up the strong racial gradient. She cites HUD data from 2015 to show that Black persons comprised 12.5 percent of the US population, yet they made up 40.4 percent of the homeless population. Moreover, 2010 data indicated that people in Black families were seven times more likely than people in white families to access homelessness shelters.

The racial disparities, in the United States at least, have barely altered since Jones's review of the data. The official statistics from the federal government show that some racial minorities are a majority of the homeless population. The 2020 data found that "people identifying as Black or African American accounted for 39 percent of all people experiencing homelessness and 53 percent of people experiencing homelessness as members of families with children but are 12 percent of the total US population" (Henry et al. 2021: 1). The official data also identified racial disparities among other groups within American society. People who identify as Latino or Hispanic make up 23 percent of the homeless population, but only 16 percent of the broader US population. Moreover, the number of people experiencing homelessness who identified as Latino and Hispanic increased by 5 percent between 2019 and 2020. Interestingly, Americans who identify racially as Asian comprise approximately 7 percent of the population, yet they make up only 1.3 percent of the homeless population (Henry et al. 2021).

The detail and precision with which race is measured in homelessness statistics in the United States are far superior than what is common elsewhere. Despite the less-developed empirical analysis from elsewhere, it is clear that being part of a racial minority in the United States means being more likely to be homeless. International evidence, particularly from the United Kingdom and Europe, focuses on migration status rather than on race, and on how migrants are more likely to experience homelessness than non-migrants.

In the most comprehensive study to document homelessness among migrants and ethnic groups across 15 European Union member states, Busch-Geertsema et al. (2014) found homelessness to be disproportionately experienced by migrants, or children of migrants. For example, the extent of homelessness among migrants in France increased from 38 percent in 2001 to 52 percent in 2012. The extent of homelessness among migrants is more starkly demonstrated in data from Paris: "In some districts 40% of young homeless people are from Eastern Europe" (Busch-Geertsema et al. 2014: 69). The same study showed that, in Italy, the figures are even more striking: survey research from 2011 with people who are homeless in Italy revealed that 60 percent "reported being of foreign origin."

In Scandinavia, which, as we showed above, was referred to as having the world's most advanced welfare systems (Benjaminsen 2016), being a migrant means being disproportionately represented in the homeless population. Migrants and their children make up 11 percent of the Danish population, yet they represent 17 percent of the homeless population (Busch-Geertsema et al. 2014). Elsewhere in Scandinavia the proportion is greater. In Finland, migrants make up 5 percent of the general population, but 26 percent of the homeless population (Busch-Geertsema et al. 2014). A study from the Swedish capital, Stockholm, found that 74 percent of the women who were homeless came from an immigrant background (Nordfeldt 2012).

In Germany, the economic powerhouse of continental Europe and another country with a comprehensive welfare system, homelessness is experienced at higher rates among migrants than among native-born Germans. In a systematic study on the prevalence of homelessness, Busch-Geertsema et al. (2020) found that the largest proportion of the German homeless population were refugees with protection status.

In England, Fitzpatrick, Pawson, et al. (2012) reported that more than half of the population sleeping rough in London were from Central Eastern Europe. They pointed out that many rough sleepers "may be refused asylum seekers or other irregular migrants" (2012: 66). Similarly, the 2014 Busch-Geertsema et al. study found East European migrants to be disproportionately represented in the population of people sleeping rough in Paris, Dublin, and Berlin. More recently, the data from England illustrates that migrants are more likely than the general population to experience the "most severe and immediate" form of homelessness, in addition to couch surfing and statutory homelessness (Fitzpatrick, Watts, et al. 2021: 69). It is not only migrants who experience disproportionate rates of homelessness in England. Drawing on official data reporting the number of people assisted under English homelessness laws, Busch-Geertsema et al. (2014) found that Black British people make up 3.5 percent of the population but 14.5 percent of the homeless population.

Albeit with less precise data, racial minorities and/or people from migrant backgrounds experience disproportionate rates of homelessness in parts of Asia. Okamoto (2007: 527) reported that, in addition to "caste-like groups" such as Eta or Hinin, "minorities such as the Ainu, Okinawans, and Koreans" are discriminated against in Japanese society and lived in accommodation that would meet mainstream definitions of homelessness.

Similarly, there is unequivocal evidence that Indigenous peoples living in settler societies experience astonishingly high rates of homelessness. This evidence comes from the four settler societies considered here (United States, Canada, Australia, and New Zealand). In the United States, Indigenous people, including American Indians, Alaska Natives, Pacific Islanders, and Native Hawaiians, make up

1 percent of the general population, but 5 percent of the homeless population (Henry et al. 2021). In Australia, Indigenous people, including Aboriginal and Torres Strait Island people, make up 3 percent of the general population, but represent 20 percent of the homeless population (Australian Bureau of Statistics 2018). In other words, Australia's Indigenous people are ten times more likely than non-Indigenous people to be homeless (Pawson et al. 2018.)

New Zealand's Indigenous people, the Māori, face similar overrepresentation in the homeless population. In the 2018 Census, Māori people were identified as four times more likely to be homeless than European New Zealanders (Amore et al. 2021). The rate for Pacific people is even greater: they are six times more likely to be homeless than European New Zealanders (Amore et al. 2021).

Although lower than New Zealand, Canada has a higher proportion of Indigenous people compared to the United States and Australia. Indigenous people comprise 5 percent of Canada's population, yet the 2018 point-in-time count found that they represent 30 percent of the homeless population (Employment and Social Development Canada 2019). In parts of Canada, Indigenous people are even more overrepresented. Sandeep Agrawal and Celine Zoe (2021) cite research from the City of Yellowknife in the North Western Territories to suggest that "almost all homeless people" in the area are Indigenous.

Given that Indigenous status, to an extraordinary extent, but also race and migrant status, so strongly predict homelessness, how can these disparities be understood? The answers presented to address this question help us further understand how homelessness as the result of unaffordable housing and poverty interacts with other forces – injustices – in society, making it a relatively predictable form of exclusion. Explanations for the racial disparities in homeless populations raise important points that have context specificities, such as migration legislation or histories of colonization. Following Jeffrey Olivet and colleagues, the explanations all generally concur that the "disproportionate rates of homelessness among people of color can be understood as a symptom of the failure of multiple systems to provide equal opportunity for all racial and ethnic groups" (2021: 96).

The literature about race explaining high rates of homelessness in the United States closely links to the literature that demonstrates high rates of other forms of disadvantage experienced by Black and African American people. Scholars draw broadly on structural racism to explain why Black and African Americans and other racial minorities are overrepresented in the homeless population. Lee et al. (2021: 16) point to structural forces, such as economic downturns, that impact Blacks more severely than they do whites, which in turn can lead to unemployment and produce greater risks of homelessness.

In an empirical analysis of lifetime prevalence of homelessness, Taeho Rhee and Robert Rosenheck seek to address the question of why Black Americans are more likely to be homeless than white Americans. They found that "81.6% of race-based inequality in past homelessness was explained by three main factors, with black adults having: lower incomes, greater incarceration histories since age of 18 and a greater risk of traumatic events" (2021: 161). This research is important for demonstrating how homelessness can be the consequence of cumulative disadvantages in life, such as imprisonment and insecure positions in the labor market. Significantly, the research illustrates that the extent to which people are likely to experience these disadvantages has a racial basis. Being Black and African American equals an increased likelihood of being incarcerated. Having been previously incarcerated equals an increased likelihood of homelessness.

Drawing on qualitative data, Dereck Paul and colleagues (2020) found that structural racism helped explain the life experiences of Black people who became and stayed homeless. Respondents in this study explained that it was engagement with the criminal justice system and incarceration that contributed to later behaviors in adulthood. In concrete terms, histories of offending and incarceration "hampered protection against exits from homelessness by making participants ineligible for subsidized housing" (Paul et al. 2020: 189). Also demonstrating how structural racism can create the conditions for homelessness, Preston and Reina (2021) examined eviction in both market-rate and subsidized housing as a "racialized process." Their analysis of evictions in Philadelphia found that racial discrimination was a likely significant contribution, "as evictions are disproportionately concentrated in communities with higher shares of Black and Latino renters" (2021: 806).

The core themes about structural racism in the United States are also engaged to explain the disproportionate rates in which migrants in Europe and the United Kingdom experience homelessness. This research has been increasingly motivated by the European Union enlargements in 2004 and 2007, which spurred concern about rising levels of migrant homelessness in Europe (Mostowska 2014). This research is significant as there is evidence that migrants who experience homelessness may not also experience the health and social problems that native-born citizens of a country who are homeless experience (Fitzpatrick, Johnsen, et al. 2012). Rather, the racism that some migrant groups face, even when they have full citizenship rights, means they are excluded from employment and are thus at a greater risk of homelessness (Kaur et al. 2021).

Sweden's preeminent homelessness scholar Ingrid Sahlin (2020) adds details to flesh out how racism negatively impacts migrants and produces homelessness. In research from the south of Sweden, Sahlin's qualitative research shows how, despite a notional commitment to provide housing to recently arrived refugees, local municipalities reframe their obligations so that people experiencing homelessness who are locally born get access to housing in front of migrant families. She concludes that it is "nevertheless remarkable that in Malmö, homeless women (born abroad) and their children by now are judged to be less 'deserving' than, e.g., homeless single men (born in Sweden) with substance abuse or mental health problems" (2020: 43).

Formal public policy, particularly welfare, housing, and labor market policy, also plays an important role in contributing to disproportionate rates of homelessness among migrants and ethnic minorities in the United Kingdom and Europe. In self-evident terms, migrants who are undocumented or people seeking asylum who have had their application rejected face barriers accessing the basic resources needed to avoid homelessness (Mayock and Sheridan 2012; Mostowska and Sheridan 2016). In the United Kingdom, this became a particularly pressing social issue during the Covid-19 pandemic, when some migrants in the homeless population were excluded from support on the basis of being categorized as having no recourse to public funds (Fitzpatrick, Watts, et al. 2020).

Mike Allen and colleagues (2020) highlight how people who are undocumented migrants and homeless blur the boundaries between homelessness and immigration policy. Writing from a European context, they argue that if an illegal migrant becomes homeless, they "should be assisted." But if migrants "have no right to live in a country, housing them, particularly in a context where citizens of that country require housing, may not be a politically or socially viable option" (2020: 143).

Homelessness as a Societal Problem

Consistent with Sahlin's analysis, other scholars have illustrated that even when migrants do have rights to access welfare services and housing, and to participate in the labor market, they nonetheless face multiple barriers that place them at risk of homelessness. These barriers include not knowing what services and resources are actually available to them (Mayock and Sheridan 2012), along with a lack of family and social support (Mostowska 2014). For people from a refugee background, past experiences of trauma and persecution contribute, in interaction with housing markets and poverty, to their high rates of homelessness (Samari and Groot 2021).

The evidence that past life traumas can contribute to homelessness – along with structural racism, housing markets, and poverty – is a critical learning from the literature that seeks to explain the societal injustices that contribute to the rates of Indigenous homelessness. The statistics noted above that an Indigenous person is 20 times more likely than a non-Indigenous person to be homeless demonstrate that fundamental societal problems exist.

A dominant theme in the literature explaining homelessness among Indigenous people is the ongoing effects of colonization that continue to systematically disadvantage Indigenous people and benefit colonizers (Peters and Robillard 2009). Referring to Indigenous overrepresentation in the homeless population, Christensen (2016) presents an analysis that urges us to examine hundreds of years of occupation and forced removal from lands to grasp the disparities that result in homelessness among Indigenous people today: "Indigenous homelessness cannot be decontextualized from the uneven economic and community development, institutionalization, landlessness, and cultural genocide experienced in different degrees and scales across Canada, Australia, and New Zealand" (2016: 3). Agrawal and Zoe (2021) offer a similar account of how the ongoing impacts of colonization interact with past and present housing policies, welfare policy, and at times remoteness, to explain the overrepresentation of Indigenous people in Canada's homeless population.

Concluding remarks

The chapter opened by introducing the idea that some people see homelessness as a choice of homeless people, albeit an indirect one, arrived at as a result of using illicit substances, refusing to engage in the labor market, or, more broadly, failing to comply with the conditions and expectations of society. Although the notion of choosing homelessness can hold resonance for some people who are homeless, as it enables them to assert agency and avoid being seen as a victim (Parsell and Parsell 2012), empirical research has largely rejected the proposition. Instead, it demonstrates that it is housing markets, poverty levels, and specific state interventions that determine whether a person becomes homeless or not.

Reflecting on this research, we are able to reframe the idea that homelessness is a choice; we propose, instead, that it is the choice of society. The compelling evidence considered in this chapter on the predictable nature of homelessness lends some credibility to the idea that societies do indeed choose for people to be homeless. This is done, for example, through policies that ensure that a not insignificant proportion of the population is excluded from affordable housing. The link between unaffordable housing and homelessness is so predictable that Beck and Twiss concluded there is a "normalization of homelessness in the United States – that is, [a] widespread acceptance of homelessness as an ordinary feature of our society" (2018: 2). Societies foster the conditions that indicate that they are choosing homelessness through the penalties that people face for experiencing predictable events – events, moreover, that are out of the control of the people who end up homeless. We saw this in particular with women and children who are penalized through patriarchal societies that make them victims of domestic violence and then inflict the compounding penalty of homelessness on them when they flee violence.

From the mounting international evidence demonstrating how homelessness is racialized, it is hard to draw any conclusion other than that society has been deliberately organized in a way to systematically disadvantage racial minorities. This is nothing new, yet the idea persists. Both the persistence and the predictability of race as a cause of homelessness suggest that societies choose for certain racial groups to be homeless.

Our choice to arrange society in such a way that homelessness is predictable of course matters most for people who are themselves homeless. We now turn to the evidence, both qualitative and quantitative, that shows what being homeless means from the perspective of people who bear the brunt of the societal choices that make homelessness a predictable, racialized, and patterned phenomena.

3
Homelessness as the Experience of Violence

Researcher: *Do you feel safe living on the streets?*
Person sleeping rough: *Yeah no worries. It's all good.*
Support worker: *What about when you were shot?*
Person sleeping rough: *Oh yeah, that was bad.*
Researcher: *You were shot?*
Person sleeping rough: *Yeah. Spent six months in hospital. They got the guy that did it. He got five years [jail sentence].*
Researcher: *So is it safe on the streets?*
Person sleeping rough: *I just keep away from everyone. Like here.*

The take-home point from the previous chapter is that homelessness is a result of societal conditions, in particular the availability, or lack, of affordable housing. To understand this societal problem fully, we must engage with the experiences of those whom society excludes from housing. The value, and the urgency, of the transformation required to end and prevent homelessness, detailed in Chapter 8, is only meaningful because of the realities of those people who experience it.

Those who experience homelessness frequently also experience an ever-present fear of physical or sexual violence. Homelessness means living in the shadow of danger. As illustrated in the conversation cited above, which I had in 2022 with a person sleeping rough in Australia, people living on the streets see violence as normal – unremarkable – yet they engage in a range of strategies to keep safe, such as staying away from others. Sometimes these strategies work, sometimes they do not. People sometimes protect themselves by committing violent acts themselves.

58 Homelessness as the Experience of Violence

Employing international evidence, both quantitative and qualitative, in this chapter we illuminate how the violence of homelessness can be understood as living in environments where people have little control. The violence of homelessness serves to deepen the meaning of home as a place of sanctuary, control, and safety. Violence is a reality for many people who are homeless, and this chapter demonstrates the way in which it is often also gendered in disturbing ways.

Violence and crime among homeless populations

> I had all my money stolen along with my spare clothes, shoes the lot. I wasn't streetwise. I kept myself to myself after that. I kept myself safe, I just told everyone I'd been inside for attempted murder and no one came near me. (Quoted in Ravenhill 2008: 166)

People who are homeless generally observe violence among others and experience it themselves at significantly higher rates than the general population: this conclusion is typically based on self-reported data. In an early US study of people who were homeless, Kevin Fitzpatrick et al. (1999) found that 22 percent of those surveyed reported having been robbed in the previous six months, and 14 percent had been assaulted, including attacks by knives and guns. They concluded that "these rates of victimization are many times higher than those of the general population" (1999: 443).

This early analysis has been supported in subsequent research from both within and beyond the United States. In a nationwide study also from the United States, Barrett Lee and Christopher Schreck (2005) report statistics showing that personal and property crime had decreased significantly among the general public. This, they point out, stands in stark contrast to the experiences of people who are homeless, who experience being robbed and violently assaulted at much higher rates than the non-homeless population. They found that 54 percent of people experiencing homelessness had been targeted while living on the streets; furthermore, 21.3 percent had been physically attacked and 49.5 percent had had property stolen. Molly Meinbresse and colleagues (2014), in a US survey conducted among 516 people with experiences of homelessness, found that 62 percent had witnessed a violent attack on another person who was homeless, and nearly half (49 percent) reported that they themselves had been victims of violent attacks while homeless.

Fran Calvo et al. (2022) conducted a study with people who were homeless in Spain. Of the 504 people surveyed, 76.2 percent reported having been a victim of violence in the past 12 months. Elise Riley and collaborators (2020) conducted a study of 300 people who were homeless in San Francisco and found that 87 percent had experienced psychological violence, 48 percent had experienced physical violence without a weapon, and 18 percent had experienced physical violence involving a weapon. They compared the results from their homeless sample to the general US population. The comparison is astounding. Namely, the "rate of gun-involved physical violence among study participants experiencing homelessness was 1800 times higher than the general population" (2020: 81).

Drawing on a survey conducted with 1,720 people who were homeless in South Korea – that is, approximately 17.2 percent of the country's overall homeless population – Gum-Ryeong Park and colleagues (2022) identified a similar pattern of high rates of violence. During people's period of homelessness, they found that 15 percent had been victims of crime, including psychological violence, sexual violence, and robbery. Whitbeck and collaborators (2001) analyzed data from young people in the United States who were homeless after running away from, or being thrown out of, home. They report extremely high rates of violence, including 42 percent who had been robbed, 38 percent beaten up, and 41 percent threatened with a weapon; 20 percent had actually been assaulted with a weapon.

From a survey with 458 people who had lived on the streets in England and Wales, Ben Sanders and Francesca Albanese (2016) found disturbing cases of abuse and crime. Not only had 45 percent been intimidated or threatened with violence or force, but 31 percent had had things thrown at them and 30 percent had been deliberately hit, kicked, or experienced some other form of violence. In addition, 6 percent reported being sexually assaulted in the 12 months prior to the survey when living on the streets.

Joshua Ellsworth (2019: 108) pooled quantitative findings from a review of the literature pertaining to the link between homelessness and violence. Referring to seven studies, he found that in the previous 12 months or less, slightly fewer than 29 percent of those surveyed had experienced a physical attack, and 46 percent had been victims of theft. Ellsworth was conscious of the methodological problems comparing the rates of physical attacks and thefts between the homeless population and non-homeless population,

60 Homelessness as the Experience of Violence

but nevertheless concluded from the limited available data that "the results suggest a startling disparity in reported incidence of victimization in comparison with the sheltered general public" (2019: 108). He concludes that, compared to the general population, people who are living on the streets are threatened with violence approximately 11 times more frequently; they are 20 times more likely to be the victims of theft (2019: 112).

Understanding, experiencing, and responding to violence

As Pamela Fischer (1992) put it, to be homeless is to endure the all-pervasive threat of violence. This is still very much the case today. A body of empirical research, both quantitative and qualitative, has sought to make sense of this violence.

How can the disproportionate rates be understood?

An immediate question we are compelled to engage with when we see the consistently high rates of violence and crime among homeless populations – consistent across time and country – is "What can we understand from these findings?" The key to this is to consider the environment that people who are homeless are forced to live in. This environmental focus downplays the emphasis that individualizes the problem of homeless people as violent and criminal individuals. Fischer's early analysis is telling: people who are homeless are compelled to inhabit environments where criminal activity is prevalent.

It is mainly in the public realm, including streets, alleyways, and parks, where people who are homeless report being victimized (Meinbresse et al. 2014). By virtue of their homelessness, people have little choice but to be in places where crime is likely. Even though the public realm is in theory accessible to everyone, the reality is different. As we will demonstrate in Chapter 6, through a range of policing and even design features, people who are homeless are forced from prime public spots and moved into marginal places. David Snow and Michael Mulcahy (2001) describe such places as being characterized by a lack of economic value to business; they are thus abandoned and largely ignored. Given the relative absence of police and social controls in these areas, they are spaces where avoiding crime is difficult.

Homelessness as the Experience of Violence 61

Ellsworth (2019) draws on the lifestyle exposure framework to aid our understanding of the prevalence of violence and crime in the lives of people who are homeless. The lifestyle exposure framework is a criminological theory that focuses squarely on the dangerous places in which people experiencing homelessness are forced to reside, where opportunities for violent crime are increased; following Snow and Mulcahy, we might refer to such locations as marginal spaces. The framework provides the conceptual scaffolding for considering how people who are homeless, including those living in shelters or on the streets, are constrained in their capacity to avoid contact with potential offenders (Ellsworth 2019).

Lee and Schreck (2005) similarly cite the marginality of people who are homeless to explain their high rates of victimization. As a marginalized population, which they explain is an active state of *being* marginalized through society not providing access to affordable housing, Lee and Schreck emphasize the way in which homelessness subverts an individual's capacity to achieve security. People experiencing homelessness are "without the protection from crime offered by a dwelling unit or residential neighborhood. The homeless-domiciled gap in victimization prevalence can be readily understood in terms of this spatial dimension of marginality" (2005: 1056).

The literature converges on the acknowledgment that the high rates of violence and crime experienced by people who are homeless can be explained by the environments in which they reside and interact. Crime is prevalent in these spaces, and, by virtue of being homeless, people have limited opportunities to avoid them. Certain individual characteristics and behaviors, which can be concealed in a home environment, contribute to the risk of incidents of victimization of people who are homeless. For instance, people in the homeless population who have a mental illness are more likely than those who are homeless without a mental illness to be a victim of crime (Ellsworth 2019). Further, those whose homelessness is chronic, or who are of advanced age, are at an even more heightened risk of experiencing violence on the streets (Meinbresse et al. 2014).

Rozelen Beck and colleagues (2022) demonstrated that the risk of violence among people who are homelessness is increased when methamphetamines are consumed. They concluded that there is limited evidence for the proposition that people experiencing homelessness who use methamphetamines are themselves likely to perpetrate violence: amphetamine use is associated with "agitation,

Homelessness as the Experience of Violence

hostility and aggression that may be perceived as, but not necessarily result in violence" (2022: 13). Notwithstanding this conclusion, there is some evidence, including from ethnographic research that we consider below, that illicit substance and alcohol use while homeless creates the conditions for being both a victim and a perpetrator of violence. Ellsworth found that "substance abuse may contribute to the escalation of interpersonal disputes from purely verbal affairs into physically violent confrontations" (2019: 100). Alcohol and illicit substance use play a role, but it is the day-to-day reality of homelessness – the lack of housing – that leads people who are homeless to become intoxicated in environments where they are subject to being the victims of opportunistic crime, including violent assaults. The state of homelessness may explain why people are in environments where violence is likely, but it tells us little about how people experience the violence, as both victim and perpetrator.

Violence experienced by people who are homeless, as victim and as perpetrator

> I take a weapon ... then I can't be forced into anything and the cunt's got to seriously think whether he wants to cut me up because he's going to cop the same thing I am. (Quoted in Heerde and Pallotta-Chiarolli 2020: 415)

People who are homeless typically see violence as an inevitability of the life they are compelled to confront. Gwendolyn Dordick's ethnographic study of homelessness in New York is telling. Referring to a large homeless shelter, she said that residents spoke of unconfirmed murders at the shelter as "common occurrences," whereas "less severe violence and robbery are virtually daily occurrences" (1997: 110). The violence occurred among residents living in the shelter, where "residents fear not only one another but also the security guards and institutional aids." As a female ethnographic researcher, Dordick provides disturbing accounts of the abuse she herself was subject to from the shelter staff. When she arrived at the shelter to conduct fieldwork each day, the security guards and institutional aids would line the stairwell making her push past them. They whistled and sometimes barked out at her. They made sexually explicit advances. When she assertively complained, she "was warned that people often had 'accidents,' such as falling down a flight of stairs or finding themselves in the middle of an unexpected brawl between residents" (1997: 111). Reflecting on the abuse she received and the violence experienced by people staying at the shelter, and in a finding consistent with Ellen Baxter and Kim Hopper's (1981) earlier observations from New York City, Dordick reports that the threat of violence and robbery is so severe in some homeless shelters that people avoid them, sometimes preferring to live on the streets. In England, Jon May and colleagues identified dangerous conditions in hostels, noting that when the only option was "traditional dormitory-style night shelter, the majority of women preferred to sleep rough" (2007: 136). As we will see, the experience of violence in homeless shelters continues to be a common theme in the literature.

Beth Watts and Janice Blenkinsopp (2022) found that the communal nature of hostel accommodation meant that some residents felt they had limited capacity and control to protect themselves from other residents. They present the account of one shelter resident from Scotland "who feared for his safety given high levels of intravenous drug use in a conflict-ridden hostel environment." As he put it: "Cunts wanted to put needles in my neck, man" (2022: 104). This fear of other hostel residents was a common theme. Another hostel resident, from Edinburgh, remarked: "I've had some scary experiences in some of these places ... Quite shocking ... Violent behaviour, self-harming. I've seen someone who self-harmed themselves really badly. In the middle of the night I was woken up to the ambulance service" (2022: 106).

Paul Cloke and colleagues (2010) carried out ethnographic research at British hostels and concluded that they were dangerous, and that residents and staff had always to be "alert to the threat of attack," stating "the need to constantly and carefully monitor their own and other people's behaviour in order simply to make it safely through the day" (2010: 169). Even when violence is not immediately present, Lynne McMordie (2021: 389) found, quoting a resident of a hostel in Belfast in Northern Ireland, "you're always on edge, you're always, constantly, on guard." However, avoiding hostel accommodation to sleep rough is not a solution to the threat of violence for many.

Although people describe living in hostels as anxiety-provoking because of the threat of harm, exploitation, and victimization (McMordie 2021: 386), many are willing to stay in hostel accommodation in order to avoid sleeping rough. McMordie quotes a resident of a hostel who had a vested interest in accessing hostel

64   Homelessness as the Experience of Violence

accommodation, despite the risks it posed, because rough sleeping meant being victimized: "I got a … bad, bad, kicking just for no reason, bottles broke on my head" (2021: 385–6)

The exposure to violence that characterizes life on the streets occurs in multiple settings. Cloke et al. (2010) illustrate how violence is provoked over territory and access to spaces to beg. When someone living on the street fails to respect another person's prime begging position, violence is the response. One male living in a hostel, but who begs on the streets of Britain, remarked: "Well if you do it [beg] prolonged in a month and it's classed as your pitch, any newcomer that comes to town that tries to take it off you, you just batter the shit out of 'em" (2010: 80–1).

Violence among people who are homeless does not occur simply in competitive situations. Megan Ravenhill's (2008) ethnographic research from England is telling. She found significant violence among people who were homeless who had formed tight-knit groups. Ravenhill concludes that living on the streets without connections is dangerous, but forming close connections – or the homeless culture, as she referred to it – could be even more dangerous. She presents observations from her research diary that illustrates the normalization of violence among members of a squat: "Last night Jim came in pissed off his head. Packer sat on Jim's box and broke it. Jim lost it. He went for him. I mean he really went for him. They were rolling round everywhere, punching each other. They broke nearly all the furniture we had. But that's how it is" (2008: 166–7). My study of people sleeping rough in Australia similarly identified that they lived in fear of other people who were homeless perpetrating violence against them. A male living in public places highlights the violence and gives a hint as to how he seeks some protection: "Like on the street, you don't camp on your own, 'cause you could get robbed, mugged, raped. You know, get your guts kicked out of you" (Parsell 2012: 165).

From the perspective of the perpetrator of violence, Teresa Gowan cites a man who was homeless as being "a menace to other homeless people." She says that this man "now raised the cash for his crack addiction by robbing weaker men and women in the shelter and out on the streets" (2010: 198). The extreme violence experienced by people who are homeless – including those living on the streets, in squats, and hostel accommodation – underlines how much of the violence *experienced* by people who are homeless is also *perpetrated*

Homelessness as the Experience of Violence 65

by people who are homeless. In some instances, as we saw above, this assumes the form of threatening or victimizing others who are homeless. This helps explain why older people who are homeless are at greater risk of being victimized than younger adults. In addition to this, we can begin to more fully understand the experience of violence among those who are homeless when we recognize that some of them are often both victims and perpetrators of violence.

Reflecting on survey data from the United States, Lee and Schreck (2005) warn us against too neatly distinguishing between victims and perpetrators of crime and violence among people who are homeless. Having property stolen may be a result of the thief having had property stolen in the first place; the difference between the thief and the victim may be a matter of timing. Lee and Shreck also suggest that people "who report difficulty controlling their violent behavior are significantly more likely to have been beaten themselves" (2005: 1076).

Jessica Heerde and Maria Pallotta-Chiarolli's (2020) Australian study of young people living on the streets provides troubling accounts of people's firsthand experiences that support Lee and Schreck's assertions. People were both victims and perpetrators: they adopt the latter role to try, as best they can, to avoid taking on the former role. Extreme violence pervades the lives of young people sleeping rough. So commonplace was the violence, Heerde and Pallotta-Chiarolli argue, that people experience it as normal behavior; moreover, they feel emotionally detached from it. On the other hand, people living on the streets do not have a disregard for the welfare of others or for social norms. Violence is required to survive, which includes the need to carry concealed weapons. But the sense of normal was discussed with a sense of unease. One of Heerde and Pallotta-Chiarolli's participants said: "If someone hits me then I'll hit them, but they'll keep hitting me, so I'll keep hitting them back" (2020: 414). Violence was seen as the appropriate thing to do to stay alive, given the circumstances of their lives. A young female who lived on the streets described violence thus: "I wasn't like I'm going to beat this person until they can't breathe, I was like I'm going to beat this person until they can't beat me anymore...they're worried about their own safety now more than beating me" (2020: 414). Judging from Heerde and Pallotta-Chiarolli's study, there can be no doubt that people on the streets perpetrate significance violence, but there can equally be no doubt

66   Homelessness as the Experience of Violence

that they are also victims of significant violence. One female hints at the violent context and her past when she finishes her point with the haunting reference to *again*: "I'd rather injure somebody else than get injured or hurt or have somebody do something awful to me again" (2020: 415)

Contemporary research sheds light on the limitations of the perpetrator/victim binary, but, more significantly, it provides firsthand accounts of how experiences of violence must be understood in the context of people's deprivation and circumstances. People feel compelled to perpetrate violence as the only reasonable and accessible way of protecting themselves. As well as evidence that violence takes place between people who are homeless, we know that these people are also subject to being threatened by the non-homeless public. Such victimization is often referred to as hate crime. In the United States, the National Coalition for the Homeless (2009) published a report that is the continuation of analysis and dissemination that began in 1999 and seeks to raise awareness about, and change, the impoverished living conditions that results in people who are homeless being subject to vicious attacks from the public. In the 20 years between 1999 and 2019, it was estimated that some 1,852 acts of violence were committed against people who were homeless, with "at least 515 homeless individuals losing their lives in the brutal attacks", including 14 people in 2019 (National Coalition for the Homeless 2020). The frightening loss of life that is documented is perhaps made even more distressing when we understand that many of the hate crimes go unreported, in part because of the way homeless people are portrayed as outside societal norms (which we discuss in Chapter 5). One of the perpetrators of a hate crime was cited as justifying their actions as, "it was just a vagrant" (National Coalition for the Homeless 2009: 10).

Hate crimes are not unique to the United States. Sanders and Albanese's study from England and Wales found strikingly similar forms of violence that were perpetrated by the general public toward people who were homeless simply because of their homeless status. They present the account of a male living on the streets who recalled: "It was some guy. He said, 'Are you homeless?' I said, 'Yeah,' and he just kicked me in the head. I was sat on the floor reading my book" (2016: 11). Another person sleeping rough described a sustained period of victimization from members of the public:

The National Coalition for the Homeless (2020) documentation of the violence perpetrated on people who are homeless in the United States is brutal yet fundamentally important. It is difficult reading. The report focuses on violent crimes committed on people who are homeless by perpetrators who are not homeless. Indeed, the violence is often inflicted on people *because* they are homeless. The National Coalition for the Homeless (2020) says that violence is committed because the perpetrators of crime express biases toward people who are homeless and because people who are homeless are accessible to the offender.

The litany of violence documented includes physical assaults, being burnt with acid, stabbings, and shootings. Even more disturbingly than the presence of these hate crimes, some of the violence is committed toward people who are homeless on the basis of brutal dehumanization. The report outlines the case of two teenagers leaving a party to "kill a homeless man for sport" (2020: 10). The offenders of a violent murder even brag about having killed a "hobo."

The dehumanizing of people who are homeless that is evidenced through murder being rationalized as a sport is also evident in less lethal but also deplorable action. In 2018 the media reported with disgust the brutality inflicted upon a Polish man who was homeless in Spain. The individual was paid €100 to get the name of a soon-to-be groom tattooed on his forehead as part of a prank allegedly by a group of British men participating in a stag party. In 2022, with funding from a local homeless charity, the individual underwent a procedure to have the tattoo removed (Finch 2022).

These actions cannot be understood without also recognizing how people who are homeless are portrayed as not only outside societal norms, but also portrayed as sub-human. This positioning of people who are homeless as "others" underpins the legislative and practice responses that marginalize and even criminalize people who are homeless in public spaces. In Chapter 6 we show the presence, for example, of draconian legislation that criminalizes homelessness in California. It is not coincidental that the majority of the hate crimes committed against people who are homeless in the United States, some 23 percent of all documented incidences nationally in 2018–19, occurred in the state of California. There are disturbing links between the othering of people who are homeless, legislation that seeks to remove them from public space, and brutal violence perpetrated against them.

The National Coalition for the Homeless documents the hate crimes perpetrated against people who are homeless for the primary purpose of bringing about societal change to end the violence. It is hoped that being confronted with people's experiences of violence will motivate the public to demand change to end it. Consistent with the core argument of this chapter, and indeed the book, the National Coalition for the Homeless sees housing as the ultimate means to end the violence endured by people who are homeless; with a home of one's own, people have the means to protect themselves from unknown offenders. In addition, to lessen the likelihood of people who are homeless experiencing violence, they advocate a reversal of laws that push people who are homeless out of public spaces. They likewise argue for the inclusion of homelessness as a status in hate crime legislation. Importantly, the National Coalition for the Homeless understands that the violence perpetrated toward people who are homeless, because of their homelessness, will not be addressed by policy and legislation change alone. To end this form of violence, people who are homeless must be seen as being beyond their state of deprivation, and as individuals who are owed the same rights and respect that we all deserve because of our shared humanity.

Oh I was beaten up once, that was a couple of weeks ago, by the same people I think that burnt my bedding up. I was in my sleeping bag because it comes around up over the shoulders, do you know what I mean? And three of them, and I was sleeping, they came over and started jumping on me, kicking me like. But I managed to get out, but to be honest, I don't know how I didn't have no marks or bruises, but I never had nothing. (2016: 15)

The nature of the violence reported is disturbing. In 2013, in Australia's third most populous city, a 51-year-old man who was

Homelessness as the Experience of Violence   69

sleeping rough was shot in the stomach with an arrow by a random member of the public as he slept in a public space (Tapim 2013). The victim had surgery to remove the arrow and survived; his comments to me open this chapter. Raegan Joern (2009) reports a case from Washington, DC, where a member of the public burnt to death a person who was homeless in a wheelchair for no other reason than because he was homeless. Such vicious crimes, and the fact that people who are homeless have little capacity to avoid victimization, lead Joern, a legal scholar, to conclude that homeless status must be added as a state-protected condition under hate crime statutes.

The calls for legislation to protect people who are homeless from violence are important, but, more profoundly, we must accept that housing is the ideal means of protection. Moreover, when we examine the experience of homelessness closely, we soon learn that the risks and prevalence of violence are not evenly distributed across genders.

Gender disparities in sexual violence

The portrait of homelessness as violent has so far been presented as gender-neutral. In reality, the violence that characterizes homelessness is anything but gender-blind. In the same way that patriarchal norms explain the significant numbers of women who enter homelessness as a result of domestic and family violence, our patriarchal society also means that women who are homeless face particular risks of physical and sexual violence.

A granular look at the data, including the data presented at the beginning of this chapter, offers some evidence of the gendered nature of violence. The study from Spain cited above (Calvo et al. 2022) illustrates the gendered dimension to victimization among the homeless. In their study of 504 people who were homeless, including 408 males and 96 females, Calvo and colleagues found that 100 percent of the females had been victims of some type of violence in the previous 12 months, while 70.6 percent of males reported likewise. Every single woman who was homeless had experienced victimization. Referring to physical violence, research from people living on the streets in England and Wales identified that 36 percent of females but only 29 percent of males reported being deliberately hit or kicked in the previous 12 months (Sanders and Albanese 2016).

70   Homelessness as the Experience of Violence

Gender disparities in sexual violence are a common yet disturbing theme in the literature. Calvo and colleagues (2022) found profound gender disparities, with 62.5 percent of females and 5.9 percent of males reporting sexual violence in the previous 12 months. They ran a regression analysis and concluded that "being a woman is an independent risk factor for suffering violence among" people who are homeless (2022: 10). Whitbeck et al. (2001) found that 25 percent of females who were homeless reported having been "forced to do sexual things," while 9.2 percent of males reported the same. In addition, 23 percent of females had been sexually assaulted or raped since being homeless, whereas 7.2 percent of males reported being sexually assaulted or raped (2001: 1188). The Korean study referred to above did not report statistical differences, but they concluded that "homeless females were likely to be victims of sexual/physical violence ... while homeless males tended to be targets of financial crime" (Park et al. 2022: 69).

Lee and Schreck (2005: 1067) found that slightly fewer than one in eight females who were homeless reported being raped; they also concluded that the probability of experiencing rape is 87 percent lower for males compared to females. Meinbresse and colleagues (2014) identified similar rates of violence among females and males who were homeless; they found that females are nearly 90 times more likely than males to experience rape while homeless.

Deeper analysis of the statistical data sheds light on the way that women who are homeless face greater risks of sexual violence, including rape, not only compared to males who are homeless, but also other females in the general population more broadly. There are multiple arguments for providing people who are homeless with housing, which we will investigate in Chapter 8. The present discussion suggests that it is hard to identify a more compelling reason to end homelessness than the evidence that demonstrates that a woman who is homeless is more likely to be raped than a woman who is housed.

Riley and colleagues (2020) show that 1.6 percent of women in the United States reported sexual assault in the previous 12 months, as opposed to 6.1 percent of their sample of homeless women. They concluded that the experience of sexual violence for women who were homeless was 44 times higher than for the general adult population in the United States.

We noted above that people who are homeless experience dispro-portionate rates of victimization because they are compelled to

Homelessness as the Experience of Violence

inhabit dangerous places. The reality of this is nowhere more stark than in instances of women's experiences of sexual violence, including rape. Whereas 21 percent of sexual assaults and rapes experienced by women in the United States (2009 data) were perpetrated by a stranger, Meinbresse and collaborators (2014) found that the comparable figure among women who were homeless was around 78 percent. They concluded: "This difference could be explained by the fact that women who are homeless are unsheltered and lacking a private residence to protect them from perpetrators who otherwise would not have access to them" (2014: 131.) Being excluded from housing means a significant risk of being exposed to sexual offenders. Even though women face violence in their homes, that risk is greater when they are homeless. Consistent with the literature on the dangers of staying in hostel accommodation, Rionach Casey and colleagues (2008) concluded that some women see hostels as male-dominated; a number of them said they had been raped in night shelters. Jana Jasinski and colleagues (2010) conducted a study of more than 700 women who slept rough on the streets of Florida. The fear of rape was a reality for the majority of these women, who feared walking the streets, especially at night. One woman, who had lived on the streets for a number of years, reflected:

> Being a homeless woman that's on the street, that's dangerous. You have homeless men, and it's co-ed when you're sleeping on the street. It's co-ed and some of them approach women and want women to give them favors sexually. Too, sometimes, they get bold enough, they try to rape the women and a lot of homeless women do be raped, raped and murdered. They will murder them in alleyways and you will find homeless women in the dumpster. Someone slit her throat. (2010: 82)

The sheer brutality of sexual violence is a recurring theme across the research. This dehumanizing reality was described by a woman from England who had been homeless for a long time: "I was raped the day I arrived [at the hostel]; in a graveyard. It was another tramp who'd not leave me alone. He was very violent and threatened me with a dog-chain and scissors" (quoted in Ravenhill 2008: 132).

The research illustrating the risks and realities of sexual assault and rape as described here helps us understand some of the ways in which homelessness is gendered; it has been pivotal in disrupting the assumption that homelessness is a problem experienced principally by men (Baptista 2010; Casey et al. 2008; Reeve 2018). Both the insights from the gender analysis of the violence inherent in women's realities of homelessness and the broader literature that demonstrates homelessness as victimization demonstrate the importance of a home and of what life is like when home is absent. The violence of homelessness is characterized cogently by the lifestyle theory and the routine activity theory. Maria Antunes and Eileen Ahlin (2017) locate these theoretical perspectives within an ecological framework to bring attention to the way that the likelihood of experiencing victimization is influenced by the activities that one engages in throughout the day. As we have seen, people who are homeless conduct their day-to-day lives both in public and in the confines of hostel accommodation. They have few alternatives. People who are homeless are often forced into marginal spaces, such as alleyways, abandoned parts of the city, or other areas of the public realm that are out of view. Combined with individual characteristics such as gender, old age, frailty (Ellsworth 2019; Lee and Schreck 2005) and a lack of protection, people become targets of victimization from motivated offenders (Antunes and Ahlin 2017) who are both on the streets and in hostel accommodation.

The lifestyle theory explains the risk of victimization by highlighting activities that are conducted outside the home: "Individuals who spend more time away from home should have higher risks of victimization because of their greater suitability as a target" (Miethe et al. 1987). Although the term lifestyle fits awkwardly with homelessness and the literature on lifestyle theory focuses on people who have a home and conduct activities outside it, the framework powerfully demonstrates what it is about homelessness that works to subvert one's capacity to keep safe.

To be without a home is to have limited capacity to exert control over one's own life, especially control over who to engage with or to distance oneself from. This is illustrated by Dordick (1997), who found that the shelter rule of having beds separated by three feet was at times ignored; instead, people were sleeping in beds that had little or no space between them. This is a jarring example that illustrates clearly how the violence of homelessness is driven by people living in environments that they cannot control and where their deprivation has the consequence of forcing interactions with others who are deprived of a space of their own. The empirical research substantiates this.

Homelessness as the Experience of Violence 73

When people who are homeless access secure and affordable housing, their rates of both perpetrating and being victims of crime reduce (Ellsworth 2021). Drawing on government official records pertaining to 37 people, I analyzed, with colleagues, violent crime data over a two-year period: in the first year of research people were homeless, and in the second year they resided in permanent housing (Parsell et al. 2017). In the second year, occurrences of criminal offenses were 24 as opposed to 50 in the first year, occurrences as a victim of crime were 11 as opposed to 24, and nights spent in police custody were 27 as opposed to 45. Neither offending programs nor even empowerment interventions are needed to reduce criminal and violent behavior: it is the provision of housing that reduces crime and violence.

In this way we can see how one core component of the ideal meaning of home is that it is a place of security (Despres 1991; Dupuis and Thorns 1996). In reality of course, the home environment is often not a place of safety; this is especially the case for women and girls (Mallett 2004; Peled and Muzicant 2008; Wardhaugh 1999). This was made clear in the previous chapter. Nevertheless, home can and often does provide a protective barrier against the outside world. When people who are homeless talk about an imagined future home, they construct it as a place of safety and security (Parsell 2012; Peled and Muzicant 2008) even if they are unsure whether they will ever achieve it (Tomas and Dittmar 1995).

Although we should be skeptical about romanticizing home as a place of unambiguous safety for all, the violence of homelessness is definitely unambiguous. People who are homeless yearn for the safety of home because the violence of homelessness is life-threatening. Data from the United States concerning hate crime and violence leading to death leaves little doubt about this (National Coalition for the Homeless 2009). In addition to physical injuries, the research on homelessness as victimization is littered with accounts of harms such as post-traumatic stress disorder (Beijer et al. 2018), medical intervention (Heerde and Pallotta-Chiarolli 2020), and even traumatic brain injuries from physical violence (Mejia-Lancheros et al. 2020).

In my Australian study of surveillance in permanent supportive housing for people who exited homelessness, I expected residents to complain about the CCTV and gazing eyes of the concierge (Parsell 2016). However, I found that people with experiences of homelessness not only tolerated but also appreciated the surveillance.

Compared to their past homelessness, surveillance was the only time they could remember feeling safe. One woman who had experienced homelessness and violence throughout her life described her situation in supportive housing as providing "somewhere safe and secure where I could go and I had control over who was going to walk to my door and who wasn't" (2016: 3198). The words "who wasn't" are indicative of homelessness as violent because people have limited control over where they are and, in turn, who they are with. Homelessness undermines control, but it does not completely eliminate it, as the remainder of this chapter will show.

How do people respond to violence?

Being without a home does mean a life of violence for many, but people experiencing homelessness are not passive victims. We saw some evidence of this above in the blurred boundaries between perpetrator and victim; some people who are homeless perpetrate violence as a means of self-protection (Heerde and Pallotta-Chiarolli 2020). Additionally, people who are homeless adopt a range of other protective mechanisms to try and keep themselves safe when they are confronted with the reality that they are excluded from housing. Here we will show the agency that people exert to try and protect themselves, even though the protective strategies are far from ideal at achieving the desired outcome.

We noted above theoretical perspectives that explain people's risk of victimization by virtue of the places they inhabit and the opportunities that these places create in terms of exposure of vulnerability, the presence of a willing offender, and the lack of a guardian as a means of protection. Simply put, being homeless means a constrained capacity to avoid dangerous places and to protect oneself within them. Despite these constraints, there is evidence that people do what they can to avoid dangerous places.

Day centers are places that provide a range of immediate resources to people who are homeless – not only food, but also an environment that is intended to be a respite from the streets. They often have a low entry threshold, meaning that they are open to anyone, regardless of addiction, illness, or migration status. Further, people are not required to comply with conditions. Rather than a respite from the streets, many people who are homeless avoid day centers for fear of assault and harassment (Cloke et al. 2010). From their research in Bristol, England, May et al. found that, "for many, day centres especially represented a space of fear rather than care. The markedly volatile atmosphere to be found in both day centres and hostels led many women to avoid them altogether" (2007: 136). Avoidance of homelessness services or hostels as a protective strategy has been noted by several scholars in the field (Evans and Forsyth 2004). Sanders and Albanese (2016: 16), for example, found that when people sleeping rough were asked what made them feel safe, responses included: "I sleep in the buses, mainly because I can't see sleeping in the street as ... safe, it's not safe because I have been harassed, I have been kicked." Another person living on the streets said that they kept safe by avoiding other rough sleepers, particularly keeping away from people consuming alcohol and illicit substances. Avoidance and keeping to oneself can help to promote safety, but it can also have a downside. Referring to avoiding others on the streets, the same person remarked: "So it doesn't really do me any good mentally because I'm on my own, but I do find it's safer" (Sanders and Albanese 2016: 16).

As well as being experienced as isolating and lonely, avoiding other people who are homeless can be difficult to achieve. It is important to consider here the way that forcibly removing people who are homeless may have the consequence of subverting their capacity to avoid others who are homeless. The capacity of people who are homeless to avoid others who are homeless relies upon their capacity to control their movements and occupation of space. There are several negative consequences that flow from forcibly removing people from certain prime public places, which we will discuss in Chapter 6. For instance, sleeping on public transport to avoid others who are homeless would not be possible under legislation such as that proposed in New York City in 2022, which would ban people experiencing homelessness from the subway system (Newman et al. 2022). This proposed legislation, along with several other proposals considered in Chapter 6, is designed to force people into homeless accommodation – accommodation that, as we have seen, is widely experienced as dangerous.

The practical challenges of avoiding others who, like them, are homeless have prompted people to employ a range of creative agentic survival strategies that seek to downplay their homelessness. These strategies have a strong gender dimension. Based on research from San

76 Homelessness as the Experience of Violence

Francisco, Vancouver, and Edinburgh, Laura Huey and Eric Berndt (2008) report, consistent with the literature above, that women who were homeless felt vulnerable on the streets after experiencing firsthand victimization. Nevertheless, some women on the streets protected themselves by performing "a set of behaviours socially constructed as 'masculine', including aggressiveness, mental and physical toughness, emotionlessness and fearlessness" (2008: 188). Women explained to Huey and Berndt that they deliberately avoided clothing that would be considered overtly feminine, "in favour of masculinized garb, including baggy T-shirts, jeans." They found that women on the streets expressed these displays of masculine toughness to avoid victimization, even though, as one woman said, "I am not really that tough, really, but just so the image like it scares people off and that seems to work" (2008: 188). In addition to downplaying their femininity and performing masculine behaviors, some women sought to protect themselves while homeless by passing themselves off as lesbian when approached by men. By asserting a lesbian identity, they were trying to politely reject male advances in a way that enabled the male to save face (Huey and Berndt 2008).

The Huey and Berndt analysis provides a deep empirical insight into the devices employed by women that enable them to survive other violent places where sexual predation is common. To protect themselves, women have to think about the potential perpetrator, and they develop protective strategies that make them cognizant of how the potential perpetrator will act. Keeping safe is an active process in which women on the streets constantly engage. This is illustrated well by one woman's comment: "If you want to survive, you've gotta learn how to play the game" (Huey and Berndt 2008: 192).

May and colleagues (2007) offer a similar account. In their research with 19 women using homelessness services across England, they found that some of them hid themselves from others (males) who were homeless, while others placed themselves in the center of groups sleeping rough and using day centers. Women strategically adopted various identities to fit in with the environment, the time of day or night, and the specific other rough sleepers present; they enacted "radically different performances of homelessness and femininity at different times of the day and night" (May et al. 2007: 133).

Women who are homeless are not simply victims of violence, nor do they just survive passively. Rather, the ethnographic literature consistently shows the active work employed by women to

Homelessness as the Experience of Violence 77

keep themselves safe. This activity must be acknowledged, but not romanticized. Casey and collaborators (2008) found that women employ a range of resistance strategies to occupy safe spaces, such as carrying a suitcase when sleeping at airports. Their survival strategies are always fragile. If they are unsuccessful in disguising their homelessness in order to occupy certain spaces, they are likely to be expelled (Casey et al. 2008). The identities performed to promote safety are nearly always about females, although Cloke et al. (2008) did report a male who was homeless expressing the importance of not presenting as frail to avoid victimization. Despite this example, the literature reporting the strategies employed by people who are homeless to keep safe frequently highlights gender.

Some scholars have noted that people who sleep rough form groups to strengthen protection; emphasis is often given to the importance of coming together as a collective (Cloke et al. 2010). Dordick (1997: 194) concludes that "homelessness transforms personal relationships into the principal currency of survival." Others have found that, rather than groups, people form relationships on the streets to protect themselves, or to protect others (women). Cloke and colleagues cite an exchange with Rob, a man living on the streets in England:

> *Rob*: We just latched onto each other basically, company for one another. Nothing sexual like, just friends. She'd help me out, I'd help her out.
> *Interviewer*: I guess she'd have felt safer with you around too?
> *Rob*: Yeah, because people take liberties with girls on the streets. It happens quite a lot. (2010: 74)

Rob's disturbing comment about the liberties taken with girls on the streets is supported by Irene Glasser and Rae Bridgman (1999: 57) who comment on the irony of women who are homeless having to cultivate "relationships with men – to protect them from other men." Reflecting on interviews with women who were homeless and moving in and out of precarious housing, Annabel Tomas and Helga Dittmar concluded: "Sleeping anywhere, without a man for protection from other men, was considered the most dangerous option in terms of both loneliness and safety. In these accounts, relationships with men were necessary relationships. Her safety was dependent on them" (1995: 509).

Women describe relationships with men as a key strategy for protection, but they also describe such relationships as not only problematic, but in fact violent. On the one hand, some women will stay in violent relationships to avoid homelessness (Kirkby and Mettler 2016); these relationships, or survival sex, must be conceptualized as gendered (Watson 2018). On the other hand, women will form relationships to escape homelessness – and the risk of violence thereof – but the relationships formed can themselves be violent. Mayock and colleagues (2015) present a sophisticated analysis of the complex ways that violent relationships maintained in order to escape homelessness often perpetuate additional traumas and lead to people again becoming homeless. Their analysis showed that when women form relationships so as to stay safe and not be homeless, the notion of stable housing is mostly an illusion. Instead, a woman might leave an overt form of homelessness, such as rough sleeping, only to engage in a hidden form of homelessness and abuse that exacerbates underlying trauma and results in a move back into overt homelessness (Mayock et al. 2015). The relationships that women enter into in order to protect themselves from the violence of homelessness are not only physically and sexually violent and traumatic in and of themselves, but they are also reflective of the violence and trauma that many women who are homeless have already experienced in childhood (Hudson et al. 2010). Broll and Huey (2020) found that multiple experiences of violent victimization and associated untreated traumas as an adult strongly predict multiple episodes of homelessness later in life.

In the same way that women exert considerable energy to survive on the streets, the literature makes clear that they also work hard to protect themselves by avoiding relationships altogether. Jasinski et al. (2010) found that a woman staying at a homelessness hostel in the United States gained great strength in staying homeless rather than engaging in sexual activities or crime to avoid homelessness. The woman's decision to avoid a relationship and stay in a shelter was "a choice she is making to better herself" (2010: 21).

Many people avoid the dangers of homelessness in its unsheltered form and in hostel accommodation by residing in various forms of informal accommodation or even in doubled-up housing (Harvey 2022). Molly Richard et al. (2022) say that to avoid shelters and rough sleeping, people in the United States are increasingly doubling up, "sharing a home with others when a home is out of reach." They estimate that in 2019 there were approximately 3.7 million people doubling up in the United States. Doubling up and residing

Homelessness as the Experience of Violence

in informal accommodation, such as a private letting of a room in a house, a garage, or even shed, may help to avoid the problems associated with overt homelessness, but it is far from safe.

The international evidence makes it clear that parents, especially a single mother, with dependent children will not sleep rough (National Alliance to End Homelessness 2021). Rather, they avoid the scrutiny of public officials, especially child protection authorities, by residing in informal accommodation. Data from the United States, for example, shows that women are overrepresented in the doubled-up homeless population (Richard et al. 2022); in 2010, it was estimated that 20 percent of children in the United States lived in doubled-up situations (Mykyta and Macartney 2012).

The research indicates that living in informal accommodation, including some boarding and doubled-up situations, can expose tenants to exploitative conditions. Andrea Sharam and Kath Hulse (2014: 302) found that families endured "sexual and physical assault, coercion, intimidation, harassment, exploitation, humiliation, hostility, vilification and cruelty." Their research highlights the vulnerable position that women and children find themselves in when living in informal accommodation. Without tenancy agreements to provide legal protection, and with little capacity to access affordable housing, women and children can be exploited by both landlords and other residents of informal accommodation.

In their landmark study illustrating how American families live on $2 per day, Kathryn Edin and Luke Shaefer (2015) show that surviving requires people to do things that they themselves believe are morally objectionable. They argue that living with extended family can help people avoid literal homelessness, but it can also be the "worst" thing to do, exposing people who are poor to violence and sexual abuse in cramped and shared housing conditions where parents cannot control or protect either themselves or their children. People take numerous steps to protect themselves when they are homeless, but, with limited power, some of their strategies fail to provide the safety they long for.

Concluding remarks

The world is safe. The international data demonstrates that it is probably the safest time to be alive in modern history (Pinker 2011).

Compared to our ancestors, many of us are far less likely nowadays to be violently robbed or violently assaulted (Sharkey et al. 2017). Debate abounds about what best explains the relative safety that our current generation experiences, but a reduction in opportunities for offending through enhancing physical security measures (Farrell et al. 2014) and promoting greater social control through community organizations (Sharkey et al. 2017) have played a key role.

The safe conditions of our modern age are of course averages. We are generally safer now than we were in previous generations. But there are many people in society whose experiences are not captured by averages. Many women and girls, for example, continue to live with the threat and experience of violent victimization (Walby et al. 2016). Further, and as demonstrated throughout this chapter, people who are homeless across the globe are not, on average, experiencing the safety that we – the housed population – now take for granted. Being homeless in today's society means being exposed to violent and dangerous living conditions. By virtue of their housing exclusion, people who are homeless are not benefiting from the elements of modern society that function to keep the rest of us living safely. We could reasonably reflect on the violence experienced by people who are homeless today and liken it to what other described homelessness was like in Skid Row of the mid-twentieth century (Caplow 1970).

As was the case in the nineteenth and early twentieth centuries, the experience of homelessness today is one of both violence and the necessity to adopt strategies to survive. A look at the survival strategies employed, such as downplaying feminine traits, or the heightened risk of experiencing sexual violence when homeless compared to when housed, forces us to confront the gendered nature of homelessness. We saw this in the previous chapter where we noted that domestic and family violence is a key trigger event for homelessness. In this chapter we have shown how violence and trauma can continue through and pervade women's experiences of homelessness (Calvo et al. 2022).

A gendered analysis must be sensitive to how women may be more likely than men to access services and be treated with sympathy (Fitzpatrick 2005), but hidden forms of homelessness, such as doubled-up accommodation, may conceal the true extent of the problem (Mayock et al. 2015), and indeed hide from public view the violent situations experienced by women and children.

Homelessness as the Experience of Violence 81

In addition to the significant harm that people who are homeless experience when living under the threat of violence, including death, we can begin to understand how homelessness chips away at citizenship, or at least a person's capacity to participate in society as a citizen. Living in the shadow of violence, as both victim and perpetrator, subverts the capacity of people who are homeless to be seen as citizens or to perform citizenship duties. Citizenship requires regulation by the rule of law (Pearce 2007). The unsafe realities that people who are homeless are forced to inhabit illustrate a failure of the state to provide the necessary resources for people to participate in society as citizens. The state responds to people who are homeless through a combination of neglect, control, and criminalization (Chapter 6).

In the next chapter we continue with our analysis of the experience of homelessness by discussing dependence and autonomy. We argue that the dominant modes of helping people who are homeless keep them locked in dependent relationships and further serve to undermine their opportunities to participate in society as citizens.

4

Being a Homeless Service User: Dependence and Autonomy

Helping someone who is homeless by giving them something that they do not have is of course positive. Pretty much all of the world's major religions teach us that giving to the needy is the hallmark of living well and in accordance with our faith. Secular ethics agrees. Richard Titmuss (2019) described the voluntary giving of blood to others for no personal reward as evidence of societies functioning as they ought. Mother Teresa was so universally loved because she dedicated her life to giving to people who were homeless. We celebrate the help that the giver provides, perhaps rightly so. We think far too little, however, about how receiving help feels. Does the benefit of receiving a bed for the night in a shelter counter the loss of autonomy that comes with it? When we give to those in need, we need to understand how it feels to be the recipient.

What are the experiences of those who access homelessness services? Focusing on immediate resources and services that people require, such as food and drink, hygiene and personal care, and homeless accommodation, this chapter examines what is provided to people to keep them alive and what it means to be reliant on these essential resources. By excluding people from housing, we push them into a position whereby they are reliant on service and care systems to meet their needs. To understand something about the experience of homelessness, we must confront the reality that the state of homelessness prevents people from controlling their lives.

Less drastic and immediately concerning than the exposure to violence that homelessness represents, it is important to critically

Dependence and Autonomy

examine what receiving services and resources to sustain life means to people who are homeless. We must engage with them and ask questions about how they feel about accessing resources and engaging with the volunteers and professionals who play significant roles in determining not only their day-to-day lives but also their capacity to survive. How do people who are homeless make meaning of the life-sustaining care they require from others? Do they, for example, think of resources such as food and drink, and access to services such as accommodation, as care? Or is the experience of being cared for by others, such as being provided with a place to sleep, a place to wash, and a meal to eat, make them feel they are being controlled? Do people feel dignified when accessing these resources?

While people who do paid or voluntary roles in homelessness services are motivated to help by providing care and improving the lives of recipients – which we can reasonably conclude from organizational mission statements and position descriptions of homelessness support roles – it is significant to examine what it is like to be on the receiving end of care and efforts to be helped. This chapter's investigation starts from the premise that it is manifestly inadequate to only consider the positive intentions of people trying to help without taking seriously the perspectives of those who are helped. It is similarly inadequate to assume help has been achieved by simple virtue of providing someone with access to a resource that they lack.

We cannot conclude a priori that someone without a bed to sleep in was appropriately helped by being given a place to sleep for the night. This chapter's investigation is broadly informed by the influential work of Joan Tronto. She reminds us that we can only assess the worth of care by engaging with "how receiving care is experienced and what it means to the person on the receiving end" (Tronto 1993: 135). Tronto's work is impressive for taking as her starting point the care receivers' perspectives and experiences. Her scholarship pushes us to challenge straightforward assumptions about what constitutes care. We cannot judge the appropriateness of care by structuring it on the basis of how the caregiver thinks they would like to be cared for. Good care – care that is meaningful and helpful – can only be determined by the person who receives it.

Tronto's work broadly, and this chapter's investigation into the experiences of accessing life-sustaining resources and services specifically, foreground autonomy. It is easy to see how the state of homelessness is a threat to autonomous action. We saw in the previous chapter how homelessness forces people into spaces where they have limited control over who they interact with, including being exposed to violent situations. In this chapter we want to push further by examining what the experience of receiving essential services and resources means for autonomy. We are guided by the work of Beate Roessler (2021). She emphasizes two critical points about autonomy that will be in the background of the analysis throughout this chapter. First, Roessler reminds us that autonomy is so important because it is constitutive of a meaningful life. Autonomy, in the form of privacy and being able to pursue our interests, is not a guarantee of a meaningful life, much less a guarantee of happiness, but it is a necessary precondition.

The second significant point that Roessler makes is that individual autonomy must be conceptualized as a social relational phenomenon. This means that we need to look at an individual's autonomy as enabled or constrained by the environment they inhabit. Roessler conveys this point when she explains that "we are never autonomous alone: we are always autonomous in social and political contexts, autonomous citizens in societies, always in interplay with others" (2021: 154). The conceptualization of autonomy as social is important for moving beyond simple assumptions about independence. Although governments like to espouse ideas of independent, and thus normal, citizens as opposed to those living in poverty who are dependent on the state and society and thus problematically abnormal (Shildrick and MacDonald 2013), conceptualizing autonomy as located within the environment is necessary for taking account of our connections with one another and the resources and opportunities that connections can open up. As Iris Marion Young (2011) illustrates, we need to think about people living interdependent lives whereby everyone owes each other a degree of reciprocal care. For our purposes, this nod to interdependence means that we must ask whether society is organized, including the way we provide resources and services to people who are homeless, in a way that enables people to be both cared for and to provide care to others (Tronto 2015). Being reliant on other people's care can be a good thing. The problem is when society is organized in a way such that people are only reliant, and cannot be caregivers. The interdependent nature of society and the social model of autonomy open the need to examine whether the care provided to people who are homeless, including the means through which that care is provided, enables or constrains autonomy.

Dependence and Autonomy

We commence the chapter by looking at the voluntary charitable services provided to people. Despite the wide moral appeal of charity in society, we draw attention to how the experience of relying on charity is less than ideal. The second half of the chapter examines the provision of formalized homelessness shelters and other forms of accommodation available to people who are homeless, and we ask how these are experienced. There are important political and moral distinctions between accessing resources through the state as a citizenry right and accessing charitable care based on the good will and voluntary compassion of volunteers (Parsell et al. 2021). These theoretical distinctions notwithstanding, we will show that, for people who are homeless, receiving both voluntary and professional modes of help are experienced similarly and in a way that replicates the experience of homelessness as subverted autonomy. People who are homeless rely on life-sustaining resources and services because homelessness means having limited control over life.

Charity

Focusing broadly on the population of people who are poor, there is mounting evidence that charity constitutes a key resource that enables them to survive. Taking charity as "the voluntary giving of money, resources, or time to non-kin or non-friends" (Parsell et al. 2021: 7), charitable responses to poverty work in tandem with deliberate government policy to wind back resources from the welfare state. From the United Kingdom, multiple studies have demonstrated that, since about 2010, the number of foodbank providers and the number of people using foodbanks have significantly increased (Garratt 2017; Lambie-Mumford 2017; Loopstra and Lalor 2017). Kingsley Purdam and colleagues (2016) suggest that food aid as a response to poverty is becoming normalized in the United Kingdom. The situation is of course not unique to that country. Charitable care to people in poverty has a long history in North America (Katz 1986). Recent research suggests that growing numbers of the US population are relying on charity to survive, including to eat (Holmes et al. 2018; Poppendieck 1999; Riches 2018).

Even in Europe, where there are traditions of comprehensive and universal welfare states, scholars have reported the increase in the use of charity by people who are poor (Lambie-Mumford and Silvasti

86 Dependence and Autonomy

2020; Silvasti 2015). The increasing number of people requiring charity to make ends meet is driven by austerity and neoliberal ideas about the role of the state in upholding citizens' social rights (Lambie-Mumford 2019). In addition, charity to people who are poor, rather than universal and adequate state provision to negate the need for charity, is part of a broader agenda that I and colleagues suggest has an objective to cultivate a society where poverty and social harms are responded to by everyday ethical citizens (Parsell et al. 2022). As we put it: "Retrenchment of aspects of the welfare state occurs alongside new investments in bottom-up charity initiatives, coupled with a commitment to grow and normalise charity as an end in itself." In this way, charity to people who are poor is seen, and has been viewed for generations, as a positive sign of a flourishing community (McKnight 1995; Smith and Lipsky 1993). Charity is widely represented as the hallmark of an engaged society characterized by citizens providing care and showing concern for others through practical actions.

Honing in more precisely on homelessness, rather than people experiencing poverty more broadly (the former is nearly always part of the latter, but the latter does not always include the former), we can observe both the significant role that charity plays in the lives of people who are homeless and the celebratory way this is viewed. Homelessness is a key site where citizens exercise *their* voluntary care and compassion. As we will demonstrate throughout the chapter, this charity is consequential for shame, othering, and constrained autonomy.

Charitable resources as key to survival

Sarah Johnsen and colleagues (2005) surveyed 165 day centers for people who are homeless in Britain. They found that 90 percent provide food and drink, with bathing and laundry facilities provided by 65 and 55 percent. Cloke et al. (2010) point to the large number of soup kitchens that operate in Britain, providing immediate relief to people who are homeless in the form of food, drinks, bedding, and clothing. They note that a majority are faith-based charities, and, although some have paid staff, mostly as coordinators, the majority are run entirely voluntarily and receive no direct government grants. They argue that some people rely on soup kitchens to survive because they can no longer access mainstream services.

Dependence and Autonomy 87

The prevalence of charity identified in Britain, in the form of food, drink, clothing, personal hygiene items, and even makeshift models of accommodating people who are homeless, is similar to what others have reported elsewhere in the world. Zsolt Temesvary's (2019) study of Hungarian nationals who were homeless in Switzerland reports that almost all used soup kitchens and many moved between different charities through the day and night to access free food and drink. Michele Lancione's (2014: 3073) study of homelessness in Italy found that churches and faith-based charities provided donated clothes free to people who were homeless "in an unlimited fashion." Moreover, some people who were homeless dedicated significant and planned aspects of each day moving around the urban environment to access donated goods.

In a US study, Thomas O'Toole and colleagues (2007) found that people presented to soup kitchens, more so than any other service, as the first stop to access support when they initially became homeless. More recently from the United States, John Barile and colleagues (2020) found that of all services used by people who were homeless, soup kitchens were the most frequently used, more so than shelters.

In Australia, reduced funding for social housing sits alongside increased funding to charities to respond to homelessness (Parsell et al. 2022). Precise numbers are difficult to access, but Australia has witnessed a proliferation of charity models that seek to meet the immediate needs of people who are homeless, including sleep buses, the temporary conversion of commercial city car parks for people to sleep in, and camping beds. These models provide resources that cover the basic necessities required to sleep, and they operate alongside other models that intend to meet the fundamental human need for hygiene through a provision of mobile showers and mobile laundries (Parsell and Watts 2017). One large Australian charity that supplies mobile laundries and mobile showers installed on the back of vehicles reports that in 2020 there were 38,125 loads of laundry provided and 5,120 showers (Orange Sky Australia 2020); this is slightly lower than what was provided the year before, pre-Covid-19.

Similar charitable models can be found outside Australia, for example in the United States (Haven of Hope on Wheels n.d.; Wright 2021), Greece (Ithaca 2019), and France (DePaul 2022). There is even a nonprofit organization, LavaMae[x], that teaches people all around the globe how to set up mobile shower facilities on the streets

(LavaMae[x] 2022). As of 2022, they assert that their affiliates have served in excess of 44,500 people. These charitable models promote their capacity to restore dignity and hope in the lives of people who are homeless (Haven of Hope on Wheels n.d). LavaMae[x] (2022) says that it "restores dignity, rekindles optimism, and fuels a sense of opportunity." Orange Sky Australia asserts that more important than the numbers of the showers and loads of laundry provided is the fact that their mode of charity "always boils down to the same thing: the people, stories, conversations and connections" (2020: 5).

Celebrating charity to the homeless

The stated aspirations to achieve connections, to value beyond anything else people and their stories, and to foreground hope and dignity unsurprisingly lead to wide political and public support for charity to meet the needs of people who are homeless. For many, support for charity is explained by the essential needs that the resources meet. Cloke et al. (2010) present soup kitchens as an important resource to help alleviate the deprivation that homelessness constitutes: "Far from being the relic of an earlier age, then, it is clear that soup runs remain a vital part of Britain's welfare landscape" (2010: 97). Furthermore, "the ethics of open acceptance practised by soup runs marks them out (on the surface at least) as the most inclusive of all the services available to homeless people" (2010: 105). This assessment is consistent with an extensive body of literature that unambiguously positions charity to people who are homeless as a good in and of itself. The positive assessment is underpinned by the straightforward analysis that being homeless is the experience of being deprived of resources, and charity is characterized as the provision of resources that go some way to reconciling this state of affairs. The reasoning goes that people who are homeless have limited access to the amenities necessary to meet their needs, such as to eat, sleep, and keep clean, and charity that addresses these gaps is self-evidently valuable.

Dana Miller and colleagues (1998: 476) argued that having soup kitchens for people who were homeless in a US city was a good thing because they provided resources that "meant support and survival. It was the only place they [people experiencing homelessness] could go, day after day, to get a free lunch." Seng-Guam Yeoh (2017) makes a similar point about the need for mobile soup kitchens in

Kuala Lumpur, Malaysia, as providing one of the only options for people who are homeless to eat. Johnsen and colleagues (2005: 805) go even further. Referring to day centers, they say these are vital for "preventing survivalist crime and facilitating the transition of homeless people into independent living." As we will demonstrate in Chapter 7, there is in fact a developed body of evidence to suggest that the most effective way of assisting people to exit homelessness is not through day centers and soup kitchens but, rather, through long-term affordable housing and, in some cases, associated support services. There is in fact little evidence demonstrating that day centers are an effective and efficient means of promoting housing access for people who are homeless, and certainly no evidence that they are more effective and efficient than a provision of housing.

Referring to a soup kitchen for people who are homeless in an exclusive London suburb, Martin Stone (2017: 158) sees the benefits of this charity as it brings together people from "different social strata" – middle-class volunteers and the homeless – so that the homeless can "develop the social skills and self-confidence to confront life more positively." For Stone, charity to people who are homeless is about more than meeting their needs for survival; it is about more than providing access to resources from which their homelessness excludes them. He argues that charity is a means to foster connections that will enable people experiencing homelessness to be better people. Charity is not only assumed to do a lot of work here, but it is also predicated on some negative assumptions about the character and capacities of people who are homeless. We will return to this negative characterization in Chapter 5.

Perhaps even more glowing portrayals of charity to people who are homeless can be found coming from politicians, the media, and public commentators. Not only do Australian governments seek out charities and encourage their volunteers to meet the immediate hygiene needs of people who are homeless, they also introduce new policy levers that ensure that charities can obtain a consistent stream of state funding to sustain their work over the long term (Parsell et al. 2022). Australian politicians refer to these charities and their volunteers as role models (Australian Capital Territory Government 2016), creating community (Moore 2016), going above and beyond (Palaszcuk 2016), and raising health standards by restoring dignity to people who are homeless (Turnbull 2016).

Dependence and Autonomy

The Australian creators of a charity, Orange Sky Australia, that provides mobile showers and mobile laundries to people who are homeless have won numerous accolades, including the 2016 Young Australians of the Year, Order of Australia Medals in 2020, and a $1 million award from the Google Impact Challenge. When Prince (now King) Charles and the Duchess of Cornwall (now Queen) toured Australia in 2018, the Duchess was so impressed with her visit to the charity that she put her hand up to be the first volunteer if the charity ever goes to the United Kingdom (SBS News 2018).

Writing about charity to people who are homeless for a US-based advocacy organization that has a mandate to fight extreme poverty, Ayesha Asad (2020) writes: "These mobile shower organizations are imperative in helping the homeless, particularly those who live and sleep on the streets. Increased access to showers links to lower rates of infectious diseases – and helping the homeless around the world is necessary for achieving a greater form of equality." Asad captures the sentiments of many: charity to people who are homeless is not simply idealized for what it is assumed to say about a caring and connected society of ethical citizens, but also because the charitable resources solve practical problems. Support for charity to people who are homeless is driven by the extreme deprivation that homelessness represents, the consequences to individuals from that deprivation, and thus charity's role in lessening harm to human life.

The experience of receiving charity

Despite the commonplace nature of charity to people who are homeless, the immediate need it can meet, and the wide support it receives, there is scant attention paid to its potential negative side. Other than pointing to the suboptimal nutritional benefits provided by some soup kitchens (Sisson and Lown 2011), commentators rarely question how charity is seen by people who are homeless themselves. Furthermore, it is controversial to point out the flaws of voluntary charity. Assertions about its limitations often result in a backlash for criticizing people who are trying to help (Parsell et al. 2021). This reaction is not difficult to understand. It is easy to conclude that the volunteers delivering charity are motivated to benefit people who are homeless: they are freely giving up their time, and sometimes resources, to help strangers who are clearly excluded from resources that most citizens take for granted. The charity offered – be it food, a

Dependence and Autonomy

place to sleep, or resources to practice hygiene – does of course meet an immediate need.

The evidence is clear, however, that even though access to such facilities as showers and laundries is necessary for good health, people sleeping rough face considerable barriers to gaining that access (Leibler et al. 2017). Because of the aim to meet immediate needs and the probable positive intentions of the charity volunteers, there is often little attention paid to what being reliant on charity actually means for people who are homeless. The positive assessments of charity are informed by those who provide the charitable acts who rarely consider what it is like to be on the receiving end of their efforts to provide care.

To understand the charitable help that is provided to people who are homeless, we must push beyond the good intentions of charities, and even the assumed aim to meet immediate needs. We must also look at the experiences of people who are homeless. If by virtue of excluding someone from housing we force them to access charity to get by, what does this mean for those on the receiving end? Engagement with how people who are homeless experience being the recipients of charity reminds us they are by no means exercising free will when accessing help. Because they have no place of their own to sleep, eat, or maintain hygiene, we must recognize that their use of these charitable resources is forced.

In my study with people living on the streets in Australia, I found that most of them relied on charities such as mobile outreach food vans to eat and drink (Parsell 2012). Accessing charity was a regular part of their lives. In my ethnographic research in the field, I observed positive interactions between people who were homeless and the volunteers providing them with sustenance. Although people who were homeless "overwhelmingly spoke positively about the volunteers and the services in general, many expressed their dissatisfaction at having to rely on others to meet their essential needs" (2012: 165). From the words of two people living on the streets, we can see how relying on charity to survive feels: "Using the charity services makes you feel stupid." "Why can't I go off and get my own food? I don't feel independent, you know, always reliant on food vans and [local service providers]. Just living like this you feel homeless" (2012: 165).

The finding that receiving charity viscerally impacts the self is a common theme in the literature. Yael Cohen and colleagues' (2017) study of soup kitchens in Israel is telling. They found that accessing food at soup kitchens came with the stripping of identity and an imposition of stigma. Food was provided in a way that separated couples, and even groups of friends, for the purposes of controlling diners and maintaining order; as a result, recipients feel demeaned, "othered."

Joe Nichols (2020) provides an ethnographic description to help us think about the way people who are homeless accessing soup kitchens are othered. He reports

> The central entrance to the kitchen is located off an alleyway where people will begin to line up at around 11:00 a.m. each day to receive their allocation of soup, bread, clothes, and other food resources as they become available. The soup kitchen itself is run by four to five volunteers. (2020: 588)

The process of queuing in public space to receive soup from volunteers is an indication of the stigmatized and dependent relationships that accessing charity as homeless fosters. People who are homeless are not only reliant on volunteers for supplies of food, etc., which makes them feel inadequate, but the process through which they access the resources, "receive their allocation," is alienating. The reality of being given an allocation – and being grateful for whatever is given without question – was central to the point conveyed in Charles Dickens's portrayal of Oliver Twist. Young Oliver's comment, "Please sir, I want some more," was provocative simply because he broke the rules by displaying independence and doing more than meekly accepting his allocation.

People's feeling of inadequacy because of being reliant on charity and dependent on volunteers was highlighted by Lancione (2014). Referring to soup kitchens in Italy used by people who are homeless, he shows how they were annoyed by the lack of space and, indeed, lack of dignity. One soup kitchen was "commonly described [as] being put in the sty with all other pigs" (2014: 3072). Lancione acknowledged the frantic work of volunteers, but, these efforts notwithstanding, soup kitchens were places where "homeless people had to fight to gain and preserve the necessary space in which to eat. Timing was strictly enforced" (2014: 3072). Reflecting on the unpleasant environment of soup kitchens, Lancoine found that most people who were homeless used them only as a last resort.

Dependence and Autonomy

Other scholars from the field have shown that, because of the shame, absence of dignity, and lack of control, some people who are homeless avoid charity altogether. In a study from Portland in the United States, Lisa Hoffman and Brian Coffey quote an individual who said "I am quite aware of the services and stuff ... and I would not touch them with a ten-foot pole. I have gone to these places for meals and it is the most degrading, impersonal, disrespectful experience in the world" (2008: 216). The mention of the degrading experience of accessing food is important; it captures the othering, the shame, and the unusual process of being reliant on volunteers to survive. The individual that Hoffman and Coffey cite also describes the experience as "disrespectful," which may indicate the approach of volunteers. Conversely, some research indicates that people reliant on charity perceive volunteers as positive (Lancione (2014; Parsell 2012), even though they experience negative emotions because of the shameful position of being dependent. Accessing charity makes people feel as though they are judged by the volunteers who are providing the resources.

Rebecca Sager and Susan Stephens's (2005) research from the United States provides a stark illustration of the judgment that some people who are homeless feel is aimed at them when they access charity. Focusing on religiously motivated charity, they draw attention to the way that help is often conditional on recipients participating in religious services, which could last anywhere from ten minutes to two hours. Accessing conditional charity was experienced by many as intrusive, coercive, and judgmental; 64 percent of their sample described it as negative. It was not only those who did not identify as religious who felt uncomfortable; Sager and Stephens cite the experience of a religious person who was homeless receiving conditional charity: "Another place I ate in the last five days was Holy Life. They try to ... it's good, I love God, I love the word, but you know, I don't like people forcing it on me before they feed me a meal" (2005: 305). They observed that in the six congregations they conducted their study, each of them held services prior to people being permitted to eat. Another person from their study described the conditional charity thus: "The preacher, you know, whoever the spokesperson is, they think we're dumb, because you know we're homeless, you know, we're nobody, and they think that they need that to be implanted in us all the time" (2005: 306).

94 Dependence and Autonomy

We also see the feelings of surveillance and judgment that come about from accessing voluntary resources in Martin Whiteford's study from the United Kingdom. He cites someone who is homeless reflecting on the proposal to charge people experiencing homelessness when they access food through charity:

> Most people agree that we should pay. It's not necessarily about being made to feel responsible but [recognizing that] the food is donated and cooked by those who give of their own time. 50p for a hot lunch is the cheapest meal in [town]; you can sit down and not feel like you're being watched or judged. (2010: 201)

The person in Whiteford's study captures a central essence about the experience of being reliant on charity: the recipient only takes, and with that they feel "watched or judged." This person wanted to pay for food because it would alter the social context whereby he would go from being a passive recipient of charitable care to a consumer. This captures the sentiments of a body of poverty research that illustrates that the shame of charity is mediated through the reliance on others with no capacity to reciprocate. Research on the deleterious impacts of receiving charity illustrate that the shame and stigma associated with receiving charity are produced through a dynamic whereby people who are homeless take resources – their allocation – but cannot give back. Andrew Clarke and I argued that it is the structural and systematic conditions of society broadly, and models of care specifically, that "constrain the capacity of people who are poor to give, and allow them only to receive, reify their positioning as passive, different, and in need of our compassion" (Parsell and Clarke 2022: 436). We argued that charitable organizations tend to label people in poverty as deficient, so their modes of help are designed to do things for the deficient. This in turn both supports assumptions that people in poverty are inadequate and makes recipients of charity feel wanting because they are not able to reciprocate.

So far, we have focused on the help provided on a charitable or voluntary basis, which people do not receive as a citizenry right, or as a right that comes with being a customer. Accessing charity is a necessity for many people who are homeless, and the accompanying feelings of shame are partially driven by their being forced to rely on accessing whatever is given to them by the goodwill of a stranger. In addition, there is a developed body of knowledge which demonstrates that people who are homeless also experience shame, othering, and a lack of autonomy when they access formalized services and accommodation as a part of state-funded welfare programs.

Shelters and formalized homelessness services

If relying on charity to meet basic needs, some of which are required to stay alive, is experienced as shameful, stigmatized, and judgmental, how do people experience formalized services, particularly homelessness accommodation such as shelters? We saw in the previous chapter that many people feel threatened in shelters, and even in day centers. Some shelters are so violent that people avoid them altogether. Do homelessness services facilitate autonomy or undermine it? As we will demonstrate here, it is often the latter.

To get a hint of the way in which formalized, and often state-funded, homelessness services subvert autonomy, we need to look briefly at how they operate. Amir Marvasti (2002), in a study from the United States, cites from minutes from shelter staff meetings about keeping clients under restrictions:

> *Tim Phillips*: Decided against lifting restriction due to drinking and causing minor disturbances; he is not acting responsibly.
> *Brandon Jones*: Decided against lifting restriction due to drinking and causing minor disturbances; he is not acting responsibly. (2002: 624)

These minutes make it immediately clear that the shelter staff judge the behavior of people who are homeless, on the one hand, and control their movements based on assessment of their behaviors, on the other. Jennifer Hoolachan's (2022) investigation of a supported accommodation hostel for young people who were homeless in Scotland came up with similar findings. Like many homeless hostels, her study site "used an array of mechanisms to monitor and control the movements and actions of the residents" (2022: 219). Her ethnographic research describes how staff control behaviors inside and outside the hostel, including whether residents are permitted to access communal areas. Hostel staff closely monitored the residents, carrying out a four-hourly room check. These checks could occur more frequently if shelter staff felt inclined to do so. Hoolachan reports that room checks involved a member of staff visiting each bedsit, knocking on the door and entering even if nobody answered. Once inside a bedsit, the staff member would spend a few minutes looking around the room, checking for health and safety risks, chatting to whoever may be in the room and ensuring that no residents were consuming alcohol or drugs as these activities were prohibited. (2022: 219)

Hoolachan's findings stand out not because the close empirical detail presented is unusual, but because it is shocking. Such methods of control comprise a reoccurring theme.

In a study of supported homeless accommodation from New York City, Anthony Marcus provides an account that illustrates the commonplace and unproblematic way that staff rationalize the need to survey shelter residents. Citing notes from his fieldwork journal where he reports overhearing a conversation between a caseworker and a resident at a homeless accommodation service, the former remarked: "You want privacy? Move. This ain't the Hotel California" (2006: 79).

Shelter environments and homeless services are structured in such a way that monitoring and controlling people who are homeless is the norm. David Snow and Leon Anderson's classic study illustrates this through two dimensions: one for promoting safety and the other to identify which people in the homeless population should be helped. They cite one manager of a homeless shelter who said: "Some people would say I'm cold-hearted, but I rule with an iron hand. I have to because these guys need to respect authority ... The experience of working with these guys has taught us the necessity of rules in order to avoid problems" (1993: 81). For another manager, monitoring was a means of distinguishing between the deserving and the undeserving: "When these people come in, you've got to size them up, see what they're really like ... it's important that the caseworker not be too cynical, though. Otherwise they would never offer services to anyone. But it's important to look for something in the individual that makes you feel they might be salvageable" (1993: 83).

The sentiments reported in Snow and Anderson's study from Texas in the early 1990s remain applicable to what Hoolachan (2022) reported 30 years later in the United Kingdom. Forrest Stuart's (2016) study of Skid Row in Los Angles depicts a largely similar situation, but with additional measures of surveillance and control. The shelter staff monitored and controlled residents in a deliberate

Dependence and Autonomy

strategy to actively intervene in an attempt to change the expectations of residents. Stuart found that in Skid Row three mega-shelters provided the majority of the accommodation and they existed for the sole purpose of rehabilitating residents; it was hard for people who needed shelter to avoid being in one of them. People staying in the shelters were required to participate in a structured rehabilitation process whereby each step in self-improvement was marked with the wearing of a different color badge. Stuart reports that these Skid Row residents were "subject to automatic thirty-day expulsion for a number of infractions, including verbal abuse, consumption of alcohol or drugs, possession of drug paraphernalia, failing to check in throughout the day, or leaving the dormitory any time after 8:00 p.m." (2016: 65).

Stuart's close ethnographic account teases out a theme in the literature that sees homelessness accommodation as paternalistic, with monitoring as part of the process that enables people who are homeless to be improved. Rodney Fopp (2002) adds a further dimension to this analysis. Focusing on Australia's shelter system, he found that, rather than the systematic rehabilitation that Stuart identified, or even the order and sorting that Snow and Anderson reported, people in homeless accommodation are surveyed and controlled simply because there is insufficient affordable housing for them to exit the shelter into. As a result, case managers, partly to justify their own jobs, engage in a futile process of dealing with the consequences, which involves monitoring people.

The international research produced from the accounts and perspectives of shelter staff draws similar conclusions. To access services, especially homelessness accommodation, people must be willing to accept certain conditions. These involve being closely monitored and controlled, often for the purpose of determining how they live, and especially for determining how they ought to live differently. An extensive body of research has been undertaken in order to understand how people who are homeless experience being monitored and controlled. It is this research that we now examine.

Surveillance and control

As might be expected from the research carried out with shelter staff, people experiencing homelessness report that shelter accommodation and the conditions that go with it are undesirable. Studies conducted

98   Dependence and Autonomy

across numerous international jurisdictions and drawing on various types of shelters have found that people who accept homeless accommodation find themselves being treated as deficient, even childlike.

Mayock and colleagues' (2015) study with women experiencing homelessness in Ireland is an illustration of this experience. They found that women felt that staying in shelter accommodation undermined their autonomy. Women felt that they were constantly surveyed and had their day-to-day lives scrutinized by shelter staff. The authors use the term "infantilization" to capture the way women experienced shelter life. One woman said that, in the shelter:

> there's people watching you, looking over you, knowing you can't do this and can't do that. That's very stressful, just horrible. We're not teenagers, we're adults in this place ... I'm not stupid, you know what I mean. When we go in it's like they're treating us like kids, like they're talking to us like kids; kids that have kids. (2015: 886)

A consistent picture emerges showing that people who are homeless feel they are being treated like children by shelter staff simply because they are homeless, and that accepting homeless accommodation means dealing with the insult of being deemed incapable of making good choices. In a study undertaken in Portland in the United States, Hoffman and Coffey illustrate this sense of being treated as deficient:

> If you get involved in the shelter, you have no life ... Your choices are taken away from you. Your self-respect is taken away from you. You are treated like a small child. It says if they think that because you are living this way you cannot make any decisions on your own, that you have no ability to ... to decide anything for yourself and ... I am not going to let them do that to me anymore. They have made too many decisions for me and ... it has gotten me nowhere. (2008: 216)

Another example can be found in Watts and Blenkinsopp's research with people who were homeless in Scotland. A person living in a shelter said "I'm nearly a 40-year-old man and I'm being told what time to fucking [be back at night] ... I should be allowed to decide when I come back, no[t] fucking somebody else" (2022: 106).

The experience of being treated like a child in homeless accommodation resonates with what was presented earlier in this chapter. Shelter staff, including managers and directors overseeing shelters, overtly describe people who are homeless as incapable, as needing paternalistic care. As a result, shelters tend to be structured in ways that significantly curtail the independence of the people who seek accommodation.

Shelters do far more than provide accommodation to meet people's immediate need for a place to sleep. Stuart (2016) found that the Skid Row mega-shelters in Los Angeles were purposefully reimagined to be places of rehabilitation in addition to simply providing accommodation. This involved, as we saw above, developing a system that monitors people, rewarding them for progress, and penalizing them, including evicting them, if they did not comply. At the same time, the literature shows again and again that people who are homeless reject the premise that they are inadequate and in need of being improved. They find the assumption, and the model of intervention that logically follows on from it, insulting.

Gowan's research with people who were homeless in San Francisco captures this feeling of being insulted by shelter staff. She reports the experience of a Mexican man who was homeless who described the Spanish-speaking shelters as the best. He said of the shelter: "The rules. You wanna think you have your own life – forget it" (2010: 197). Gowan described how the shelter staff focused more on rules than on humanity or even common sense. The Mexican man quoted above described an interaction he had with a shelter staff member when he was forced to discard the food he was carrying prior to entering the shelter, or he would face eviction. He described the inter-action as being "embarrassing, being treated like a kid … No one talks much to each other. They all embarrassed. They are humiliated" (2010: 197–198).

People who are homeless are not simply embarrassed about their homelessness; rather, they are embarrassed and frustrated with how they are managed when they are homeless. Sometimes this is explicit, as, for instance, when Marcus (2006) found that people have to take medication or pass drug tests as a condition of continuing to receive accommodation. Marcus's research is consistent with the literature that shows it is the structure and rules of shelters that subvert autonomy, even if shelter staff are not overtly punitive.

McMordie (2021) found that shelters in Northern Ireland outlawed alcohol consumption, for example, which curtailed individual autonomy and people's capacities for self-determination. The rules of hostels, and the unpredictable nature of complying with them depending how shelter staff enforced them, meant that people were in "a profound and continuous sense of unpredictability." A person living in a shelter described the atmosphere as "you're always waiting on somebody calling you, or somebody moving in who you've argued with ... You're always on edge, you're always, constantly, on guard" (2021: 389).

Because living in homeless accommodation involves being guided by shelter staff, people have little control over their own lives and little knowledge about how shelter staff will respond to them. Watts and Blenkinsopp (2022) found that the rules and day-to-day realities of living in shelter accommodation undermined people's wellbeing by preventing them from forming intimate relationships or even contact with children. Such experiences offer little support for the aspirations of shelter managers that a controlling environment is a successful way of improving people who are homeless. Perversely, having one's life controlled in homeless accommodation is, overall, experienced as stressful. Watts and Blenkinsopp (2022) acknowledge that hostels and other forms of homeless accommodation do require rules, but they argue that the stringent practices and close monitoring that characterize most shelters fall short of enabling people's capabilities. This is particularly the case in communal hostel accommodation, where rules are required to respond to environments that are unacceptable. As Watts and Blenkinsopp (2022: 112) recognize, the subverted autonomy and undesirable experiences in shelters are a product of both paternalistic rules that govern behavior as well as the communal living that forces "vulnerable strangers [to live] cheek by jowl."

So far, we have largely focused on single adults. There is also a recognition in the literature that parents with dependent children who experience homelessness find their autonomy being subverted as their parental status is undermined. This has two dimensions. First, being seen as deficient and childlike is particularly felt by adults who are themselves trying to parent. Living in homeless accommodation with dependent children brings into sharp focus what it means to be controlled by shelter rules and staff and the way this conflicts with parental authority. To retain a place in family homeless accommodation, parents are required to not only undergo the scrutiny identified above (such as drug tests), but also participate in therapy sessions, parental programs, and other interventions that assume homelessness to be synonymous with being a bad parent (Carr 2011; Tomas and Dittmar 1995).

People who are homeless not only receive specialist homelessness services, such as temporary accommodation and charity to meet hygiene needs, they also access a broad range of care services from the welfare state that are available to all citizens. These include primary healthcare, mental healthcare, and drug and alcohol support. Although this broad range of services is not provided to people because they are homeless, the experience of accessing these services while homeless influences how the care may be provided and how it is experienced as a recipient. Because being homeless is believed by many in society to be the fault of the individual, for example, through a misuse of alcohol or illicit substances, the delivery of services to people who are homeless can be premised on the assumption that people need to be changed. E. Summerson Carr (2011) provides a brilliant empirical analysis of the nature of social work intervention with women who are homeless. Drawing on a three-and-a-half year ethnographic study at an outpatient drug treatment program for women experiencing homelessness in the United States, Carr demonstrates that therapists set the clear expectations about how clients are required to refer to themselves and their addiction – to take full responsibility for their failings and need to change. Women, in turn, work hard to ensure that they portray themselves as addicts in precisely the way that therapists mandate. The language demanded by the therapist and articulated by the good client was so central to service provision, Carr argued, that language was more important than reconfiguring people's relationships with drugs.

Carr's study serves as an important reminder that the language people who are homeless accessing services are required to adopt, such as scripts about personal responsibility and self-sufficiency, are politically and culturally normative. To continue accessing services, people learn to represent themselves and their problems in ways that accord with existing cultural and political narratives. It is not coincidental that the drug treatment facility that Carr studied was in a city with a lack of affordable housing. Therapists in the treatment facility, which was funded by federal and state governments, worked hard to ensure that homeless women saw their addictions and homelessness in terms of personal failings rather than societal problems.

To continue to receive treatment, which for most women was obligatory and thus to fail to do so was to breach their parole conditions, women refer to themselves as the problem. Part of the brilliance of Carr's analysis is the manner in which she shows that women did not passively take on these narratives or internalize their oppression. They rather agentically adopted language that they knew was needed. Women in the treatment program engaged in what Carr referred to as "flipping the script" – that is, "formally replicating prescribed ways of speaking about themselves and their problems without investing in the context of those scripts" (2011: 3).

Flipping the script was an act of agency that shows that people who are homeless can take on language and outwardly appear to embody the belief that they are responsible for their homelessness even when they do not in fact believe that to be the case. Adopting the language is not only important to avoid breaching bail conditions, for example, but in the site Carr studied, like many services for people who are homeless across the globe, active participation in the program was required as a condition of receiving resources such as a (temporary) roof over their head. Ultimately, Carr's study adds great depth to the literature by teasing out what it can mean to be homeless and the recipient of what a practitioner (and the state) sees as help, and how this form of being helped is not necessarily considered helpful for the person on the receiving end. It is the emotional work that people who are homeless endure as clients of social services that helps illuminate why many find them undesirable, to the extent that people who are homeless avoid accepting the available resources and care services. Being homeless means handing over control and authority to others, as Carr shows, including the authority for others to determine how people express the nature of their own problems.

The literature concerning parenting while homeless disproportionately focuses on women (Baptista et al. 2017). Drawing on qualitative research from France, Nathalie Thiery (2008) shows that women experienced being in homeless accommodation as undermining their authority as parents; women were concerned that their homelessness would mean a "loss of control over the child" (2008: 8). Being a parent living in homeless accommodation, as Lisa Cosgrove and Cheryl Flynn found in a US study, was stressful "because the parenting rules of the shelter were not always congruent with participants' previous ways of parenting" (2005: 133).

Many women who are homeless with their children do not access formal homelessness services; rather, they draw on informal networks to access accommodation (Baptista et al. 2017). Even though doubling up with friends or even strangers does not involve case managers or professional staff along with shelter rules and regulations, women experiencing homelessness in these informal arrangements still find their parental capacities undermined. Hope Harvey's (2022) study of low-income mothers living as a guest with their children in someone else's home found that the forced housing arrangements prevented them from parenting as they would like. Women see that being a mother requires them to have access to independent housing where they have the control to parent in a way consistent with their values and expectations. One participant in Harvey's study described doubled-up housing with her father as limiting her authority to parent her children. In contrast, moving to her own public housing unit meant "just being able to set the standards and the order in the house is, oh, I love it" (2022: 273).

It is not only mothers who suffer; the consequences for children are multiple and profound. A major study from the United States observed that homelessness among children "may lead to changes in brain architecture that can interfere with learning, emotional self-regulation, cognitive skills, and social relationships" (Bassuk et al. 2014: 7). The literature on childhood homelessness shows that the development needs of children are impaired as a result of homelessness, particularly the impacts from reduced social networks and an inability to access safe places to play (Murran and Brady 2022).

Qualitative research among children experiencing homelessness illustrates how exclusion from housing disrupts life and taken-for-granted aspects of childhood. The constant movement that

104 Dependence and Autonomy

homelessness often constitutes means that children become disconnected from family, friends, and education. Children who miss out on these opportunities experience sadness and loss. Maggie Kirkman and colleagues report the words of a child experiencing homelessness: "It's kind of sad, because then you miss all your friends that you've just made, and they're like really nice and friendly, and then all of a sudden you lose your friends, like your best friends, and then you feel really lonely when you get to the new school 'cause you don't know anyone" (2010: 999).

In addition to the multitude of ways that homelessness negatively impacts people described throughout this book, including the way in which they feel controlled, the literature on childhood homelessness is significant for demonstrating how exclusion from housing works to exclude children from basic, yet developmentally critical, aspects of life (Murran and Brady 2022).

Housing, home, and autonomy

The diverse experiences presented thus far illustrate a central theme: excluding people from housing pushes them into dependent positions where they are reliant on the good will or control of people who intervene to meet their needs. Homelessness is characterized as forced deprivation (Busch-Geertsema et al. 2016); people in this situation have no place of their own or control over their lives. Homelessness equally means forced dependence. Jeremy Waldron (1991) explains that we have to think about homelessness as an experience whereby people have no place in which they can truly be free; they have no capacity to exercise the rights and freedom that are theoretically available to all of us as citizens of liberal democracies.

In a state of forced deprivation, people who are homeless have limited control over their food consumption, and over hygiene and personal care, and little control over where they sleep. Voluntary charity and professionalized services might respond to some of their needs, but, as we have seen, this has the consequence of stigmatizing recipients, positioning them as childlike and other, and forcing them into potentially dangerous physical environments and unequal relationships with service providers.

The experiences of homelessness as subverted autonomy, not to mention shame and othering, dovetail with both the conceptual

Dependence and Autonomy 105

literature on the meaning of home and the empirical literature about people who move from homelessness to home. As opposed to the fluidity and unpredictability of the public realm, the idealized home is theorized as a place of sanctuary; a place where people can control both mundane and intimate aspects of life (Douglas 1991). For Mallett (2004: 82), the privacy of home "means a space where one has the capacity to establish and control personal boundaries." It is the control one has in the home that contributes toward the experience of home as a place of ontological security (Dupuis and Thorns 1996).

We saw in the previous chapter that home is valued because it provides people with safety and the ability to exert control over their own lives, in contrast to the experiences of violence that characterize life when homeless. Deborah Padgett's (2007) important work from New York City illustrates this compellingly. Focusing on people who moved from homelessness into independent apartments, she found that ontological security was realized because housing provided people with the resources to achieve self-determination. Responding to the interview question, "What do you like about it being your own apartment?", one of Padgett's participants describes how housing promotes control and autonomy: "Just having it ... Stay over anytime you wanted to. You know, things like that. Go shopping. You don't have to ... People can't tell you what to do in your own place. You have your own say-so. What goes on in your own apartment. Things like that" (2007: 1930–1931). We can only grasp the meaning of self-determination and control that Padgett's participant articulated by reflecting on the experience described above about relying on charity to survive or living in homeless accommodation where people felt shamed, watched, and controlled. Padgett's participant valued being in their own apartment because, among other reasons, "people can't tell you what to do." Others have found likewise. A Canadian study found that people who moved from homelessness into permanent supportive housing appreciated the autonomy they experienced as a result. One resident even declined to eat meals that were paid for as part of his rent because preparing his own food at a time convenient to him was an expression of autonomy that he valued and that he was only able to achieve because of housing (Burns et al. 2020). People in homeless accommodation appreciate the help provided by staff, particularly when it involves giving them the opportunity to make their own decisions (Parsell, Stambe, Baxter 2018). In an

Australian study, it was shown that gaining housing after periods of rough sleeping meant gaining the capacity to control one's own healthcare, through, for example, storing medication and the routine required to attend regular medical appointments (Parsell, ten Have, et al. 2018).

The literature on the experience of subverted autonomy while homeless is unambiguous. The salience of the theme is brought into even sharper focus when we reflect on what home means to people who exit homelessness. In ways that are perhaps self-evident, people appreciate housing for providing them with what was missing in their lives when they were homeless. What is missing is not simply housing, but the limited control over life that comes from housing exclusion. The experiences of people who are homeless resonate with Roessler's social model of autonomy. As she observes, "individuals conceive of their life as good, meaningful, and well-lived only when it is in fact their own life, when their decisions are respected" (2021: 113–114). Autonomy means being free to pursue what one wants in life; homelessness, at least living in homeless accommodation and being reliant on charity, makes autonomous action difficult to achieve. Homelessness is the experience of being controlled in homeless accommodation and reliant on charity that prevents people from exercising their own choices. Rather, they are forced to queue for an allocation, eat in places likened to pigsties, or participate in religious services in return for food.

Autonomy is the state of being provided with the resources that enable people to pursue their own choices. This means, and we saw this from the research examining the experiences of people who exit homelessness and move into housing, having a private space of one's own. In Roessler's terms, these people experience their housing as home, in direct contrast to their homelessness, because "something is private when a person is able and fundamentally entitled to control access to it" (2021: 137).

Concluding remarks

The experiences of subverted autonomy that have been reported here are similar to those endured by people who are poor. As Lister's (2021) comprehensive review of the evidence illustrates, being poor means having an inadequate income to control the conditions of one's own life, including getting out of poverty. The experience of homelessness amplifies the conditions that subvert control and autonomy in ways that extend beyond being only poor.

By virtue of being homeless, people do not have a space of their own. It is the lack of a space of one's own, in addition to living below the poverty line, that creates the conditions where people are forced into dependent relationships. The state of homelessness means people are reliant on others for simple yet basic life necessities, such as using the toilet or having the amenity to wash oneself. People who are poor but who have access to housing do have the capacity to wash themselves, and even to store, prepare, and consume food under conditions of control. For people who are homeless, this is not the case. The state of homelessness means, on the one hand, that control over basic elements of life is prevented and, on the other, that people become dependent on others, including charitable volunteers and paid professionals, to provide them with these basic elements of life.

This chapter has illustrated the subverted autonomy that homelessness represents through analysis of three perspectives that converge to illustrate the same picture. First, we saw that many service providers and even volunteers perceive people who are homeless are in some way deficient, and thus design their model of care on this basis. Second, we showed the mounting evidence from people who are homeless that the controlling and paternalistic care models, predictably, subvert not only their autonomy but also their sense of self as capable individuals. Third, we illustrated how homelessness is the experience of subverted autonomy by engaging the experiences of people who had moved from homelessness to housing; the latter is valued for the material conditions it provides, which enable autonomy.

We started the chapter by asking a range of questions about what it means to help people who are homeless, and by taking their perspectives and experiences as the starting point. The evidence presented raises challenging questions about how help and care can be provided. The simple assumption that giving someone who is homeless something that they do not have was rejected. Although, as Cloke et al. (2010: 93) observe, "for those wanting to do something to counter the problem of street homelessness, soup runs offer an immediate and highly visible expression of their desire to help," we have shown that this desire *to help* may be incongruent with the experience of *being helped*.

Dependence and Autonomy

Attempts to help people are experienced as particularly deleterious, as we have shown, because the recipients of help are positioned as inadequate. Their state of homelessness is taken by those trying to help them as indicative of underlying incapacities. It is this positioning of people who are homeless as deficient, as the other, that we examine in greater depth in the next chapter.

5

The Experience of Homelessness: Identity and Identification

When natural disasters hit, such as the huge devastation wrought by Hurricane Katrina in and around New Orleans in 2005, the media join the chorus of those who count and even lament the number of people who were made homeless. Following natural disasters, people who lose their homes are framed as people who have been "left homeless." They are not framed as "homeless people." As people left homeless by conditions outside their control, the homelessness they experience is not in any way linked to their identities. They are simply normal people *who happen to be without homes. All the media and public attention focuses on rebuilding, insurance payouts, and government intervention into building. There is no suggestion that people without homes after natural disasters are homeless people. This is in stark contrast to those whose state of homelessness is assumed to say something about their identities.*

This chapter builds on the extensive body of work about the experience of poverty and identity and asks what the state of being homeless means for how people are thought about. What is it about homelessness, other than living in poverty, that shapes and drives the identities of people who are homeless? What identities are imposed on them by others? And how do they assert their own identities? Being labeled is the reality of being homeless, but that is only part of the story.

In thinking about this, we must consider what the effects of living or interacting in the public realm – and thus having one's day-to-day life on public display – have on people's identities. For many of us, a home enables us to feel ontologically secure, as it is an

110 Identity and Identification

observable means by which we can anchor our identities (Dupuis and Thorns 1996). The control and security that home represents are resources that we can draw on to construct a sense, or senses, of self. In contrast, the state of homelessness is a symbolic and practical challenge to maintaining normal identities; homelessness poses a challenge for people to be able to name their identity claims and have those claims socially validated.

We have seen in previous chapters that exclusion from housing risks people being exposed to violence and to relationships characterized by control and a loss of autonomy. Building on this, here we examine what exclusion from housing means for the way we make sense of the identities of the excluded. The chapter engages with the broad body of sociological literature on identities, which provides four key lessons that will help frame the analysis of identity and homelessness.

The first core finding from the sociology of identity threads through the entire chapter. This can be briefly introduced as the identities that make people feel validated, along with the identities that are imposed upon them by others, which are not equally distributed across society. Identities are exercises of power. There is a close relationship between access to resources and power and the ability to define who we are (Bauman 2004). This is paramount when thinking about a homeless *identity* and the way we *identify* the homeless. Second, the sociological work on identity reminds us that identities are not singular or fixed. Identity is not a concept used to represent a true self. Rather, identities are multiple, fluid, and malleable (Brekhus 2020; Lawler 2014). Third, when we think of people's identities we must think too about agency and people's capacity to express their identities. The role of power in asserting and having one's identity claim recognized does not mean that people who are poor or homeless have no agency in the identities they assert and make meaning of.

Finally, we always have to think about people's identities within their environment. This can include the immediate environment (Lemke 2008). It is important to consider people's identities – either expressed or imposed – with reference, for example, to their position in homeless accommodation, or their interaction with a care provider. These contexts matter for identity, including which identities people can display and which ones we assume to be salient. The environment also includes the macro or societal level. The identities we assume that people have, especially deviant identities, are mediated through social norms about what constitutes the right way to live in society. A personal identity is always social, as Wayne Brekhus (2020) says, in its formation and implications.

This chapter illustrates the significant problems of the stigmatized and all-encompassing negative identities that are imposed upon people. It engages the empirical work that shows that people who are homeless identify in often non-stigmatized ways that have nothing to do with their homelessness. There are even benefits of doing so. This chapter aims to achieve a balance that ensures the literature presented challenges the negative stereotypes attached to people who are homeless, on the one hand, but does not ignore the predictable, systematic, and structural problems that they disproportionately experience, on the other. People who are homeless may well identify as normal, but they have disproportionately experienced exclusion and poverty at some point in their lives, and, for some, throughout their lives. Just because people may feel normal, and just because they have the moral right to be seen as such, it does not mean that society has given them an equal chance to live a normal life.

The historical portrayal

We begin our investigation into the portrayal of homeless people's identities with a focus on the people who lived on Skid Row. The term "skid row" describes the inner urban locations where accommodation and services to people experiencing homelessness were concentrated; it derives from the United States and the skidways that were used by lumberjacks (Bahr 1973). Samuel Wallace wrote about Skid Row in the mid-twentieth century, describing it as the "most deviant community in the United States." His portrayal of people who were homeless in Skid Row, which at the time was inhabited almost exclusively by men without dependent children, reflects a consistent picture from the period that linked homelessness to the most profound inadequacy and immorality. According to Wallace, a person living on Skid Row "did not bathe, eat regularly, dress respectably, marry or raise children, attend school, vote, own property, or regularly live in the same place. He does little work of any kind. He does not even steal. The Skid Rower does nothing, he just is. He is everything that all the rest of us try not to be" (1965: 144).

112   Identity and Identification

It would be difficult to find more extreme words than those used by Wallace to represent a person as other: "He is everything that all the rest of us try not to be." These sentiments were nevertheless consistent with the scholarly picture depicted at the time. The Skid Row areas of the United States were synonymous with the people who lived there. Theodore Caplow reported that the cost of living on Skid Row, for instance of accommodation and food, was actually higher than in other parts of the urban world. The homeless person lived on Skid Row because they were believed to desire a certain type of life. This is important, as it goes to the heart of ideas that the homeless are a distinct type of people. They were not simply materially deprived or poor: there was something different about them. Caplow depicted the inhabitants of Skid Row as people "whose major components are isolation from women, wine-drinking, the free disposition of one's time, and the absence of compulsory obligations" (1970: 5). He went on to argue that their distinct way of life was driven by a back history that was similarly deprived. He said that there is wide agreement that the typical homeless man had endured a life of "social undernourishment which has discouraged him from seeking satisfaction in family relationships, self-improvements" (1970: 7). This abnormal life leading into homelessness along with the deviance that characterizes life on Skid Row, Caplow argued, meant that rehabilitating the homeless man is challenging because he was never had a normal life.

Donald Bogue's (1963) study of Skid Row similarly reported the alcoholism and "ambitionless bums," but he also suggested that not everyone there was an alcoholic. Moreover, he pointed to the failures of the labor market and the social safety net as producing a population of people with wasted lives on Skid Row.

Although no other part of the world ever developed areas approximating to Skid Row, or defined tracts of urban society dedicated to homeless populations, the depiction of the homeless person by scholars in the mid-twentieth century outside the United States is similar to what was written about in the United States. Writing in Australia in the mid-twentieth century, Alan Jordan says that people who are homeless are childish, dependent, and neither motivated nor able to improve their lives. He goes as far to say that if a physician was to label a homeless person, it would be as an "inadequate personality" (Jordan 1965: 27). What the homeless needed, according to the thinking at the time, was a "firm benevolent father figure to guard

Identity and Identification 113

them from the pitfalls of their own limited intelligence" (Linsell 1962: 9).

The portrayal of the homeless person as deficient and as a group distinct from the mainstream population did not emerge from a vacuum in the mid-twentieth century. As Beate Althammer (2014) notes, people whom we would now define as homeless have been cast as the deviant poor since at least the Middle Ages throughout Europe. In the United States, representations of the tramp in the nineteenth century portrayed them as drunk and lazy. But most concerning, they were portrayed as a threat to hard-working people and societal order because of their contempt for social norms (Kusmer 2002).

In Britain in the early nineteenth century, some of the homeless population, referred to as vagrants or rogues, were seen as so deviant and such a threat to public order they could be whipped or imprisoned (Freeman and Nelson 2008). In 1906, a report from the Local Government Board in Britain concluded that so-called tramps lived "an unsocial and wretched sort of existence with no object in life and little hope for an improved future" (Humphreys 1999: 114). The local government report said that men who slept at shelters or on a staircase were "often verminous and always filthy." In Ireland as well as elsewhere in Europe in the nineteenth century, as Eoin O'Sullivan (2020) shows, the people whom we would now define as homeless were institutionalized in the hope of making them ready for the labor market. We return to this idea of deviant identity and rehabilitation at the end of the chapter.

The historical literature reporting on people who are homeless does more than represent them as deviant and deficient. It implies that people's state of homelessness says something about their identities. It is worth noting here that the focus of research into homelessness in the nineteenth and first half of the twentieth century was on the homeless man, even though many women at the time did also experience homelessness. Their experiences were largely concealed because researchers had both a limited gaze and a gendered understanding of the type of problem that homelessness represented (O'Sullivan 2016). The image presented at the time indicated that people not only *experienced* homelessness, but they *were* homeless people. The efforts to respond to homelessness thus focused on changing the people who were homeless rather the circumstances around them. This is important. Although the language and some

114 Identity and Identification

of the underlying theories have changed, the idea that homelessness constitutes an identity has endured through time.

As we will show, in the last decades of the twentieth century, some scholars argued that it was not the problematic characteristics of the homeless – for example, the deprived life histories and labor market failures – that explained their state of homelessness; rather, homeless people's distinctive identity was driven by their homelessness.

Identity change

We now look again at the studies conducted among people living on Skid Row, because this important early work on homelessness constituted a shift in understandings of identity. Howard Bahr (1973) provided seminal work in this area. His thesis is that people on Skid Row became disaffiliated from mainstream society, describing this as a weakness or absence of bonds to the general population, including family, friends, and employment (Bahr 1970). Important in Bahr's analysis is that disaffiliation is not because of something inherently problematic about the individuals living on Skid Row, but rather that the identity shifts associated with disaffiliation were socially produced as homelessness endured. The problems on Skid Row, according to Bahr, were that (1) its inhabitants had no valued roles, ties, or obligations, and (2) society, both workers on Skid Row and the population outside, viewed the Skid Row inhabitants as inadequate and distinct. What this meant, he argued, was "the imputed defectiveness, validated in interaction and internalized, acts to prevent the establishment of new affiliations or the reactivation of old ones" (1973: 286).

He went on to assert that the problem with Skid Row is not to do with the people as such: there are more alcoholics, unemployed, and mobile people outside Skid Row than there are inside. Rather, the fundamental problem is the way the people are judged negatively by the outside world, and that this judgment is internalized. We can see how this was anchored in labeling theory and symbolic interactionism in that people come to see themselves as others see them. Central to Bahr's analysis was the idea that people become disaffiliated because they begin to see themselves as society sees them. He speculated that the Skid Row man can be rehabilitated, but if "he has never really found himself before coming to Skid Row, the Skid Row

Identity and Identification 115

identity may be particularly hard to shake, especially if the labelling process has been set into motion by the social control agents of Skid Row" (1973: 287–288).

Wallace went further with the idea of disaffiliation. He proposed that more than individual behaviors, people on Skid Row constituted "a community of deviants, a deviant community" (1965: 141). The inhabitants of Skid Row were believed to be a subculture. This idea was significant for the identities that people who were homeless were believed to adopt. Wallace stressed that the subculture on Skid Row was necessary for people to survive; he similarly stressed that it was a subculture or community that many of its members no doubt did not enjoy. It was a survival strategy: they needed to form a community because they had no contact with kin, no relationships with women, and few associations outside Skid Row. They were thus reliant on the community of Skid Row, and as they became more reliant, they also became more detached from mainstream society. This then meant, according to Wallace, that they began to identify themselves as "Skid Rowerers," a shift that signaled that they were "completely acculturated in Skid Row subculture" (1965: 181) – which actually meant to be a drunk. For Wallace, being a drunk was quite different from being an alcoholic: "The drunk has rejected every single one of society's established values and wholly conformed to the basic values of Skid Row subculture" (1965: 181–182). There was no doubt for Wallace that life on Skid Row was distinct from mainstream society, and not only geographically distinct. He believed that the longer people survived on Skid Row, the more they no longer saw themselves as part of society. Furthermore, expressing a view that has profound practical implications, he also believed that people on Skid Row actually had norms and values that materially differed from the rest of society. Surviving Skid Row, he argued, produced a "totally deviant individual" (1965: 187–188).

Nearly 30 years after studies began to emerge on the subject of Skid Row, Snow and Anderson (1993) picked up on the idea of a subculture of street life. This idea was important for the conceptualization of many subsequent scholars' arguments that homelessness triggers identity changes. The model put forward by Snow and Anderson included engagement with the subtleties that were identified through sustained ethnographic engagement. They realized that the subculture was not characterized by a distinctive set of shared values; it was instead a subculture rooted in the behaviors

116 Identity and Identification

and patterns that people adopt to manage life while homeless. Many of these behaviors are carried out to respond to the homelessness and wider systems that people engage with to survive. Because of the realities required to survive homelessness, the social bonds are often superficial and characterized by distrust. Snow and Anderson described an encounter during fieldwork on the streets where three men who were homeless met and shared money to buy and consume beer: "The three men had known each other for only a few hours when we encountered them, but already they talked of their close friendship and were planning to go hiking together" (1993: 175). After drinking together, the men split up. Snow and Anderson described this as being characteristic of superficial relationships. People come together to share resources, for protection, to survive homelessness. These survival strategies contribute to the developing personal identities of people as homeless. Even though the relationships were often superficial, and although some people distanced themselves from the social identity of a homeless person, others embraced it. Those who did so tended "to lose their antipathy for other homeless people and begin to identify with them" (1993: 195). People who embraced the homeless identity accepted "street-role identities such as tramp and bum" (1993: 220). Most individuals who developed personal identities as homeless people were what they referred to as "outsiders." Outsiders were people who had been on the streets the longest and people who "have developed relatively stable material, psychological, and social patterns of adaption" (1993: 195). As part of the outsider identity, Snow and Anderson found that people presented themselves as self-sufficient, and not in need of the services that were on offer. In fact, they constructed their outsider identity in opposition to other people on the streets that rely on charities and services. One person whom they categorized as an outsider remarked: "It wouldn't be right for us to be using the Sally [Salvation Army] because we don't really need it. Not like the people down there. We can always find a place to crash – some empty building or something" (1993: 188).

Research on how people's identities change as they endure homelessness has spurred a cognate body of work on what this means for people's capacity to exit homelessness. The idea that people construct their identities as non-services users is important for exiting homelessness. If there were good reasons and benefits to identifying as a homeless person and becoming members of a homeless community

Identity and Identification 117

(Wolch and Dear 1993), what were the downsides, particularly over the long term? Researchers argued that the communities that people formed while homeless, or the adaptive identity strategies they took on, represented something of a double-edged sword (Grigsby et al. 1990; Osborne 2002).

This body of work assumes that the social processes that benefit people as they endure long-term homelessness actually serve to entrench them in homelessness. Jennifer Wolch and colleagues (1988) said that people who are long-term homeless are inhabiting a culture of chronicity, the last stage of the "downward spiral of despair and deprivation from which escape is difficult or even impossible" (1988: 443). Randall Osborne (2002) added to this by arguing that the homeless identity that people adopt to survive also means they are more likely to stay homeless because the identity is characterized by a non-use of services and fewer attempts to transition out of homelessness.

Charles Grigsby and colleagues present a line of argument that goes even further. They draw attention to values and belief, arguing that: "Membership in a network of other homeless people may promote psychological well-being and afford a degree of protection from some of the hardships of life on the street. But this can also encourage entrenchment in homelessness" (1990: 143–144). For Grigsby et al., people become entrenched in homelessness not simply because they lose contact with people who are not homeless from whom they may draw support, but because "as a group they exhibit nontraditional attitudes and behavior patterns – e.g., they are less interested in employment and are more likely to have problems with alcohol" (1990: 152). Here we see a view arguing that the processes people undergo when they become homeless involve changing their values and beliefs.

Drawing on the idea that people adopt an enduring homeless identity, characterized by deviant values that differ from mainstream society and make entry into the mainstream difficult, David MacKenzie and Chris Chamberlain (2003) argued that homelessness should be thought of as a career process. They theorized that people develop self-identities as homeless people as they progress through the career. In so doing, they adopt a normative acceptance of criminal and amoral activities (Chamberlain and MacKenzie 2006). Moreover, taking on the homeless identities means rejecting other elements of life; people who adopt the homeless identity "no longer express a strong disposition to change their lifestyle" (Chamberlain and MacKenzie 1998: 57).

118   Identity and Identification

These theories are consistent with the purported shelterization thesis. This thesis has been challenged for not taking account of the diverse experiences within shelters or of people's rejection of the shelter model (see Lee et al. 2010; see also Chapter 4). It assumes that staying in a homeless shelter creates dependencies and undermines people's attempts to exit. The connection between homelessness and shelters reflects the supposed relationship between poverty and welfare that scholars have drawn attention to. A long line of scholarship and political theory has assumed that people in poverty have a deviant set of attitudes (Mead 1997). Similarly, there is a wide body of work that asserts that welfare creates barriers to employment by supposedly eroding the work ethic (Murray 1984).

Like the poverty and welfare arguments, the homeless identity and shelterization theses are imposed on people without there being any evidence that they are relevant. Further, these theories are underpinned by assumptions about homeless people's immorality and differences from what is presented as a taken-for-granted mainstream society. Abby Margolis (2008) argued that because work and home are so central to the Japanese identity, the public perception is that people who are homeless simply cannot exist in Japanese culture, or even in Japan. Or, if they do, they cannot actually be Japanese; they are so deviant, they must inhabit a realm outside Japanese culture.

Stigma and the feeling of being othered

When scholars assert that people who are homeless do not have a desire to participate in the labor market or exit homelessness, or assume that they are alcohol- or illicit-substance-dependent, we must consider how this is received by those we identify in such ways. The homeless identities imposed on people matter to them; when people who are homeless are assumed by society to be deviant others, they feel shamed and devalued.

The feeling of being cast out as other than a normal citizen was conveyed by the participants in Jasinski and colleagues' study from the United States. One captured the sentiments of many, when she remarked:

> Being homeless is abusive [in] that people look down on you. They look at you as dirty or someone bad. They don't look at you and say, well, maybe they had a problem, maybe they house burnt down, maybe they

Identity and Identification 119

had too much pride to live with they family, maybe they trying to do it on they own. They don't look at that. They look and say, wow, look at this. This person don't want to work. This person is lazy. This person just want to be a menace to society. (2010: 140)

This constant feeing about being devalued and unaccepted by society has an impact on people's sense of self. Muhammed Asadi (2013) found that people who were homeless blamed themselves and their poor choices for their condition. He argued that this self-blame – the feeling of being at fault for not living up to the ideals of having a home, or a family based in the home – was produced as a result of the process of being managed and treated in the homelessness system. The reader will recall from the previous chapter the common experience that people living in homeless accommodation have of feeling devalued and treated like children. Asadi found that the people who had been institutionalized in the homelessness system the longest expressed the most self-blame.

Jessica Gerrard and David Farrugia argue that the public see people who are homeless as distasteful. This, they argue, is not simply because the public avert their eyes from people who are homeless or demand that "they get a job." Rather, people who are homeless are positioned as other, as inadequate, "as figures of helplessness and despair" (2015: 2230). For Farrugia, this positioning of the homeless in a lamentable light, or the symbolic burden that they carry because of their homelessness, viscerally impacts them. His research with young people who were homeless found that they widely believed that society looks down on them and judges them for being lazy, immoral, and irresponsible. Young people who are homeless "are positioned as less than other people," which results in their feeling "low self-worth, shame, anger" (2011: 78). Farrugia cites the comments of one of his participants who gives a sense of the day-to-day processes that contribute to people who are homeless feeling judged, and at the same time ostracized, by society:

Well it's definitely the looks. And it's a feeling you get. Because when you sit down next to someone they kind of, you know, put their purse aside or briefcase and kind of just give you a dirty, well I keep saying dirty looks but that's one big part and also they glance at you and then they cough or pretend like you're making this kind of offensive odour or whatever. Or they stand away from you too. (2011: 79)

The homeless identity is thus far more than a construction of researchers to make sense of adaptive strategies deployed by people on the streets. The identity, which is premised on people living outside societal norms, is felt by people who are homeless as encapsulating their totality. People who are homeless feel that they are seen as the embodiment of their state of deprivation, which includes deviant norms, but also includes filth. The homeless identity is an amalgam of stereotypes which act as a "defining feature of a person's character, overshadowing all other axes of identity" (McCarthy 2013: 46).

The homeless identity is stigmatized, imposed upon people who are homeless. At its core, it assumes that homelessness is the defining attribute of the person who is homeless. When we impose a homeless identity on people, we are not only drawing on stigmatized attributes to say something about the other, we are closing down opportunities for people who are homeless to construct their senses of self in ways important to them.

It is, as we have seen, the interactions that people who are homeless have with the non-homeless that makes the former feel judged by and outside of mainstream society. The homeless identity is felt by people when they are looked down on, or, even worse still, looked through. It is also produced and felt because people who are homeless have their lives on public display. Living in public space, or spending significant parts of the day interacting in public spaces because many shelters require residents to vacate the premises during the day, means that people have little option but to display what we with houses conceal within the privacy of our homes. This is particularly the case with the display of behaviors that are stigmatized.

When people who are homeless display their alcohol use or effects of alcohol and illicit substances, their psychiatric illnesses, or conflict, it reinforces public perceptions of the homeless person as different. Don Mitchell's (1997) classic research is informative. He argues that when people who are homeless sleep in public places, they are both seen as deviant and "threaten the proper meaning of that place" (1997: 321). Having one's life on public display contributes to the validity of the homeless identity because it serves to signify and reify the person's difference. The identities of people who are homeless, because so many aspects of their lives are openly visible, are assumed to be widely shared by the public (Parsell 2011). The assumed identity intends to convey fundamental elements of who a person

Identity and Identification 121

is. This identity is based on a deficiency; we expect to know what a person is like as an individual based on what they do not have.

Being named and having identity imposed

The singular identity imposed on people who are homeless jars with what we know from the sociology of identity. At the beginning of this chapter, we noted that there is no single identity; rather, people have multiple identities. They act out their multiple identities in order to respond, for example, to the given social context. They present different senses of the self, depending on who they are interacting with, or what environment they are in. They may, for example, present a radically different sense of who they are when socializing with peers, interacting with parents or grandparents, or employed at work. The multiple identities people present and feel are important to convey the complexities and nuances of life.

One's capacity to present different and unique elements of the self is mediated by the resources an individual has at their disposal and also their position in society. The fluidity of identities that Giddens (1991) conceptualized in late modernity relies upon resources. It is consumerism, mobility, and opportunities that derive from engagement in the modern economy that enable people to take on and adopt multiple identities (Hamilton 2010). Gidden argued that the modern world means that people get to choose who to be, but, given that resources are important for the choices they make, including whether they get to make them at all, the capacity to independently display different identities is distributed unevenly in society, along with the unequal distribution of resources.

It is not just about resources, however. People's position in society matters for how their identities are recognized. As we have seen, the reality of homelessness is the reality of being defined by what one lacks. Steph Lawler (2014) makes this point by reflecting on the way in which working-class people are identified in the United Kingdom. She argues that it is taken for granted that they do not even know themselves. Instead, their true identities are mistakenly assumed to be self-evidently known by the middle class. The working class and other marginalized groups are collectively known as the mob, whereas middle-class identities "silently pass as normal" (2014: 141). Lawler's work is significant for illustrating how material poverty impacts identity in two ways. First, being poor is assumed to be all one needs to know about the poor: their identity is constructed in terms of what they lack. Second, being poor means the constrained social legitimacy to have a voice that is heard that can challenge the identities imposed upon them.

Being homeless means having only limited power to project any identity beyond what is imposed by others. As Brekhus (2003) observes, some attributes are not only socially stigmatized, but they are also assumed by society to be indicative of the identities of people. People are not simply homeless; society assumes that this is an identity that says something about the person on individual and collective levels. Bauman makes this point well with reference to people who are marginalized in society for whom "access to identity is barred – they are given no say in deciding their preferences. They are burdened with the identities enforced or imposed by others; identities which they themselves resent, but are not allowed to shed" (2004: 38).

The experience of homelessness results in people's limited ability to have their identity claims socially accepted. We need to critically reflect upon the way that the non-homeless characterize homeless identities as an act of power. This point is articulated well by Lister (2021), who argues that poverty should not be seen exclusively in material terms. Poverty must be seen as relational, with a recognition of the profound power imbalances in the relationship. This is manifested in who gets to decide the identities that are constructed about the poor. As Lister recognizes, people experiencing poverty are far from passive victims in the power struggle. They assert agency and present counter-narratives about their own identities, even though these may have nothing whatsoever to do with their state of impoverishment.

We see this too among people who are homeless. Although identified as the other by society, and with constrained power to counter the identities imposed upon them, people who are homeless do indeed articulate and express their identities in ways that challenge dominant characterizations.

Self-identities

The weight of knowledge that we have about the homeless identity is generated by people who are not homeless. How do people who are homeless identify themselves? What does homelessness, if anything at all, have to do with the identities people who are homeless construct for themselves? There is a body of research that finds that people who are homeless reject the homeless identity.

Surveys undertaken in Canada (O'Grady et al. 2020), in the United States (Winetrobe et al. 2017), and in Australia (Walter et al. 2015) all depict a largely similarly story. Focusing on both young people and adults who were homeless, these surveys find that many people who were objectively defined as homeless, often because they were residing in homeless accommodation, did not actually identify themselves as homeless. Hailey Winetrobe and colleagues found slightly fewer than half their sample of 448 people did not identify as homeless; Bill O'Grady and collaborators' survey of 1,103 people who were homeless found that approximately two-thirds did not identify themselves as homeless; Zoe Walter and colleagues found 31 percent of their sample of 114 residents of a homeless shelter did not identify themselves as homeless, whereas 12 percent were ambivalent about the category.

These surveys align with in-depth qualitative research. People who are homeless recognize that society sees them as stigmatized (McNaughton 2008), but they themselves feel normal and resist the homeless identity (Preece et al. 2020). In addition to the identity strategies reported in Chapter 3 that women carry out to keep safe, the literature shows that they go to considerable trouble to distance themselves from a homeless identity.

Some scholars have argued that people who are homeless construct social comparisons to maintain favorable identities. They make intragroup comparisons to both differentiate themselves from others who are homeless and to articulate a positive sense of self. Katherine Boydell and colleagues' (2000) Canadian study reports an identity hierarchy, where people who are homeless asserted their sense of self at the top of a group of people who were socially stigmatized. They did this by referring to past experiences of work, and imagined future selves engaged in helping others. Participants in Alice Farrington and W. Peter Robinson's study portrayed themselves positively by emphasizing their skills and coping abilities, and even the esteem in which they are held. One person in their study highlighted how he was different from the others who were homeless as he was one of a "select few homeless people allowed to have his post sent to the shelter" (1999: 184).

124 Identity and Identification

In a more recent investigation from the United Kingdom, Jenny Preece and colleagues (2020) found that people who are homeless asserted their normality and distance from a homeless identity by highlighting their hygiene practices and avoidance of begging and behaviors associated with the stigma of homelessness. Others reframed their homelessness, not as a form of deprivation, but as a travel experience. The analysis of downward social comparison and efforts to emphasize positive aspects of identity are consistent with Snow and Anderson's (1993) findings that people engage in identity strategies to salvage the self.

It is not simply the case that people who are homeless reframe their deprivation as something positive, or engage in negative comparisons to present themselves favorably. People who are homeless do not necessarily see homelessness as part of their identity that they need to avoid or challenge. They draw sharp distinctions between what they are experiencing in terms of being without a home and who they are as individuals. Services can facilitate this. Anne Roschelle and Peter Kaufman's (2004) research with young people who were homeless in San Francisco showed that volunteers and services created conditions for people to rise above their homelessness and to assert identities unrelated to their housing exclusion. They achieved this by encouraging young people to form friendships and engage in activities and behaviors that rejected their positioning as distinct from society.

Rather than their state of homelessness, ethnographic research illustrates that people who are homeless construct their identities in ways that have deep and personal meaning. Shiloh Groot and collaborators' (2010) study from New Zealand drew on photo-elicitation to show that Māori living on the street firmly located their identities with relation to family (whanau) and meeting grounds (marae), even those who had been homeless for many consecutive years. The authors argue that it is important to realize the diversity in both Māori and homeless identities or "we risk dehumanising both groups by reducing their lives to the problems they face without recourse to their own understandings and strengths" (2010: 130).

In my research undertaken in Australia, I found that people experiencing unsheltered, often long-term, homelessness primarily defined themselves in terms of family, such as their status as a parent, grandparent, aunt, or uncle (Parsell 2010). People did not ignore their homelessness or romanticize their relationships with family. Many who were homeless acknowledged fractured relationships

Identity and Identification

with family, including having no recent contact with them at all. They similarly recognized that their day-to-day lives were deviant, especially those who had drug problems and resorted to crime to fund their addictions. They distinguished what they did in life from who they were. Despite what was wrong in their lives, including having no recent contact with family, their sense of who they were did not change: "I'm Keely's father. That's who I am. This ain't changin' no matter where I'm staying" (2010: 190).

Although not linking to family relationships, Leslie Irvine and colleagues' (2012) research from the United States found that people who were homeless constructed their moral identities based on being responsible pet owners. It was as responsible pet owners, and thus just like normal citizens, that people wanted to be known, not as homeless people.

The research focusing on the firsthand accounts and meaning-making of people who are homeless brings to light the subtleties in identities. It shows, for example, that people living on the streets and in shelter accommodation draw sharp distinctions between their day-to-day lives and their sense of self. The people in Toolis and Hammack's (2015: 56) study went to great lengths to decouple their homelessness from their sense of self; one person remarked, "we are not bad people, but we're in a bad situation."

People who are homeless widely recognize that living as homeless, along with the consequences of it in terms of forced dependence, is abnormal, but they distinguish this way of living from how they see themselves. Even after living as homeless for many years, they construct their identities in ways that they see as mainstream, and, as I have illustrated, they anchor to their notions of traditional family norms and aspirations for participation in the labor market. Rather than a remembered identity from a pre-homeless existence in which people felt attached to the mainstream, they described life histories where they had never felt connected to traditional institutions such as family, school, or employment. One participant, who had experienced long-term unsheltered homelessness, conveyed this, saying: "I've been on my own all my life ever since I was born ... Me days have just been hell mate, not good at all" (Parsell 2010: 190). The commitment to mainstream identities and rejection of homelessness as constituting a core element of identity is part of a search for a valued and recognized role in a society that people on the streets have rarely felt part of (Parsell and Parsell 2012). People are physically detached from what they see as mainstream society, but they still strongly identify with mainstream society.

People do not adopt identities as homeless people, nor do they see homelessness as representing an important feature of their sense of self, because homelessness is often the continuation of a life excluded from mainstream institutions. Homelessness is not an event that is triggered by an identity-defining moment or a state distinct from early life experiences, but is, rather, part and parcel of a life that involves multiple forms of exclusion and trauma since infancy (Fitzpatrick et al. 2013).

It is important to consider the independence that people exert when presenting their identities. A significant concern with the homeless identity is that it is one-dimensional; it assumes that the state of homelessness is all we need to know about the identity of people who are homeless. Ethnographic work shows that people who are homeless present multiple identities, which are contextually bound. Preece and colleagues (2020) found that people displayed a homeless identity when residing in shelters. It was but one identity, expressed in response to the socio-spatial context.

Gender, identity, and homelessness

What does the homeless identity, particularly the identity of a stigmatized state of living outside societal norms and institutions, mean for women? To this point, we have illustrated how gender matters to homelessness. It does so, for example, in terms of domestic and family violence as a dominant trigger into homelessness and the increased risks of violence while homeless. We also saw, in Chapter 3, that women who are homeless display certain aspects of themselves, and downplay others, as a means of protection.

Engagement with gender and the identities of people who are homeless is critical to help counter the dominant historical narrative that homelessness is almost exclusively experienced by men. Are there specific dimensions to gender that shape the homeless identity, and does gender have anything to do with the experience of being identified as a homeless person? O'Grady and colleagues (2020) offer a hint when they analyzed their sample of homeless young people to find that females were less likely to identify as being homeless than males. Adding to the broader analysis of homelessness as gendered,

Identity and Identification 127

In an Australian ethnographic study, I illustrated how the people who are homeless not only exercised agency by expressing multiple identities, but they also did so by anchoring their identities to the norms and social context of their environments. People displayed multiple identities, and were conscious of when and where they highlighted one identity over the other. One example comes from those on the streets accepting food from volunteers:

> Approximately 25 people, mostly male, a number presenting as disheveled, some carrying large plastic bags full of personal belongings, line up waiting for hot drinks and sandwiches from the van. The line is impeccably orderly; no one pushes or speaks loudly. Nearly all of those lining up have little expression on their faces, and their heads are slightly bent down. For the most part, people are appreciative as they take their drink and food from me (and my co-volunteers). Nearly all say thank you, those who don't, take what is given to them gently. Some people make eye contact and mention the weather, but most don't make eye contact, and keep their head lowered, without speaking. (Parsell 2011: 449)

The identities on show here were passive and meek, characterized by people presenting themselves as being in need of care and support. This presentation was enacted with routine consistency when people who were homeless accessed charitable resources in public space. Moreover, my interviews with volunteers suggested that they expected people accessing their care to present as humble and meek; volunteers complained about young people who were homeless who failed to conform to this passive identity.

I also conducted sustained participant observations in a café, which, although directed toward people who were homeless, also provided food and drink for purchase. As opposed to being a recipient of someone else's voluntary care, people in the café accessed food and drink as customers. I observed that a starkly different identity – an assertive, empowered customer identity – was presented in the café by people who were homeless, including the same people who at other times accessed charity:

> Customers debating merits of rugby league team with staff, as another enters café, interrupts, and makes derogative joke to staff member about music being played, and the type of person he is. A number of people walk in and out talking on mobile phones before returning. A different customer speaks with social worker about expected dividends from compensation about to be received. After loud comments from a friend, another customer explains to staff member how he would not ask her out, as she is married. (2011: 453)

> In the café, people displayed an aspect of their identity distinct from their homelessness. This identity was the antithesis of the passive, meek identity. People who were homeless, just like anyone else, showed multiple elements of the self. No single identity was more or less true; rather they were presented purposefully depending on the environment in which people found themselves.

here we demonstrate how being identified as a homeless other is not gender-neutral.

In an outstanding early account from the United States, Elliot Liebow (1993) shows what homelessness means for the identities that woman actively avoid and construct. She simply says that women who are homeless are neither more nor less normal, neither more nor less virtuous, than women who are not homeless. However, day-to-day life while homeless, both inside shelters and on the streets, means that homeless women are seen as unusual. They are perceived by society as out of place and the undifferentiated other. With ethnographic data, Liebow shows that women respond to this positioning as other by engaging "in a titanic struggle to remain human in an unremittingly dehumanizing environment" (1993: 222).

Julia Wardhaugh (1999) builds on this to further tease out gender norms and what this means for how homeless women are thought about and judged. Her work illustrates what being homeless means for the identities imposed upon women and the implications for their positioning in society. The homeless woman is perceived to "have not accepted, or sometimes have been refused, their place in the world" (1999: 92). Because of gender assumptions about woman's positions as mothers and carers, and as having a natural place in the home, woman experiencing homelessness are cast as even more deviant and transgressive than homeless men. Being homeless and unbound to the home, family, and domesticity is a threat to "home as a source of identity and as a foundation of social order" (1999: 106). Those who stay tied to the home and gender norms represent goodness, whereas those women who are homeless are the epitome of badness.

Reflecting on the idea that homeless women are perceived to represent badness, Judith Gonyea and Kelly Melekis (2017) examine the way older women who are homeless engage in identity work. This is important because the combination of age and gender mean that older women's homelessness is particularly unconforming. They found that older women who are objectively defined as homeless exerted agency: they saw themselves as neither homeless nor old. Conscious of the negative stereotypes that otherwise encapsulate their worlds, the older women experiencing homelessness identified themselves as good by emphasizing the care they provide to family and others living in shelters with them. In this way, homelessness is not simply a dangerous form of deprivation for women; it is not simply a stigmatized identity as other. For women, homelessness is perceived as especially transgressive as it unsettles gendered identities that center on home, care responsibilities, and parenting (Casey et al. 2008).

The threat that homelessness represents to feeling like a mother and being seen by society as a mother is a consistent theme. We saw in the previous chapter that the reality of homelessness is the reality of constrained autonomy to be a parent. When the experience of homelessness means that mothers are living apart from their children, they experience psychological suffering "with the stigma of spoilt motherhood ever-present" (Bimpson et al. 2022: 274). Mayock and colleagues (2015) refer to this as the erosion of motherhood. In their study, of the 22 women who were homeless and had children, 18 reported having at least one of their children placed in the care of the state or a relative. For these women, there was a pervasive sense of powerlessness.

Even when living with their children in homeless accommodation, women are concerned that, with the loss of autonomy that comes with being managed as a client, there is a threat that their parental identities will not be valued by their children (Thiery 2008). Women who are homeless express concern that their children will not even see them as legitimate mothers. Lois Takahashi and colleagues' (2002) research found that mothers who were homeless ensured their children were well-dressed and ready for school so as to avoid being seen by society as homeless. We can see how homelessness and gender intersect to doubly disadvantage mothers: on the one hand, homelessness is resource depletion that threatens their capacity to act as a parent, and, on the other, it is a symbolic burden that challenges women's ability to be seen as a worthy parent.

The impact of identity on homelessness

It is perhaps uncontroversial to assert that imposing an identity on an individual based on a deficit is morally unacceptable. In addition to this, the identities imposed on people who are homeless, along with the ways they identify themselves, have a range of material impacts. The research suggests that people who do not see homelessness as part of their identity are likely to experience benefits.

For instance, in their sample of young people who were homeless in the United States, Winetrobe et al. (2017) found that those who identified as homeless, compared to those who did not do so, were 1.9 times more likely to access shelters and housing services. In a study with 114 people residing in an Australian homelessness shelter, Walter and colleagues (2015) did not find that identifying as homeless predicted service use. They did, however, find that people who rejected the homeless label as part of their identity reported both greater wellbeing and lower negative moods. Josie Parker and colleagues' (2016) study from the United States adds an important dimension to this with reference to avoiding a homeless identity and identifying with family. They found that identifying as a parent, whereby the person downplays or discounts their homelessness when constructing a sense of self, promotes feelings of self-control and self-efficacy.

Anchoring one's identity to favorable elements of life, such as family rather than homelessness, may be associated with wellbeing, but identifying in such a way can be easier said than done. O'Grady and colleagues' (2020) study with young people who were homeless found that the identities people present are shaped by past and present life problems. Young people who identify themselves as homeless are more likely than those who do not identify as homeless to have no or little contact with family. They concluded that young people experiencing homelessness who "see themselves as being 'family less' also consider themselves to be homeless" (O'Grady et al. 2020: 506).

The way that homelessness services operate represent opportunities for either promoting wellbeing or perpetuating the homeless identity. If rejecting the homeless identity predicts wellbeing, and if framing one's identity in terms of family is associated with self-control and self-efficacy, homelessness services have a role to play. Walter and colleagues argued that homelessness services should be delivered in such a way that people do not need to identify as being homeless: "Our results highlight the importance of not tying people's needs, for example, their need for housing, with categories and identities that are based on assumptions of who the people are and how they see themselves vis-a-vis what their needs are" (2015: 352).

The necessary changes can also include the nature of language used by staff, for example ensuring that people are not referred to by what they lack. These changes are significant. Writing in the United Kingdom, McNaughton says that entering the formal homelessness system requires that people "explicitly identify themselves as a homeless person" (2008: 140). Drawing on research from the United States, Gonyea and Melekis report that, to gain resources and access to shelters, older women who were homeless were required to "take on bureaucratic definitions of homelessness" (2017: 79).

Providing services and resources in a way that does not reify the homeless identity, and the idea that homeless people are deficient, can also be progressed through the design features of homelessness accommodation. Parsell, Stambe, and Baxter (2018) found that the renovation of a homeless shelter that involved the removal of safety screens that separated homeless people from workers, along with the removal of de-humanizing dormitory-style accommodation, was predicated on the belief that people who are homeless have the same rights as all people in society. Moreover, as capable citizens with the capacity to make choices about their own interests, they should be given the choice as to which case workers to engage with, if, that is, they want to engage with a case worker at all.

There are other examples where a homeless identity based on the purported distinctiveness and deficiencies of homeless people shape what society does about homelessness. This helps us think about identity in terms of how people who are homeless see themselves and how society sees and labels them. The previous chapter's reflection on some charitable approaches to homelessness are telling. The models of support that aim to accommodate people in carparks, sleep buses, or other contraptions such as backpack beds and sleeping bags, are premised on both a poverty of ambition and a belief that the homeless are indeed different from the rest of society. It is hard to justify the adequacy of charity that enables people to sleep in urban carparks if they are seen as individuals with inherent worth, capacities, and a humanity that transcends their state of deprivation.

These contemporary approaches to homelessness build on a long history of seeing homeless people as deficient. From the United States, Bahr cites an important report that takes this idea of deficiencies, combined with undeserving status, to an extreme level:

> We do not recommend extensive or elaborate attempts at rehabilitation for the men nor do we favor a permanent municipal shelter or halfway house for all the men that has been proposed from time to time. Such major private and public social service funds that are available to the Philadelphia community should be expended on families with children or persons with greater promise. (1973: 241)

We can see from this report that the assumption of a distinct homeless identity can have profound implications for what society is prepared to do about homelessness. The assumed homeless identity, underpinned as it is by the belief that there are things wrong with the homeless person, has throughout history shaped homelessness services that seek to change people; to make them less inadequate. Edward Snyder (2014) shows that rehabilitation was at the center of efforts in Europe in the nineteenth century, particularly through rehabilitation that was motivated by, and sought to achieve, religious ends. Noting concern expressed at the time about the limitations of halfway houses and agriculture worker colonies in Germany in the late nineteenth century, Desiree Schauz wrote: "The homeless found only temporary refuge there. Combined with a continuing programme of discipline encompassing a strictly regulated day, regular working hours and a prohibition on alcohol, they did not offer their inmates any long-term prospects" (2014: 200).

An observer of homelessness policy or practice in the contemporary world will note that the ideas from the nineteenth and twentieth centuries are not entirely absent from today's discourse. We saw evidence of this in the previous chapter, where staff at homelessness

Identity and Identification 133

services see part of their role to be rehabilitating and changing the attitudes of the homeless. Stuart (2016) found that, in Los Angeles, the mega-shelters had made a recent move toward explicitly trying to rehabilitate people rather than providing only a bed and a meal. The assumption is that the deficient homeless person needs more than material resources. Even more recently, the United States federal government proposed that sobriety should be a measure for success in homelessness service provision (United States Interagency Council on Homelessness 2020).

There is something of a romanticized view of the homeless person as distinct that can also shape what society does about homelessness. Just as attempts to rehabilitate or to accommodate people in make-shift environments are predicated on deficiency, so leaving the homeless to endure their deprivation can also be grounded in an idea that they are a different type of people, who have chosen homelessness. It is difficult to know how prevalent this view is across society, but the public statements of elected officials and media coverage do indeed show that some at least endorse the idea that homeless people are different from others (see Chapter 2). This purported difference is manifest in their choice to be homeless (Parsell and Parsell 2012). These assumptions about homeless people's distinctness feeds into the belief that they are actually at home on the streets, and they are living among homeless communities.

The view that people are choosing homelessness supports the belief that society needs to do nothing at all about it. Why intervene to prevent people's free choices? Instead, the only thing society needs to do is respect these people's choices, and let them live as they choose. As Bahr said long ago, "if Skid Row men prefer the quality of life which characterizes Skid Row, then the rest of us are absolved guilt" (1973: 8).

There is a final practical implication that merits brief reflection. The theory that homelessness constitutes a shift in identity, one that is characterized by people holding values and norms that differ from mainstream society, shapes the expectations of what society should do to respond to homelessness. We should remember that the homeless identity means that people neither see themselves as belonging to the family unit nor express a strong disposition to change their lives (Chamberlain and MacKenzie 1998). This is consistent with the broad idea that people are choosing homelessness. The assumptions underpinning this theory feed directly into, and provide a moral

134 Identity and Identification

justification for, interventions or charitable acts that both perpetuate a person's homelessness and provide suboptimal resources while they are homeless. It is not an improbable step to move from (1) the assumption that homeless people have different values to (2) they do not need normal affordable housing like the rest of us. When, for instance, homeless people are positioned as distinct from society, it is justifiable to provide dormitory beds in shelter accommodation, to provide them with charitable care so that they can eat and clean themselves on the streets, or even villages where it is assumed that homelessness says something meaningful about their personal and, especially, their collective identities.

Concluding remarks

The language used to define people who are homeless in the twenty-first century differs from the language used historically. Reflecting changed societal norms concerning what language is acceptable and how it used to define people, today's homelessness literature no longer defines people as ambitionless bums, as lazy, or with limited intelligence. These changes notwithstanding, the contemporary literature still gives credibility to the idea that homelessness is an identity of distinct people, rather than simply an experience.

The multiple identities that we are able to employ, and the number of opportunities available in the modern world allowing us to choose who to be, are largely absent for people who are homeless. Their identities are instead defined by us; they largely consist of an all-encompassing identity that constructs a sense of self that is based on what we see is lacking for people who are homeless.

Homelessness is assumed to be an identity that says something meaningful about the people who are homeless. They are no longer seen as individuals, and they are no longer given a say in identifying themselves in ways that matter to them. Their individuality, including family position, voting preference, or even interest in sports or hobbies, is overlooked. As one of Gonyea and Melekis's participants said, "the only thing you are is ... one of the numbers ... I want to be back to being Smitty" (2017: 79). The scholarship on identity is interested in the multiplicity of identities (Brekhus 2020). Being homeless conceals these other identities – at least in the public imagination. Homelessness marks people's identity, whereas people

Identity and Identification

with homes get to decide what their identities are, even as they make judgments about people who are homeless.

When people who are homeless are asked about how they identify themselves, many do so with reference to family. Even those who have fractured relationships with family members still see them as the anchor for their identities. People often do not romanticize their family relationships or ignore the material deprivation that their homelessness amounts to; they just do not see homelessness as a salient feature of who they are. For people who have experienced chronic homelessness, this was routinely part of a life characterized by other forms of exclusion and trauma. Thus, homelessness did necessarily define who they were because it was a continuation of already being failed by society in multiple ways.

The identities that we assume people who are homeless have also matter for what society does about homelessness. Social policies do not simply respond to objective social problems; rather, social policies reflect deliberate problematizations. Social policies rely on a set of assumptions about what is wrong and what needs changing, and these assumptions are produced through subjective and political processes (Head 2022).

When homelessness is problematized as an issue of distinct, and even defective, people, we avoid looking for deficiencies in the organization of society. Even as we define *the homeless* by what they lack, we ourselves lack a focus on how housing markets fail to produce affordable housing for all of the population. The distinctness of the homeless person is a cover for the failures of society that produce homelessness. We take this proposition up in the next three chapters, where we examine, first, what society does about homelessness (Chapter 6 and 7), and then, what society ought to do about homelessness (Chapter 8). To set in motion the societal change required to prevent and end homelessness, we need to move our gaze from the assumed identities of people who are homeless and look instead toward the institutions, policies, and societal arrangements that prevent people from living in a way that would make them feel included in and accepted by society.

6

What Can Societies Do about Homelessness?

When confronted with the despair and waste of human life that homelessness amounts to, we are compelled to do something. For many of us, this something is just theoretical. When we see a person who is homeless on the street in front of us, we make meaning of their situation in terms of illness, bad choices, and even pity. Some of us respond with anger: anger at the state for its failures; anger at modern society for its callousness, or anger at the disrespect that the homeless represent for bringing their deprivation to our neighborhoods. Even if we cross the road to avoid the person who is homeless, we are doing something: we are trying to avoid the way homelessness unsettles us. Of course, many people respond through trying to help. Our shared humanity means that deciding what we should do when we see a person who is homeless is a decision that will exist for as long as homelessness does.

Homelessness is never a problem that simply occurs; it is a problem that societies always respond to, dedicating significant thought, effort, and funding to respond to people who are homeless. These societal responses include both state and nonstate actors. The latter frequently operate with the support of state funding, and their work with people who are homeless is often directed to address or counter inadequate state responses.

Because homelessness is experienced by people across the life course and in varying situations – and because homelessness is the result of a range of different structural and immediate triggers (see Chapter 2) – the responses to homelessness vary enormously. They vary to such a great extent that it is meaningless to talk about a

What Can Societies Do about Homelessness? 137

homelessness response that has relevance within a single country, let alone across international borders.

As we will illustrate in this chapter, the diverse homelessness responses reflect the many different interpretations of homelessness and what to do about it. This includes the supposition that people who are homeless need to be moved, cared for, and sheltered, and even that they need to be changed. In many societies, we see these competing ideas and multiple responses occurring simultaneously.

Never far from these approaches is the idea of a homeless identity, as discussed in the previous chapter. This identity is underpinned by ideas of both differences and deficiencies. Homelessness responses are often targeted at remedying the problematic individual and bringing people back in to an assumed mainstream from which they diverge. Underlying the many homelessness responses is the obvious assumption that they are most frequently directed toward the individual who is homeless. As we will identify in this chapter and then develop in subsequent chapters, responses that focus on the individual are by their nature unable to address the societal conditions that leads to individuals ending up homeless in the first place.

Abolishing homelessness

This chapter is deliberately focused on how societies respond to people who are homeless, rather than how societies actually help people who are homeless, because societal responses are often not intended to help. The aim of some societies is simply to eliminate homelessness by coercively removing people from public spaces or entrapping them in the criminal justice system. The dominant narrative is that their removal is part of a revanchist agenda, whereby the public realm is cleansed of poverty and despair.

Don Mitchell's work from the United States is an archetypical demonstration of the revanchist thesis. The title of his article, *The Annihilation of Space by Law*, gives a sense of the extreme criminalization of homelessness as he saw it. Referring to laws that, he says, are being passed "in city after city," Mitchell presents a dystopic analysis. According to him, the laws are "in effect annihilating the spaces in which the homeless must live, these laws seek simply to annihilate homeless people themselves" (1997: 305). Mitchell was clear that the laws did not simply negatively impact people who

138   What Can Societies Do about Homelessness?

were homeless. They were actually "anti-homeless" laws, intended to remove people who were homeless from the public realm because the state was trying to redefine the public space as a place only for the housed. From this revanchist perspective, annihilation of *the homeless* was part of an agenda to take back the streets for workers and the middle classes (Smith 1996). The revanchist view assumes that homelessness is a barrier to attracting the capital and skilled workforce that cities need to stay competitive in the global world. From this perspective, removing people who are homeless is the necessary means to benefit the city's development and growth.

In a characterization that perhaps out-does Mitchell in terms of moral panic, Randall Amster argued that the criminalization of homelessness – the forced removal of homeless people from desirable public places – has existed throughout modern history. His assessment of the United States suggests that efforts to first demonize and then criminalize the homeless have increased. He proposes that people who are homeless are presented as filthy and diseased, at risk of contaminating the public and the public realm. For Amster, criminal legislation that targets people who are homeless does more than remove them from desirable places: it works to erase their existence altogether. Presenting the most extreme picture of the state's brute force to remove, he remarks: "unsurprisingly, the 'extermination' scenario is never far from the surface of the homeless experience, since it is the logical aim of these myriad policies and practices of criminalization" (2003: 214). Although the sort of language used by Mitchell ("annihilate") and by Amster ("extermination") is no longer commonly used, the criminal laws continue to directly impact the capacity of people who are homeless to survive in public places. Although never passed into law or formal policy, President Donald Trump evoked the revanchist thesis when he threatened to take federal intervention to eradicate homelessness in parts of California. This threat of federal intervention was couched as necessary because, Trump claimed, cities were being overrun with homelessness, homelessness ruins the prestige of cities, and people in homes were being forced to leave because of this (Rucker and Stein 2019).

Chris Herring (2019) provides a detailed and nuanced analysis of the legislation that impacts the capacity of people who are homeless to be in public spaces. He shows that the number of laws enacted that essentially ban homelessness – including camping, living in a vehicle,

What Can Societies Do about Homelessness? 139

or even sitting or lying in a public space – significantly increased in the United States between 2006 and 2016. He refers to these as anti-homelessness laws, which are underpinned by the intention to remove homelessness from the urban realm.

Hungary is one of the few countries outside of the United States where removal is enabled through severe laws that criminalize homelessness. Hungary is unique for being the only national jurisdiction where penalizing homelessness is encoded in the constitution (Udvarhelyi 2014). Following the mayoral enactment of a "homelessness-free zone" in a district of Budapest, Hungary passed laws that prevented people from using public spaces in "a way that is different from its original designation," which included sleeping or storing personal belongings (Bence and Udvarhelyi 2013: 138). People in breach of this law could be fined, and if fines are unpaid, people could be incarcerated.

Removal through design

Evidence for the relevance of the revanchist thesis and concern that people who are experiencing homeless are being aggressively removed from the public realm are animated by examples of hostile architecture. This is a broad concept that "describes the various structures that are attached to or installed in spaces of public use in order to render them unusable in certain ways or by certain groups" (Petty 2016: 68). By virtue of its function to exclude, hostile architecture is not an "innocent description; it is an allegation" (Rosenberger 2020: 884).

A recent example that galvanized deep public outrage were the London so-called "anti-homeless spikes." The spikes, which were actually steel studs, were first implanted in the alcove of an expensive London apartment building to prevent people who are homeless from sleeping or sitting there. This was private property and therefore contravened no law, but they provoked so much public outrage that they were removed by the apartment owners within a week (Petty 2016).

The spikes received significant publication attention, but they are by no means an outlier. Johannes Lenhard's (2022) ethnographic research provides an example from Paris where structures were erected to prevent people who were sleeping rough from gaining warmth from hot air vents. By shutting off access to the vents, people's capacity to survive on the streets during the winter was similarly shut off. Steel grates to block vents or steel spikes to prevent anyone from lying down or sitting are extreme and visible forms of hostile architecture, but more common forms exist to exclude people who are homeless that may go unnoticed. In many cities of the world, *public* benches and seats are designed with metal dividers (armrests) that prevent a person from lying down; the picture on the cover of this books illustrates this form of hostile architecture. These are referred to as anti-sleep benches (Rosenberger 2020). Another example that is not immediately obvious includes irrigation systems randomly operating in parks throughout the evening to prevent sleeping. Albeit rationalized by public officials as a necessary means to protect people who are living on the streets (Lenhard 2022), it is difficult to explain hostile architecture in a way other than as part of a longstanding attempt to forcibly remove people who are homeless from the public realm because their presence is at odds with the image of a city that is attractive to consumerism.

James Petty (2016) argues that the London spikes comprise an aggressive form of coercion toward, and disregard for, people who are homeless, but they are consistent with long-held public sentiment and responses to homelessness. What the spikes did was provide an impetus for the public to reflect upon the subtle exclusion that people who are homeless typically face. For the public, the London spikes meant that ambivalence about homelessness was "temporarily ruptured: compassion for the body denied shelter by these spikes momentarily outweighed the apathy, futility and resentment that often characterises encounters with, and understandings of, homelessness in the urban landscape" (2016: 77).

The presence of overt hostile architecture is controversial because it grates with any notion of inclusion or universal rights to public space. It is difficult to know precisely whether these tactics to discriminate are on the rise, as some scholars suggest (Rosenberger 2020). It is nevertheless important to consider how hostile architecture and criminal legislation that is used to remove people who are homeless from public space sit alongside responses that aim to provide care. When we consider and become enraged by the way societies force people from public space, we need to also examine what else they could do.

As we will explain throughout this chapter, the ethicality of responses to homelessness rest on their capacity to benefit people who are homeless themselves, and provide the benefits that they themselves want. Beth Watts and colleagues provide a theoretical model that challenges the simple assumption that less assertive intervention equates to more ethical homelessness responses, with coercive responses to alter behavior simply assumed to be the least ethical. They adopt a consequentialist framework and argue that the ethicality of homelessness responses should be informed by effectiveness, proportionality, and balance (Watts, Fitzpatrick, Johnsen 2018). For the present discussion, we work from the premise that the desirability or otherwise of efforts to remove homelessness depend on what removal achieves and who gets to determine its achievement.

A more nuanced criminal justice response?

Alongside the extreme revanchist image portrayed in the United States and Hungary, or the myriad examples of hostile architecture designed to remove people who are homeless from public space, a more nuanced picture is emerging. This shows that although legislation and policing do have a negative impact on the use of public space by people who are homeless, these are not the only strategies adopted.

Gordon MacLeod (2002) stresses that it is important to highlight the differences between, for example, the hard criminalization tactics adopted in New York with the less coercive approach to homelessness deployed in Glasgow. This is not to romanticize the Glasgow response. The push to promote Glasgow's urban entrepreneurialism has led to policies that seek to control, remove, and purify the unsheltered homeless. MacLeod observes that the removal of homelessness through criminalization in that city cannot be said to be widespread, and there are myriad forms of care and support provided in addition to punitive measures (see below).

As in Glasgow, so elsewhere in Europe (apart from Hungary) the picture of criminalization as a means of removing homelessness is also a mixed one. There is little evidence for the assumption that dystopic criminalizing of homelessness has been exported from the United States to Europe. O'Sullivan (2012), who is editor-in-chief of the *European Journal of Homelessness*, observes that punitive responses to homelessness have existed for hundreds of years in Europe, originating in Belgium and Switzerland. These punitive measures negatively impact people who are homeless. However, in

142   What Can Societies Do about Homelessness?

Europe, "the evidence that this is part of a strategy of punishing the poor or annihilating public space is scant. Homelessness policy is still largely driven by the politics of social inclusion rather than the politics of social exclusion" (2012: 89).

The Canadian punitive approach to eliminate homelessness also differs from what is found south of the country's border. Gaetz's (2013) Canadian analysis shows that the punitive turn in homelessness governance followed neoliberal changes that reduced levels of both welfare and affordable housing. Canada's criminalization of homelessness occurred in some cities but not all, and it took place alongside support services. Geoff DeVerteuil sums up the differences well, noting, as a Canadian, that he found the "punitive thesis to be rather narrowly American" (2014: 878).

The criminalization of homelessness in Australia is similar to what has been identified outside the United States. Tamara Walsh (2005) is clear that legislation does negatively impact both people who are homeless and their rights to simply be in public space. On the other hand, the legislation cannot be said to attempt to erase or annihilate the homeless. Statutory provisions are conscious of a person's homelessness status and this must be taken into account when, for example, determining whether a person who is homeless has the capacity to pay a fine.

The more complicated picture is also evidenced through examination of why police remove people who are homeless. The extent to and manner in which police intervene to enact existing legislation is shaped by public sentiment and the public's acceptance of homelessness. It is not only the presence of a law or how that law is drafted to take account of homelessness that influence whether police can and do act to remove people who are homeless; it is also whether police are pressured by the public to take a punitive approach. Herring (2019) focused on the way that, in the United States, complaints received via calls from the public on 911 – which he refers to as complaint-oriented policing – drive the police to punitively remove people who are homeless from public spaces, something that he demonstrates with data. Although unsheltered homelessness in San Francisco grew by about 1 percent between 2013 and 2017, there was a 72 percent increase during the same period in calls from the public concerning homelessness. He argues that increased criminalization of the homeless happens, in part, because of an increased number of public reports to the police about homelessness. It is an important analysis, because he shows that although the police do contribute toward the temporary removal of homelessness, they do so by acting on the wishes of citizens who want people who are homeless removed. This is in contrast to the police being pushed to criminalize homelessness as a way of reaching arrest targets, or even because of officer discretion.

The negative impacts of this policing on people who are homeless most frequently come not from incarceration or even court appearances or fines, but instead from being constantly moved on, or even having personal belongings removed and destroyed (Herring et al. 2020). Unsurprisingly, being moved on by the police does not resolve a person's homelessness. Rather, being moved on means that people's homelessness is dispersed throughout the urban environment and shifted from one police jurisdiction to another (Herring et al. 2020).

In Australia, a community organization provides street outreach to move people who are sleeping rough on from public space so as to prevent them from being harassed by the police. The outreach service receives funding from a state initiative to reduce Indigenous deaths in custody. As an outreach worker described it, they aim to keep one step ahead of police: "We move Aboriginal people around from one temporary spot to another. And then later on we move them on again. We move them on 'cause of the public's concern of Aboriginal people being in public. But there is nowhere to move them to" (Parsell and Phillips 2014: 196). The futility and frustration of being moved on by the outreach service and police is demonstrated by those on the receiving end:

> *Researcher*: What do they [police] do?
> *Person sleeping rough*: Spill your grog [pour alcohol onto the ground] – spill your grog and walk away and laugh, or either spill your grog and lock you up.
> *Researcher*: Do they ever move you away?
> *Person sleeping rough*: Oh of course yeah.
> *Researcher*: Where do they tell you to move?
> *Person sleeping rough*: Just move, just get away, move somewhere, three parts of the trouble is caused through police harassment. (Parsell and Phillips 2014: 197)

Being moved on from one place to another and having their belongings destroyed means that a person who is homeless has an increased vulnerability to both violence and crime (Herring 2019).

144 What Can Societies Do about Homelessness?

We saw in Chapter 3 that people living on the streets are likely to experience violence either as a victim or as a perpetrator when they are pushed into marginal public spaces where there are few guardians and a high proportion of potential offenders. Moving people who are homeless from one public place to another is a strategy that aims to benefit the non-homeless population. It is an example of the way in which the citizen rights of people who are homeless are denied.

Coercive removal to realize care?

Removing people who are homeless through coercion – be it legislation, policing, or design – is controversial. It is an affront to legal premises of proportionality and people's right to the use public space. Despite some rhetoric about aspirations to benefit people who are homeless, not only is moving them from place to place perceived as punitive (Robinson 2019), research also demonstrates that there are negative consequences. These include disrupted sleep, anxiety about police harassment, and ending up in concealed and thus more dangerous places to avoid police contact (Westbrook and Robinson 2021). At the highest level, the limitations of criminalizing homelessness have been demonstrated and the alternative care and support responses have been articulated (United States Interagency Council on Homelessness 2012).

It is unusual for societies to only forcibly remove people who are homeless from public space; the deleterious impacts of the criminalizing approaches have informed a broad suite of responses that aim to couple care and coercion. DeVerteuil (2014) argues that a solely punitive approach to removing people who are homeless without joined up forms of care would be unbearable and untenable. Criminalizing homelessness is only part of what happens in practice. Much more frequent is the reality that states fund and oversee the delivery of both care and coercive measures. This includes, as was the case in England in the early 2000s, coercive street outreach that explicitly aims to achieve social inclusion and benefits to people sleeping rough. Although the evidence for a coercive approach to benefit people making long-term changes was not strong, this did form part of a broader welfare agenda that did not intend to engage the criminal justice system (Fitzpatrick and Jones 2005).

Empirical research shows that there are mounting challenges to the idea that governments and societies simply want homelessness

What Can Societies Do about Homelessness? 145

Against the backdrop of the increasing number of legislative responses that seek to forcibly remove people who are homeless from public space, Herring and colleagues (2020) provide a detailed empirical analysis to illustrate how anti-homeless laws reinforce poverty. Drawing on a study conducted in San Francisco, they interpret the criminalizing of homelessness as a form of pervasive penalty, which they conceptualize as "a punitive process of policing through move-along orders, citations, and threats of arrest that largely remain hidden from public view and official scrutiny because such policing falls short of official booking" (2020: 134). Perversely, the anti-homeless laws were framed by legislators as quality-of-life measures.

The negative impact upon people who are homeless is evident even when these laws do not lead to arrests. Analysis from San Francisco shows that – taking the swathe of anti-homeless practices collectively, such as bans on camping, move-on orders, and disposal of personal items – these measures exacerbate inequities in terms of gender, race, and health disparities among people who are homeless.

A significant insight developed by Herring and colleagues is the frustration and emotional turmoil that people who are homeless experience at constantly being moved on from one public space to another. Even in the absence of arrest, as conveyed by one person, "[it felt] like a constant pestering that keeps you from ever feeling relaxed or belonging just about anywhere" (2020: 139). Important to consider here is that these consequences of being moved on are felt not only by those who sleep rough. Because many shelters require residents to vacate the premises during the day, people staying in shelters are also moved on when they have no other place to (legally, legitimately) be. The emotional impacts of being moved on were made worse, as Herring and collaborators demonstrated, because the process was often felt as dehumanizing. People felt they were being treated as mere objects; they likened the process of being moved on to that of rubbish being disposed of.

The emotional impacts of being moved on sat alongside a range of direct practical implications. On the one hand, it pushed people into fringe public places that were dangerous and where the risk of violence was higher. On the other, the anti-homeless legislation facilitated a raft of public sanitation practices that led to people's belongings being destroyed. People living on the streets often lost irreplaceable items such as family photos, as well as critical items such as medication and personal identification, the costs of which were often too high to replace. The financial consequences of paying fines place people in extreme financial hardship, but for those who cannot afford to pay, the consequences may be worse. A failure to pay is noted in people's histories and can count against them when (and if) they apply for employment or housing.

The significant contribution of the Herring study is to demonstrate that the multiple and interacting mechanisms involved in legislative measures designed to move people who are homeless on from public places entrench their marginalization. Moreover, these legislative measures are often concealed from public view and criminal data, since many of them do not lead to official arrests, much less imprisonment.

When moving people who are homeless from one public space to another is framed in terms of quality-of-life legislation, it is clear that the quality of life referred to is not that of people who are homeless. In fact, anti-homeless legislation contributes to, rather than reduces, homelessness, given that it is so deleterious.

criminalized. In England, government policy certainly aims to prevent begging, street drinking, and rough sleeping through assertive means. These homelessness responses do, as Johnsen and Fitzpatrick (2010: 1705) point out, "appear at first glance to be symptomatic of revanchist attempts to sanitise public spaces." But the homelessness responses that seek to move people from public space are not simply revanchist; they actually involve care, compassion, and a desire to enhance people's welfare. Alongside the delivery of antisocial behavior orders and police practices that prevent some people sleeping rough from using certain spaces is the enhanced responsibility of both the state and voluntary organizations to provide support and resources to people who are experiencing unsheltered homelessness. In England, care and coercion occur in parallel, and, under certain conditions, enforcement – through minimizing

What Can Societies Do about Homelessness?

147

exposures to harm, for example – is intended to directly benefit people who are homeless.

Challenging the extermination and annihilation claims, Johnsen and Fitzpatrick assert that responses to homelessness must be examined to avoid emphasizing "rhetorical drama over a more complex and less sensational reality" (2010: 1718). Penelope Laurenson and Damian Collins (2007), make a similar point about New Zealand, where although enforcement and overtly punitive measures are sometimes used to respond to people who are homeless, welfare and housing measures are more often adopted. They assert that criminalizing homelessness is not common in New Zealand. In the United States, there is, likewise, evidence of enforcement and care working in unison, although the findings are less optimistic about the extent to which people who are homeless derive benefit, or, at least, choice.

Forrest Stuart's research from Los Angeles depicts the complex and coordinated ways that police enforcement and the provision of shelters work in concert. These two approaches are designed to come together to constitute the dominant form of homelessness governance. Underpinned by the assumption that people who are homeless are deficient, the combination of care and coercion present in Los Angeles is referred to as a velvet fist in iron glove (Stuart 2016). According to this view, people are not only deficient, they are also likely not to be aware of their deficiencies, and certainly will not voluntarily access interventions to address them. Police patrol the streets of Skid Row and engage with people who are homeless, but they do so to persuade them to use the available mega-shelters. If people do decide to use the shelters, the police refrain from issuing fines. Once in the shelters, people are actively confronted with therapeutic measures in an attempt to address their inadequacies.

Because of this form of paternalistic intervention, many people on the streets of Los Angeles' Skid Row prefer to stay put. The police thus play a critical role in encouraging them to enroll in a shelter; this encouragement takes the form of people sleeping rough being given the choice between a criminal justice response or a shelter response. Police in Los Angeles thus no longer simply criminalize people experiencing homelessness, they "now work chiefly to 'shepherd' wayward citizens toward more approved lifestyle choices and eventual reintegration into conventional society beyond Skid Row" (Stuart 2016: 33).

148   What Can Societies Do about Homelessness?

It is impossible to think about the therapeutic policing that Stuart identified without also considering the homeless identities presented in the previous chapter that assume that people who are homeless are both inadequate and inhabit a social world outside mainstream norms. Contemporary literature, particularly that based on empirical research, shows that, although the dystopic image of criminalizing homelessness is not the full story, efforts to respond to homelessness often intend to change people who are homeless. Rather than change through the criminal justice system, it is change through therapeutic intervention. In practice, we can conclude that a Hobson's choice is offered. People who are homeless can accept shelters and the therapeutic intervention that goes with it, or they are criminalized. There is a range of care services on offer, but the links to coercive intervention mean that we cannot think about these care offerings as completely voluntary.

A similarly paternalistic but not exclusively punitive approach to managing and changing people who are homeless can be observed in Singapore. There, people sleeping rough are subject to laws that include policing, rehabilitation, and compulsory care. The approach is overtly underpinned by the belief that homeless people need intervention to improve, and this intervention is not offered as a choice. This model of compulsory care means that "any idle person found in a public place, whether or not he is begging, who has no visible means of subsistence or place of residence or is unable to give a satisfactory account of himself can be picked up by MSF [Ministry of Social and Family Development] authorities and admitted into any of the 12 welfare homes for care and rehabilitation" (Tan and Forbes-Mewett 2018: 3584). The Singapore approach is stark because of the state powers deployed to rehabilitate a person who is homeless, against her of his will. Without recall to mental health legislation or the courts, it is improbable to imagine this type of forced intervention occurring in other countries examined in this book. The Singapore example is similar to many countries examined in that there is a coupling of care and coercion, whereby the latter is employed to try and achieve the former. As Brian Hennigan and Jessie Speer (2019) say with reference to the United States, the boundaries between care and coercion are blurred; this "is a hallmark of contemporary homeless policy across the United States" (Herring 2021: 265).

In Australia too, coercion and care overlap. In a regional city, CCTV is used to actively monitor people who are experiencing

What Can Societies Do about Homelessness? 149

unsheltered homelessness. This surveillance feeds into practices that seek to forcibly remove people from public spaces. At the same time, it is used as part of the homelessness governance system that contributes to ending a person's homelessness. Street outreach workers who have permanent housing allocations for people sleeping rough use CCTV to locate them to ensure that they are able to take up offers of permanent housing before those offers expire. Andrew Clarke and I concluded that the state's imposed use of "surveillance can also be deployed to facilitate supportive responses that aim to help people who are homeless overcome the barriers to accessing services and resources" (Clarke and Parsell 2019: 1964).

Shelter and change

If coercion is deployed ostensibly to achieve a range of care objectives, what do the care responses consist of? In previous chapters we have seen that shelter or hostel accommodation, along with charity that provides sustenance, are essential elements of the homelessness governance system. They provide people who are homeless with shelter and food, and sometimes with hygiene facilities too. Along with being essential, these responses are also frequently experienced as subverting people's autonomy and promoting feelings of shame. Furthermore, there is little evidence that they end homelessness; indeed, they may well perpetuate it. Developing this latter point, here we look more closely at shelters and temporary means of accommodating people who are homeless. We examine what these types of care try to achieve and their function in society.

Shelters, hostels, and emergency homeless accommodation

Shelters are the oldest form of institutional care provided to people who are homeless, commencing from at least the early nineteenth century (Busch-Geertsema and Sahlin 2007). They existed well before the concept of homelessness did. Prior to being referred to as shelters, they were called workhouses, poorhouses, or almshouses. The country-specific evolution of shelters means that there are variations in what they are called, what they try to achieve, who in the homeless population they work with, and their physical features. What might be called a shelter in one country differs from what is called a shelter in another. In the United States, the word "shelter" is frequently used, whereas, in the United Kingdom the term "hostel" is more common, or, in some circumstances, bed-and-breakfast accommodation. The terms are generally used interchangeably; other terms employed are generic homeless accommodation, temporary accommodation, and crisis/emergency accommodation.

Shelters and common forms of homeless accommodation have some characteristics in common; they both (1) are temporary, at least in theory, (2) have some shared amenities such as bathrooms, toilets, and kitchens, (3) have communal sleeping quarters, (4) have onsite supervision and restrictions, and (5) provide occupants with no legal tenancy rights (Busch-Geertsema and Sahlin 2007). Not all homeless shelters have all these characteristics, and, indeed, their features and function in society can change within a short period of time (Herring 2021). Nevertheless, the above characteristics represent a fair overview of what most shelters look like.

Support for shelters, and thus their prevalence in society, has shifted over time. After the closure of many shelters in Europe with the expansion of welfare states in the decades following World War II, their numbers began to increase across the continent in the 1970s (Busch-Geertsema and Sahlin 2007). In Scotland in 2018, there were nearly three times more people staying in homeless temporary accommodation than were in in the early 2000s (Watts, Littlewood, et al. 2018). Emergency shelters are in use in all the 35 European countries where the homelessness service system has recently been examined (Baptista and Marlier 2019).

In the United States, Christopher Jencks (1995) reports the development of at least 35,000 new shelters in the mid- to late 1980s. The growth in shelters follows demand. In 2006 in the United States, there was a 9 percent increase in demand for shelters, although 23 percent of those requesting shelters did not have their needs met (Mitchell and Heynen 2009). In 2020, there were 301,589 beds in emergency shelters in the United States, which is a 43 percent increase since 2007 (Henry et al. 2021). Given that shelters are intended to be for short-term use, this number of beds can accommodate in excess of one million citizens annually.

O'Sullivan (2020) argues that the shelter model is seen as the default response to homelessness, which, despite its many limitations, discussed below, remains popular throughout the Global North (O'Sullivan 2020). Allen and colleagues argue that "congregate

What Can Societies Do about Homelessness? 151

accommodation remains the single most significant intervention in the lives of people experiencing homelessness in a majority of Western countries" (2020: 14). In most countries with an advanced welfare state, a person who is homeless will likely rely on food from charities, have their access to public space shaped by the state, and spend at least some time living in shelters.

Critique

Alongside the dominant role played by shelters in the lives of people experiencing homelessness are damning and long-term critiques of their value in society. In Chapter 4 it was demonstrated that many people who stay in shelters feel that they are treated like children because they do not have the capacity to make decisions about their lives. As a result, some people find homeless accommodation so undesirable that they decide instead to sleep rough. Scholars have lamented the stigmatizing effect on people who are homeless being congregated in inadequate shelter accommodation that is physically separated from the remainder of society.

Designated and discrete shelters, especially those with shared living quarters, raise concerns that people who are homeless are being physically separated from society in ways akin to nineteenth-century institutions. This lends support to the misconception that people who are homeless have a distinct identity consisting of deviant values and norms (see Chapter 5). On the other hand, regular housing in the community is advocated because this helps people who are homeless feel "more human and less part of a category of persons" (Markowitz and Syverson 2021).

There are other damning critiques of homelessness shelters, hostels, and crisis accommodation, some of which are complicated. On face value, responding to people who are homeless by providing temporary accommodation is eminently reasonable because it overtly addresses their immediate need. In some cases, of course, this is true. But when societies rely on shelters as the dominant and ongoing force – as is currently the case across the globe – we have to question whether they are actually addressing the conditions that led to people becoming homeless in the first place. We need to broaden our gaze when evaluating shelters as a response to homelessness by taking into account the system failures that explain why people need them; we need to scrutinize shelters in ways that extend beyond their meeting a

152   What Can Societies Do about Homelessness?

person's need for a place to sleep. We should first ask: What actually is the need, or the problem, that shelters try to address? This question then leads to another: How does the use of shelters in society conceal the underlying problem, yet make us think that it is actually dealing with it?

The first problem with many shelters is that they try to do more than accommodate people; many operate on the assumption that homeless people need to change. That is, it is the role of shelters and hostels to facilitate change – to change people so that they become ready to move into more permanent housing. Once people have changed during their spell in shelters, the assumption goes, only then will they be ready for housing. This idea is premised on a staircase model, or what is also referred to as a "linear continuum of care" (Padgett et al. 2016). According to this model, shelters are at the bottom of the staircase/continuum, and housing is at the top. Through therapeutic intervention, shelters work to push people up the staircase so that they can graduate into – and be rewarded with – housing. Some argue that the undesirable conditions of shelters are actually intentional (Sahlin 2005). Providing people with inadequate conditions in controlling environments is thought to act as a motivating force for people to propel themselves up to housing. Certainly, the evidence presented in Chapter 4 indicates that people who are homeless would agree that shelter operators are successful in making them unpleasant.

The staircase model was informed by the straightforward and unsophisticated observation that many people in shelters exhibited individual health and behavioral problems, and it was these problems that caused people's homelessness (Allen et al. 2020). This reasoning then informed the belief that, first of all, people's problems needed to be resolved, and then their homelessness could be remedied. Housing is "the end product of rehabilitative success" (Kertesz et al. 2009: 500). Through the objective to facilitate rehabilitation, shelters perform a role not unlike that played by institutions toward vagrants in the nineteenth century (O'Sullivan 2020). The staircase continuum-based model is likewise consistent with long-held American values of personal responsibility and behavioral change (Padgett et al. 2016). Throughout history, especially in the United States, a dominant narrative has been that it is the poor who need to change, since the system itself is working just fine (Katz 1986). Trying to change people to prepare them for housing is not just an historical quirk. Reporting on

What Can Societies Do about Homelessness? 153

a comprehensive analysis, Isabel Baptista and Eric Marlier (2019: 77) conclude that "a staircase model of service provision seems to prevail in the overwhelming majority of European countries." Although its dominance is challenged by permanent supportive housing approaches such as Housing First (see Chapter 7), the continuum approach continues to prevail in shelters in the United States.

While the staircase approach continues the world over, the evidence raises serious questions about the effectiveness and appropriateness of this approach, and the shelters that facilitate it. The staircase model relies upon conditionality: shelter residents comply with conditions – such as curfews, abstinence, sobriety, and medication – and doing so ensures that they retain accommodation and progress upwards. In reality, the conditional approach rarely works. Instead, many people who are homeless stay on the bottom rung or are evicted for noncompliance. Conditionality and the evictions they produce trigger a continuation of cycling through homelessness, on the one hand (O'Sullivan 2020), and a confirmation that the deficient and noncompliant homeless person was indeed not ready for housing, on the other (Padgett et al. 2016). Failure to progress up the conditional staircase model is taken to be a failure of the individual rather than a failure of the model.

Below we challenge the staircase approach and its underlying premise of trying to change people. Before we even get to that, we can see that it is problematic also because the means through which people are intended to be changed – i.e., the conditionality aspects of the model – do not have a clear evidence base supporting their effectiveness (Watts and Fitzpatrick 2018). The type of change they are trying to realize is unlikely to be achieved: threating to evict a person with addiction for not overcoming that addiction might sound like tough love, but it is unlikely to promote the desired behavior change. The same challenges exist in telling a person with a mental illness simply to take their medication. By evicting or excluding people from shelters because they will not do what they are told, the staircase or linear continuum of care approaches that underpin them "have furthered the social exclusion of many people experiencing homelessness who have a mental illness or use substances" (Kerman et al. 2021).

Aside from addiction and mental illness, the staircase approach also assumes that it can make people housing-ready by teaching them how to be responsible tenants. The limitations of shelters to

154   What Can Societies Do about Homelessness?

facilitate individual change was vividly conveyed by Volker Busch-Geertsema, the long-term coordinator of the European Observatory on Homelessness. Evoking the basic requirement to have water in order to learn to swim, he makes the point that housing, not shelters, is the best place for someone to be made ready for housing. Highlighting the serious limitations of trying to make someone ready for independent housing by intervening and placing a range of conditions on them through a staircase approach, he observes:

> Support to enable tenancy sustainment is more effectively provided if people are quickly provided with a tenancy, just as learning to swim is much easier when practising in water. The principle is also called "learning by doing"! It seems so obvious that managing a tenancy, getting on with neighbours, paying the bills and turning a house into a home is best practiced under "real" conditions in a self-contained permanent tenancy with the perspective of staying there, rather than in a communal or other institutional setting, where other requirements have to be met. (2013: 324)

Shelters do not succeed in helping people to become housing-ready because the conditions necessary to sustain that readiness require people actually to be in housing. Moreover, while people can be evicted from shelters for not complying with curfews, abstinence, sobriety, or medication, none of these conditions necessarily needs to be complied with in order to remain in housing. As we demonstrate in Chapter 7, there is significant evidence that many people successfully exit homelessness and remain in housing even with active addictions and a range of behaviors that shelters try to unsuccessfully change.

But there is an even more potent critique against shelters and the models adopted to change people. The staircase approach is most controversial and, even, flawed because, by focusing on the inadequacies of and need to change people who are homeless, it ignores the deficiencies within housing and broader welfare systems. The reality is that many shelters actually function as a long-term option because accessible long-term affordable housing does not exist (Busch-Geertsema and Sahlin 2007). Fopp (2002) referred to this as bottlenecks and backlogs: people in shelters cannot exit because there are no affordable housing options, thus they stay in shelters even after they are ready to move on. This is not because of personal inadequacies, but rather because there is nowhere for them to go.

What Can Societies Do about Homelessness?   155

This is unhelpful both for people in shelters and for those who, in an emergency, could potentially benefit from crisis accommodation; the latter cannot access it because it is full with people who do not need it. Shelters then end up becoming de facto inadequate housing.

Shelters, and the housing-ready approach, reaffirm the normality of the housing market, and simultaneously reify the deficiencies of people who are homeless. As such, they can work to reaffirm the broken housing and societal conditions that produce homelessness in the first place. The validity of shelters as a response to homelessness is based on the perpetual myth that homelessness is a crisis rather than a systematic problem within society (Hopper 2004). The evidence clearly demonstrates that what people who are homeless need is affordable and secure housing, and it is these structural conditions that push them into homelessness and make exiting hard. Therapeutic intervention in shelters is unlikely to provide people with what they actually need.

An important analysis from the United States demonstrates this well. Culhane and Metraux (2008) found that approximately 50 percent of shelter beds were taken up by a small fraction of the homeless population, about 10 percent. If that small group of chronically homeless were provided with permanent housing rather than shelters, the need for the latter would drastically reduce. Culhane and Metraux recommended that money be redirected from shelters toward housing, including measures to help people to stay in housing or to access it rapidly once homeless. The Australian Institute of Health and Welfare (2019) collects data on all Australian homelessness services such as shelters; it reported that 95 percent of clients did not have their need for long-term housing met. The chorus of scholars asserting the ineffectiveness of shelters (Allen et al. 2020; Busch-Geertsema and Sahlin 2007; Culhane and Metraux 2008; Hopper and Baumohl 1994; Kerman et al. 2021; O'Sullivan 2020) are essentially pointing to the lack of affordable housing: shelters are ineffective because they cannot address people's need for affordable housing.

We therefore have to think about the value or otherwise of shelters – and why there is a need for them – in the context of the broader society in which they operate, including the conditions and availability of housing, labor, and welfare. Kim Hopper and Jim Baumohl (1994) argue that shelters play the role of containing and warehousing people who are homeless; they manage a surplus population but without any capacity to address the underlying societal conditions that produce that situation to start with. Shelters can make it look as if society is doing something about the problem of homelessness, whereas their presence actually works to distract attention from the housing and societal failures that drive people to reside in shelters.

On this reading, Dambisa Moyo's analysis of aid to the so-called developing world is apt. For Moyo, aid is the disease for which it pretends to be the cure. Shelters are presented as the cure for homelessness, particularly through teaching people to be housing-ready, but they are actually part of the problem. This parallels with Moyo's analysis of aid: "The problem is that aid is not benign – it's malignant. No longer part of the potential solution, it's part of the problem – in fact aid is the problem" (2010: 47). She goes on to argue that the donors have a greater need to give aid than the recipients do of receiving it. The analysis from Stuart (2016) in Los Angeles, discussed above, may suggest that the need to provide shelters is greater than the need for people to access them. O'Sullivan sums this all up well: "There is no convincing evidence that the provision of large congregate shelters for people experiencing homelessness achieves anything other than a temporary, and generally unpleasant, respite from the elements" (2020: 31).

Even in an ideal society, or a society that is demonstrably trans-formed (as discussed in Chapter 8), some people will end up homeless and in need or emergency or temporary accommodation. As Busch-Geertsema and Sahlin (2007) suggest, temporary accommodation to meet the needs of people who are homeless must meet two critical criteria. First, it must be temporary. This means that we can only ever think about homeless accommodation in relation to the broader housing and welfare system. If shelter accommodation is used for more than a crisis, it means that the housing system has failed, and the long-term presence of homeless accommodation works to both normalize and conceal these failures. Second, temporary accommo-dation should resemble normal living as much as possible, such as hotels. In other words, temporary homeless accommodation should not manage, control, or try to change people, nor should it require people who are homeless to live in inhumane shared conditions on the basis that it will motivate them to be better. As we explain in more detail in the next chapter, it is appropriate to provide a range of supports and interventions for people who are homeless, including those with addiction and mental health issues. It is important to

What Can Societies Do about Homelessness? 157

recognize, however, that accessing housing should not be conditional on a person receiving treatment. Support services are most effective when provided to people after they have been housed.

There is no more compelling reason to critique the function of shelters, hostels, and the many forms of homeless accommodation in society than pointing to the evidence showing that providing housing actually works to end homelessness. Analyzed in light of the existing evidence, we can conclude that shelters used for anything more than an immediate crisis play at best a superfluous function and at worst a counterproductive function if the objective is to provide affordable and secure housing to all citizens.

Concluding remarks

One could appreciate that a person who is homeless may be bemused by the constellation of responses they are subject to. They are likely to be supported by volunteers who provide resources, perhaps companionship, and who exhibit a desire to help them. At the same time, in many parts of the world people who are homeless in the public realm may feel harassed, pushed away, and even coerced by public officials, police, and even hostile architecture. In some places at certain times, people who are homeless are pushed – nudged – into interventions and accommodation that seek to change them. The extreme criminalization that is widely reported in the United States, and for that matter Hungary, cannot be generalized the world over. What does appear to transcend international borders is the coupling of coercive measures with care: coercive responses are often activated to promote care objectives. Some would refer to this as tough love, or, as Stuart termed it, a velvet fist in an iron glove. In these circumstances, what is ostensibly care is imposed upon people who are homeless with the intention of changing them.

The evidence suggests, however, that the desired changes rarely happen. Rather, the efforts to realize such changes themselves perpetuate housing exclusion. People generally do not want to be changed; they want housing. They may be willing and able to consider changes after they are securely housed. When societies exclude people from housing, they create the conditions for those people to be subject to the responses of a host of state and nonstate actors. Exclusion from housing rarely means exclusion from some

158   What Can Societies Do about Homelessness?

type of intervention, but the interventions adopted do little to meet the housing needs of people who are homeless.

Inspired in part by the overwhelming evidence that moving people, temporarily sheltering them, and trying to change them does little to end their homelessness, societies are experimenting with, and even rolling out, significant investments in models of housing and support. As we will examine in the next chapter, these integrated housing and support models – permanent supportive housing – represent a positive progression at the individual level.

7
Supportive Housing Models

All of us receive support. At least we would hope to do so. We live in our homes with support from family, both those who live with us and those who live elsewhere. We might be supported by our neighbors, or broader friendship and social circles. It would be the extreme exception for people living in the countries considered in this book not to receive some form of professional care, particularly from medical and allied health practitioners. Wealthy people receive lots of support in their housing, from cleaning, to childcare, to general home mainte- nance. When people who are homeless access support, it is presented as something different from what the rest of us receive. The help they receive is conceptualized as supportive housing; the assumption is that they need support to keep their housing. We need to reflect upon support in our own lives when we are thinking about supportive housing as a unique and different response to those who are homeless.

We might be puzzled to learn that the provision of housing to people who are homeless is presented as something of an innovation. But, as we enter the third decade of the twenty-first century, the reality is that providing people who are homeless with housing – through models of permanent supportive housing such as Housing First – are seen by many as novel. The novelty of providing housing to people who are homeless through the Housing First approach is conveyed powerfully by Padgett and colleagues (2016). They refer to it as no less than a paradigm shift. Drawing on Thomas Kuhn's notion that a paradigm shift in science happens as a result of profound jolts, they argue that Housing First "has acquired the gravitas of a paradigm

160　　　　Supportive Housing Models

shift. Its widespread adoption has inspired systems change well beyond what a model could accomplish" (2016: 12). We should note that the third author of the Padgett et al. (2016) publication is the person who developed Housing First, Sam Tsemberis. Nevertheless, their characterization of Housing First as being seriously innovative is consistent with a chorus of others. Writing in England, Pleace and Joanne Bretherton say that "Housing First is a breakthrough in ending homelessness" (2019: 5), while Busch-Geertsema (2014) observes that it constitutes a radical diversion from other approaches. Housing First is hailed everywhere as a radical idea for proving housing to people who are homeless, often chronically homeless and with addictions.

With everything that has been considered until this point, it is obvious that we should be excited by moves to provide people who are homeless with housing and linked support services. In contrast to the responses examined in the previous chapter, along with people's experiences receiving homelessness services presented in Chapter 4, it is clear that models that link affordable housing with support services are what many people who are homeless require. The evidence strongly suggests the effectiveness of these approaches to ending a person's homelessness. This notwithstanding, toward the end of this chapter we will consider how models of permanent supportive housing, although effective and meaningful at the individual level, are insufficient on their own to address the housing needs of the vast majority of people excluded from housing. This critical reflection on the limitations of permanent supportive housing represents a segue into the final chapter where we then consider the required and ideal societal changes needed to end and prevent homelessness among the many.

Housing First and permanent supportive housing

What does it mean to provide someone who is homeless with housing through permanent supportive housing models such as Housing First? Housing First can be thought about at the program level or at the higher-order principle level. Although there is no agreement in the use of terms, especially across international borders, at both the program and principle level Housing First consists of the integration of affordable housing with health and social care. At the program level, Housing First was established through the Pathways to Housing program developed by Sam Tsemberis in New York in the early 1990s. The program aimed to end homelessness for people whom the existing mental health and associated systems had failed, or, as Tsemberis (2010: 38) puts it, "the chronically homeless and severely mentally ill." With the credibility generated through robust evidence of success (see below), by 2016 guidelines were being provided for how services funded by the US federal government could implement Housing First as the preferred response. Since the George W. Bush administration, Housing First has been promoted at the federal level, and government funding has moved away from transitional (and conditional) responses to homelessness toward Housing First models (Eide 2020).

In the United States, Housing First programs, both Pathways to Housing and most subsequent programs, often rely on accessing housing from the private rental market through a head lease model that is funded by federal government housing vouchers. It is critical to understand that Housing First programs in the United States – and, to some extent, in Canada – focus on people in the homeless population who have diagnosed disabilities, often psychiatric disabilities. This group is important because they are eligible for funding that is used to underpin the Pathways to Housing program. In addition, the focus on people with mental illnesses, which are often severe and persistent, explained why some Housing First programs are linked to Assertive Community Outreach teams, including psychiatrists.

The resources in Pathways to Housing mean that many programs that are referred to as Housing First do not faithfully follow the model exactly (Johnson et al. 2012). Some jurisdictions say they are enacting the Housing First model because it sounds good, even though that is not actually what is happening (Clarke et al. 2020). Moreover, the New York City and US policy context means that complying with the Housing First model in different jurisdictions is challenging and perhaps not even meaningful. At the program level, Housing First can look very different outside North America, particularly in countries that have large supplies of social housing which is allocated based not on strict ideas of diagnosed disability, but rather on citizenship. There is some evidence that the principles of Housing First are embedded within the broader housing and homelessness system in the United Kingdom (Johnsen and Teixira 2012). The diversity in how the Housing First approach has been implemented has inspired a literature that identifies and measures Housing First program fidelity (Goering et al. 2016).

162   Supportive Housing Models

Beyond the program domain, Housing First can be thought about as a set of principles for how societies should respond and provide housing to people who are homeless. Housing First has three integrated normative principles. First, housing is a human right (Tsemberis et al. 2004). Second, choice is preeminent; this means that the provision and ongoing receipt of housing is not conditional on certain behaviors such as compliance with medication (Tsemberis 2010). Third, harm-reduction should be pursued, which means that abstinence and sobriety are not required (Padgett et al. 2016). These principles are closely aligned to the features of permanent supportive housing more broadly (Rog et al. 2014).

The principles of permanent supportive housing, including the Housing First approach, represent the antithesis of staircase or linear continuum models that characterize shelters as described in the previous chapter. Permanent supportive housing models such as Housing First can be considered housing-led, as opposed to staircase/ linear approaches, which are housing-ready. The positioning of housing as a human right is at stark odds with the model adopted in shelters whereby people have to earn the right to housing by progressing up the "staircase." One of the significant contributions from the permanent supportive housing and Housing First movements is the idea that people need housing immediately, rather than intervention while they are homeless. Moreover, these models of housing with linked support directly challenge the paternalism approach adopted in shelters by prioritizing choice, including people's choice to engage, or not, with services, and to consume, or not, alcohol and illicit substances. An array of different support services is critical to permanent supportive housing and Housing First, but use of services is not mandated and nor are they conditional on the continued provision of housing.

The normative principles that honor autonomy and self-determination are celebrated by some, while for others they represent a failure to deal with what are thought to be the critical problems. In a critique of Housing First written for the Manhattan Institute, the conservative think-tank, Stephen Eide (2020) reports that 23 Republican Congress representatives lobbied the federal government to end the policy that punished programs that sought to advance work, education, and sobriety in their responses to homelessness. Eide is worried that staircase and continuum-based models will no longer be considered in policy and government funding schemes.

Supportive Housing Models

But his main critique of permanent supportive housing models such as Housing First is that they do not lead to less homelessness at the community level. This perspective highlights how Housing First is critiqued because it challenges ideas of who is and is not deserving of housing. The infrequent challenges notwithstanding, the approach of Housing First and permanent supportive housing has received a groundswell of support for achieving a range of successes.

Evidence

Sometimes we need the best scientific research to discover new things; other times we require rigorous research to empirically prove what is otherwise intuitive. When it comes to Housing First and permanent supportive housing models, or even the less well-researched approach of providing people who are homeless with access to affordable and secure housing, research makes it clear that housing ends homelessness. If it were not for the dominant tradition of responding to people who are homeless with a combination of removal, paternalistic care, or shelter accommodation, one might wonder why research is needed to substantiate that this is the case.

Against the backdrop of many responses to homelessness that do not involve the provision of permanent affordable and secure housing with linked support services, or the direct challenges Housing First receives (Eide 2020), this research is critical. The research on housing as a solution to homelessness contains three important insights. First, permanent supportive housing models enable people to exit homelessness and remain in housing. Second, these models achieve superior housing outcomes compared to staircase models deployed in shelters. Third, people who have experienced chronic homelessness, often with significant health problems, retain their tenancies in permanent supportive housing.

In a systematic review of research from high-income countries, Aubry and colleagues (2020) found that permanent supportive housing, most often Housing First programs, significantly improved housing stability for people exiting homelessness with severe mental illnesses, and the outcomes remained statistically significant at a six-year follow-up. Studies have demonstrated that the majority of people who exit homelessness with the help of the Housing First program stay housed: 80 percent after two years (Tsmberis et al. 2004), 78 percent after four years (Stefancic and Tsemberis 2007), and 88 percent after five years (Tsemberis and Eisenberg 2000). Some of the research compares Housing First approaches to treatment as usual – that is, staircase and linear continuum of care models; Housing First consistently resulted in people spending more days in stable housing conditions and fewer days homeless. Aubry and colleagues (2020) found that 74 percent of people who took part in the Housing First program were securely housed after 24 months, whereas the figure for those who received care under previous systems was only 41 percent. More recently, in a French study following people for four years after access to either a Housing First program or earlier staircase models, Sandrine Loubière and colleagues (2022) found that Housing First participants achieved greater housing stability – more days in a house or flat – than what was achieved by others.

The group in the Loubière study who had not benefited from Housing First included people sleeping rough, so it is hardly surprising that better housing stability is achieved in a comparison group who were provided with housing and integrated support services. Nevertheless, the evidence is abundantly clear that responses to people who are homeless that involve the provision of affordable and long-term housing do end homelessness. The evidence likewise demonstrates that the same result is achieved for people with psychiatric disabilities and active addictions. Some permanent supportive housing programs target those with the longest experiences of homelessness and the worst health. Experimental research shows that Housing First has a more significant impact on housing stability for people with high needs compared to people with moderate needs (Stergiopoulos et al. 2019). This is an important finding for the cost-offset research described below, and it is worth noting that focusing on people who have been homeless the longest is a positive step forward compared to former practices that sought to address only the easiest cases and those for whom the outcome was most likely to succeed (Quinn et al. 2018).

There is, however, less clarity about the extent to which people who exit homelessness and remain housed also go on to report other improvements in life. Although the evidence for the social determinants of health demonstrates that homelessness is bad for health, and that being homeless impinges on people's ability to integrate socially, enroll in education, or participate in the labor market, it also shows that, even when people exit homelessness, many of them make no substantial improvements in these domains.

Supportive Housing Models

Andrew Baxter and colleagues' (2019) systematic review identified unclear short-term health and wellbeing outcomes among people who exited homelessness and accessed housing through Housing First programs. Moreover, they found no clear differences in mental health, quality of life, or substance use between those who benefited from the Housing First program and those in treatment-as-usual models. The Aubry et al. (2020) review came up with similar conclusions.

Substance use and misuse, of both illicit drugs and alcohol, have been the focus of research both among people who exit homelessness and those who do not. This is an important area of investigation, as staircase or continuum-based models often require sobriety and abstinence, whereas permanent supportive housing models promote choice. The former model is underpinned by the assumption that substance misuse, especially addiction, is a barrier to exiting homelessness. The latest research has significant practical implications: it indicates that people with addictions are able to exit homelessness on a long-term basis. In addition, the substance-related harms reported by people in both Housing First models and continuum-based models are broadly consistent (Kerman et al. 2021).

The diverse permanent supportive housing approaches provide evidence that ending homelessness for people is possible, especially for individuals who are assumed to be not housing-ready under the shelter model. This evidence creates a challenge to the treatment-first and sobriety approaches advocated by some (Eide 2020). Referring to Housing First specifically, but in a sentiment that speaks to the broader permanent supportive housing and housing-led efforts across many countries, Tsemberis rightly argues that they have "expanded the range of what is considered possible for people who are homeless and suffer from mental illness and addiction disorders" (2010: 43).

Through an array of approaches that essentially boil down to the provision of affordable housing with integrated health and social care services, it is clear that ending homelessness requires a change in our existing systems. In stark contrast to staircase or continuum-based models that explicitly focus on changing people who are homeless themselves, analysis of the broad literature demonstrates that when the way in which housing and support are allocated is reshaped, homelessness outcomes are much more effective. In other words, to end homelessness, societal changes are needed. One reading of

166 Supportive Housing Models

the research that shows less than dramatic improvements in health and addiction among people who exit homelessness is that health and social problems do not in fact need to be addressed prior to exiting homelessness, as is assumed by the staircase model. People who are homeless, just like anyone else, experience health and social problems, and they need to be treated and supported like everyone else. Although people's health can be negatively impacted by the experience of homelessness and although they are more likely to have experienced various social difficulties in their life, these issues are not in and of themselves problems of *homelessness*.

Cost benefits and their limitations

If the evidence presented in the preceding chapters about the significant and multiple harms that homelessness constitutes is anything to go by, then the compelling evidence generated since the late 1990s about the models that successfully end homelessness do provide optimism. Alongside our optimism, we need to inquire a little more deeply into permanent supportive housing models such as Housing First that undoubtedly change people's lives for the better.

Central to this critical evaluation are the cost motivations. The costs of homelessness, and the cost offsets achieved through ending it, were highlighted in one of the first influential studies in this area, conducted by Culhane and colleagues (2002). The costs of homelessness refer to the financial costs attributed to people using a disproportionate amount of publicly funded services, such as acute healthcare, shelters, and the criminal justice system, as a consequence of their homelessness. Based on analysis of government data from multiple departments in New York City, Culhane and collaborators estimated that a small group of the homeless population – people who were chronically homeless – costs the taxpayer approximately $40,000 annually given their extensive use of public services. However, and this is a significant however, they found that when people with severe mental illness were allocated permanent supportive housing – and thus exited homelessness – there was a corresponding reduction in their use of health and criminal justice systems. As a direct consequence, "supportive housing intervention significantly reduces these costs" (2002: 138). Specifically, and focusing on people who are chronically homeless with severe mental illnesses, "95 percent of the

Supportive Housing Models

The Housing First approach has reshaped how many governments and service provider organizations across numerous countries think about, or at least talk about, homelessness. And there is little doubt that the impact of Housing First is backed by rigorous and compelling quantitative research. This quantitative research has shown not only that Housing First is successful at ending a person's homelessness, but also that it results in a range of cost benefits. Less influential and well known, however, is the important body of qualitative research, which illustrates what Housing First means to people who have moved from homelessness to secure housing. Engaging closely with recipients of Housing First, the qualitative research helps us understand how people make meaning of their housing and the services provided through Housing First initiatives.

Control, autonomy, and home are key ideas to come out of the qualitative research. It is one thing to provide people with housing; it is another thing for people to experience that housing as home. Padgett (2007) argues that people do in fact gain a home when provided with housing through Housing First. Critically, she shows that people experience their housing as home because it provides them with control over their lives, including whether to consume alcohol or to invite and, importantly, restrict visitors. Padgett dew on the notion of ontological security to denote the meaning of home for people who exit homelessness. A woman who moved from homelessness to housing in a Housing First program captures what home means to her: "I don't want to have nobody controlling me and nobody telling me what to do and when to come. I just want to live my life the way I am now" (Padgett et al. 2016: 67).

As the pages in this book disturbingly illustrate, the reality of homelessness is all too often the reality of an absence of control. Understanding how homelessness equates with being controlled helps contextualize what it means to experience home when housing is provided.

In addition to housing as a means to gain control over life, the qualitative research illustrates how people who moved from homelessness to their own housing through Housing First feel pride. They feel pride at having achieved housing, but also at having overcome life challenges associated with their past homelessness (Padgett et al. 2016). This is an important finding, because it takes us far beyond the quantitative research that illustrates the value of Housing First in terms of the number of days housed. Of course, that matters too, but this quantitative picture can gloss over what it means psychologically to be housed: the notion of pride is something that matters deeply to us all, but it is a notion that we rarely consider when examining homelessness (or poverty).

The qualitative research also gives a sense of how Housing First is experienced in practice. Responding to the literature that refers to housing outcomes as if people have no choice about being moved into housing, I found, with colleagues, that this was not at all the case (Parsell et al. 2014). Housing First outcomes were not imposed on people; they make their own choices. The availability of affordable housing is critical, but people understand that their engagement with Housing First is contingent on the resources being made available in a way that does not undermine their sense of self. Moreover, people who gained access to Housing First described their determination not to return to homelessness to be part of a broader life project in which they had committed to make life changes.

The qualitative research helps us understand what Housing First represents in terms of supporting life changes; like any program or intervention, it is a resource that people actively engage with, or avoid. The program has been successful because it provides people with an outcome they want (affordable housing), and in a way that reflects what they want (control, autonomy, dignity).

costs of the supportive housing (operating, service, and debt service costs) are compensated by reductions in collateral service attributed to the housing placement" (2002: 138).

This finding has proven to be extraordinarily influential. It has spearheaded a body of subsequent investigation that has sought to monetize the costs both of homelessness itself and of ending it. The Community Preventive Services Task Force (2019) reviewed the evidence from the United States about Housing First. This

Supportive Housing Models 169

independent government body reported that when communities ended a person's homelessness through Housing First, "there was a societal cost savings of $1.44 for every $1 invested." On the basis of the available evidence, they concluded that "the economic benefits exceed the intervention cost for Housing First Programs." A similar result from a systematic review found that Housing First in the United States achieved $1.80 *worth of* benefit for every $1 invested (Jacob et al. 2022). Other reviews have provided a more mixed interpretation of the cost benefits.

Eric Latimer and colleagues (2020) evaluated the cost-effectiveness of a large Housing First trial in Canada. They found that 69 percent of the costs of the trial were offset by other savings associated with housing outcomes achieved. Aubry and colleagues (2020) provide a more cautious analysis of the cost-effectiveness claims, but still report the cost offsets that permanent supportive housing can achieve. Further, because cost offsets are attributed to averted costs mainly from healthcare and even the criminal justice system, they will invariably differ from country to country depending on, for example, whether people who are homeless are excluded from or included in mainstream health and social institutions. Perversely, if people who are homeless are excluded from healthcare, the costs associated with their homelessness will be less. Moreover, if accessing housing enables people to overcome barriers to accessing healthcare – as the evidence suggests (Parsell, ten Have, et al. 2018) – there may well be substantial cost increases in ending their homelessness. Cost benefits claims need to be closely embedded in empirical analysis of the specific circumstances of individuals and service systems in local contexts.

There are fewer studies from outside of the United States on the cost benefits of ending homelessness. Of the research that does exist, Busch-Geertsema (2014) says the indications are that Housing First will realize cost benefits to ending homelessness in Europe. Similarly, from both England and Australia, the research points to cost benefits of ending homelessness through Housing First compared to shelters or continuum-based approaches (Johnson et al. 2014; Pleace and Bretherton 2019). Drawing on rigorous analysis of the long-term costs of Housing First in France for people who were homeless with severe mental illnesses, Coralie Lemoine and colleagues (2021) found that, in terms of housing stability and reduction in some resource use, Housing First was cost-effective in the long term.

There are significant differences across the cost-effectiveness research. Some is based on randomized control trials, some on systematic reviews; some draws on less robust pre- and post- self-report surveys; some include criminal justice systems and some exclude them; some focuses exclusively on people who are homeless with diagnosed disabilities, whereas other research does not specify this, or it focuses on homelessness more broadly. The differences must be taken into account, but they do not negate a prevalent conclusion: homelessness, especially if it is chronic and experienced by people who are extremely sick, is a drain on the public purse. Models of permanent supportive housing enable people to escape homelessness, and, as a result, there are many cost offsets.

There is clear evidence that homelessness represents a cost burden to the taxpayer. This evidence spurs action for change. In the United States, it is estimated that homelessness costs society $3.4 billion annually (Jacob et al. 2022). Research conducted by the London School of Economics indicates that London boroughs spent £900 million responding to homelessness in 2017/18, and this figure will increase in subsequent years (Scanlon et al. 2019). Even if we can somehow overlook the consequences to human life, the costs that homelessness constitutes mean that it is hardly surprising that moves toward ending homelessness through permanent supportive housing models such as Housing First garner political and public support. When actors across the globe advocate Housing First and policies to address homelessness, they frequently refer to the cost-effectiveness research to underpin their credibility. Culhane (2008) argues that the cost benefits analyses and their use by advocates have achieved substantial policy impact, including funding for permanent supportive housing.

What could possibly be concerning about efforts to end homelessness being inspired by evidence that there are cost offsets, in addition to human benefits? It is surely the responsibility of governments to ensure the efficient use of public resources. This is hardly new. Michael Katz (1986: 54) reports that in the nineteenth century a public official advocated renting a room for a widowed mother and her children because an "orphan asylum" would cost more. Given the clear evidence that some people are frequent and costly users of services because of their homelessness, and that ending their homelessness impacts the government-funded services they use, there seems little point in criticizing programs to end homelessness that are motivated by cost rationalizations.

Supportive Housing Models 171

Or, one might reasonably argue, who cares what motivates governments to end homelessness, just as long as they do so. There is something intuitive about this consequentialist argument, but, as we will tease out now, there can be some unintended negative consequences when we frame ending homelessness as a cost-saving endeavor. In fact, the cost motivation can materially shape the nature of our efforts to end homelessness and, in particular, whether it is a permanent end at the societal level or an end at the individual level, and perhaps not so permanent an end after all.

The most significant concern is a moral one. It is important to reflect on the cost arguments when ending homelessness is framed as a means of reducing the burden on the taxpayer. We should be instantly concerned that homelessness becomes a policy problem only because it harms the well-off. It is of course a very profound burden on people who are homeless when societies exclude them from housing, as Chapters 3–5 have demonstrated. It is problematic, to say the least, if societies are only interested in ensuring that citizens have access to safe housing because this benefits the housed. We ought not to ignore the costs of homelessness and potential cost offsets of ending it, but our focus must be driven by the interests of the excluded, irrespective of what their exclusion might cost the included.

Inherent in the evidence that homelessness is financially costly to society, and thus that there are cost benefits to be realized by ending it, is the fact that certain groups of people who are homeless, albeit a small proportion, are very high users of government services. The focus on ending homelessness because it costs too much therefore ignores the majority of people who are excluded from affordable housing. As Culhane (2008) has stressed, the cost arguments are probably not going to stack up for most people who are homeless. A focus on ending homelessness among a small cohort because of their costs also runs the risk of benefiting some in the homeless population by making the conditions for others worse (Beck and Twiss 2018). The cost arguments are about rationing resources that do exist; if there is no increased funding for additional affordable housing, prioritizing the costly inevitably means the non-costly are de-prioritized.

Housing people who are the sickest in the homeless population because of the potential cost offsets distracts from the failures within the entire housing and social systems that produce homelessness among the many. In fact, Padgett and colleagues (2016) make this point when they observe that the health focus, with its emphasis on reducing costs, may let governments off the hook when it comes to their responsibility to build affordable housing to address the underlying structural problem. Craig Willse goes further by arguing that the framing of housing deprivation among a small cohort of chronically homeless as a burden on public budgets is a "textbook example of neoliberal post-social thinking in action" (2015: 157). By focusing on a minority of the homeless population and for motivations that derive from benefits to the taxpayer rather than to people who are homeless (people who, we often forget, also pay tax), Willse believes that Housing First and related programs work to "extend neoliberal economic industries that produce housing insecurities in the first place" (2015: 159).

By excluding most people who are homeless from the analysis because their deprivation does not cost society anything, the focus on the sickest in the homeless population, and as result the heaviest users of public services, is a way of reducing governments' responsibilities to the overall problem. The cost motivations mean that housing is not considered a resource and entitlement that citizens deserve, but something governments give for clinical or health economic reasons. It leads to a pathologizing of poverty (Padgett et al. 2016). In this way, as Helena Hansen and colleagues (2014) put it, the medicalizing of poverty that characterizes the post-welfare era means that the stigma of disability and mental illness is recast as the only legitimate way for citizens who are poor to draw sufficient resources from the state to survive. Cost rationalizations change the nature of the relationship between the state and the citizen, and the role that housing is assumed to play in society. In classic political theorizing, the state provides basic resources to all citizens to enable their social rights. The state delivers on this responsibility and citizens have the opportunity to then exercise their responsibilities to contribute to society and the collective good. When the state provides housing only to the sickest so as to divert them from more expensive intervention, society as a whole is undermined.

This focus on the sickest not only damages society, it is also short-sighted from a health and public expenditure perspective. Longitudinal research shows that, as homelessness endures, so health deteriorates (Johnson and Tseng 2014). The social determinants of health literature illustrate how homelessness makes people sick. If the logic is that we should house people because of the attendant cost offsets, and that those offsets are derived from reduced health service use because of people's extreme sickness, it is not hard to see that withholding housing from the healthy homeless is likely to set them on a downhill trajectory of poor health. The longer people are homeless, the sicker they become. At the end of this downward spiral, they will then become costly service users and will, only then, be prioritized for housing. By withholding housing to someone who is homeless because they are not sick enough, we perpetuate their homelessness, which means they will inevitably end up sick, and probably sick enough to be housed at some point in the future. The question is not whether people who are homeless are sick enough to house, it is a question of whether they are sick enough *yet* to house.

Furthermore, the cost-effectiveness rationales provide a framework for us to identify who in the homeless population is deserving. Interestingly, this is not about morality or compliance with mainstream norms, as it has historically been in the poverty and welfare spheres (Katz 1986). Almost the reverse is true. To be deemed deserving of housing through an economic analysis, one needs simply to behave in ways that cost society too much. Many of these costly behaviors may in fact be immoral, such as substance abuse and behaviors that generate a criminal justice intervention.

The focus on ending homelessness to realize cost offsets can also shape the nature of permanent supportive housing. It can shape what permanent supportive housing tries to achieve, and, ultimately, represents a challenge to its permanency. Referring to Housing First in Scandinavia, Cecilia Löfstrand and Kirsi Juhila argue that, despite the rhetoric on choice and self-determination, the recovery focus underpinning Housing First does indeed intend to change people. They conclude that Housing First functions "to monitor and reshape the conduct of these citizens" (2012: 62). Hennigan (2017) concludes likewise with analysis from the United States. He believes that Housing First is an instrument of disciplinary power that aims to reform people so that they can be reintegrated back into the capitalist marketplace. The prevailing cost offset can be read as changing people to reintegrate them – to promote their recovery – to ensure that they become less costly to society. When permanent supportive housing has done its job of changing people, the resources can be put to work on other people. This may seem like a cynical analysis, but there is evidence of governments using so-called permanent supportive housing in just this way.

In Alberta, Canada, Housing First is not permanent supportive housing in the definitional sense of permanent; rather, it is time-limited. Sophie Stadler and Damian Collins (2021) demonstrate that Alberta Housing First is premised on the need for clients to graduate out of the program, ideally within three to eighteen months. The support services provided in Housing First are not only to help people sustain their tenancy, they are actually to encourage "self-sufficiency and empowerment" to maintain "tenancies once clients graduate from HF" (Stadler and Collins 2021). This evidence suggests that Housing First works to reduce not only immediate costs, but also long-term costs by changing people. Analysis of what is happening on the ground in the United States likewise puts pressure on the notion of permanency. The federal government has incentivized service providers to encourage tenants of permanent supportive housing to participate in the Moving On initiative. As the name suggests, this initiative is designed to get people out of permanent supportive housing, an approach that Emmy Tiderington and colleagues (2022) say has proliferated across the United States.

The policy that seeks to move people out of permanent supportive housing renders permanent an idea that is, instead, operationalized as transitional. This subversion of the nature of permanency fits the logic that housing should be provided to people on the basis that their homelessness costs too much. The US Department of Housing and Urban Development (2022) says that "as part of its strategic priority to end homelessness, HUD encourages communities to explore Moving On strategies." Ending homelessness is reframed as ending the burden on the taxpayer that the chronically homeless – the sick – represent. The focus on cost offsets overwhelms the assumption that housing is a right. In an analysis from Canada, Damian Collins and Madeleine Stout show the limitations of the right to housing in Housing First policy. This limited notion was particularly apparent when it was linked to economic reasons: it "weakened the moral basis for HF by linking it to something contingent – cost containment in the public sector" (2021: 353). In this way, rather than people who are homeless having a right to housing, it is the taxpayer who has a right to change their situation so as to minimize the financial burden.

Housing First and permanent supportive housing initiatives in Europe and Australia are small scale (Baptista and Marlier 2019; Parkinson and Parsell 2018). In the United States and Canada there is a significant difference between the number of people who require permanent supportive housing and the amount of available stock (Stadler and Collins 2021; Tiderington et al. 2022). This means that there are pressures to ensure that this cost-saving mechanism is used efficiently. It follows that, because ending homelessness is motivated by the need to avert costs to the taxpayer, rather than by society's responsibility to provide housing to all, cost-saving interventions will be under constant pressure, not to permanently house citizens but to save money. The push to permanently end a person's homelessness because of the attendant costs can become a little shaky when the person is securely housed, assumed to be recovered, and thus no longer deemed to be too costly. Employing permanent supportive housing programs to offset costs is about helping the chronically homeless into permanent housing and even back into the workforce.

Concluding remarks

If people's exclusion from housing persists, particularly when they have a diagnosed illness, they may well be responded to with housing, alongside a suite of health and care services. In many parts of the world, models of permanent supportive housing are implemented or being put forward as part of the solution to homelessness.

The movement toward ending a person's homelessness with models of permanent supportive housing certainly represents progress vis-à-vis models that function to keep people accommodated in shelters. For those in the homeless population lucky enough to access permanent supportive housing models such as Housing First, there are life-changing implications (Padgett et al. 2016). The word "lucky" is used ironically here. People can be considered lucky because demand outstrips supply, and those who are able to use Housing First – many of whom have likely been systematically failed by society for all or most of their lives – end up experiencing profound life changes.

In addition to dampening our optimism about models of permanent supportive housing because they successfully assist people whom we otherwise systematically fail, we need to consider their role in the broader society. When we rightly celebrate the success of our housing and support models to provide exits for the long-term homeless and for those who are the sickest, we need to also ask what are we doing to stop future generations from also needing these evidence-based integrated housing and support interventions. This means, and we will pick this up in the next and final chapter, that when we get excited about an intervention because it ends a person's chronic homelessness, we should also ask what needs to be done to alter society so that these specialist housing initiatives have no future client base.

8
What Should We Do about Homelessness?

If the job of a scholar, or, as Marx said, a philosopher, is to not simply interpret the world but to change it, then the past seven chapters offer the scholar or student of society an awful lot to get busy with.

In some ways this is the easiest chapter to write. What we should do about homelessness is, demonstrably, increase the supply of affordable, accessible, and permanent housing. While we are at it, we should also eliminate poverty. In other words, we need to transform society so that the structural conditions that produce homelessness are eradicated. To this point, I have outlined the moral reason for making these changes, which is evidenced through the profound harms that homelessness causes. The argument that homelessness is the largely predictable outcome of how we choose to organize society similarly constitutes the basis for our assertions about what we should do to tackle it. The proposal put forward in this chapter is that homelessness can be eradicated if we choose to organize society differently.

Articulating the necessity for and appropriateness of these transformations is the easy part. Now for the hard part: how do we, in practice, actually transform societies? What would these transformations look like? Making societal changes is a challenge we must confront in order to realize the conditions in which all people have access to housing because of our shared humanity.

We first look at current innovations that are emerging the world over that intend to solve homelessness. Although these innovations look promising and represent positive progress on the suboptimal

178   What Should We Do about Homelessness?

responses considered in previous chapters, they generally frame homelessness as a technical and discrete problem within society that can be addressed while leaving fundamental structures of society in place. They assume that homelessness can be solved as long there is better evidence to drive better practice. We will look at these innovations and identify their limitations, which lay the groundwork for the recommended societal transformations. Some proposed transformations are more radical in one country than in another, but they all assume that people cannot exit homelessness, or stop themselves from becoming homeless, alone. Rather, "the ability of homeless people to fulfill housing, health, and sustenance needs likely depends on the capacity and accessibility of the local service environment, not just individual perseverance" (Lee et al. 2021: 17).

This chapter outlines these required changes, illustrates where these conditions exist or are being progressed, and speculates on how other societies can be helped to realize them. This includes consideration of what role people who are homeless, as well as those trying to help them, can play in transforming society.

The myth of solving homelessness through more evidence and better practices

In the first decades of the twenty-first century a movement began to emerge that looks, prima facie, both sensible and optimistic. It is not the sort of movement that represents a cohesive collective; rather, it consists of a range of actors in numerous countries who are all committed to innovation to achieve a similar set of ends. This movement has three core components. First, societies should set specific targets for ending a certain type of homelessness among a specific population in a specified time and place. Second, the targets can be realized through changing our practices, including data, measurement, and collaboration. Third, evidence of what works should underpin all activities.

Lígia Teixeira's work is a good place to start. As the founding chief executive of the United Kingdom's Centre for Homelessness Impact, she certainly knows a lot about the problem of homelessness and about what societies have done – or not done – about it. She laments the continuation of homelessness, despite years of passionate speeches

What Should We Do about Homelessness?

by public officials and massive public investment. She correctly says that "these efforts have helped. But they are not enough" (2020: 1).

Teixeira is no doubt correct: if good intentions and money were all that is needed, homelessness would not persist. Her concern is that there are programs that may be effective at ending a person's homelessness, but these or other activities on which public money is spent do not lead to a sustained reduction at the population level. In fact, referring to the United Kingdom and beyond, Teixeira argues that the vast majority of government-funded programs and interventions directed at homelessness are largely ineffective because they are not backed by evidence. This is one of her key areas of concern and focus. She argues that the lack of evidence informing homelessness responses means that good taxpayers' money is thrown after bad. Teixeira worries not only that responses are ill-informed by evidence and thus not a good use of the public purse – similar to the harms done by physicians prior to the advent of evidence-based medicine in the nineteenth century – but that the dominant mode of delivering untested homelessness responses may actually do harm.

We cannot reasonably question the problems that Teixeira identifies in the continuation of homelessness and the assessment that current spending is ineffective. These sentiments are supported by much of what has already been discussed in this book, particularly the harms caused by forcibly moving people around public spaces or providing paternalistic shelter accommodation that people actually try to avoid. All the evidence suggests that there are profound limitations with what we currently do. It is reasonable, therefore, to lament the ineffective responses to homelessness across the globe even as the problem persists or, in some places, grows.

Teixeira's mantra, and that of the Centre for Homelessness Impact, is that societies must focus "on 'what works' – by finding and funding solutions backed by evidence and data and by seeding experiments with the potential to produce outsized social returns" (2020: 2). Our responses to homelessness should be like evidence-based medicine, where we prove what works and what does not work, ideally with randomized control trials, and we cease funding the latter and invest heavily in the former. The Centre for Homelessness Impact exists to be "a catalyst for evidence-led change" (2020: 6). At first glance, it is hard to argue with this. One does not want to be on the side of putting forward responses to homelessness that are not based on evidence. The Centre for Homelessness Impact values evidence, arguing that it provides the necessary means to achieve the fundamental goal of living in a world without homelessness.

Linda Gibbs and colleagues (2021) examined the efforts of ten international cities that have embarked upon a strategy to end unsheltered homelessness. The authors are all consultants who played a role in designing these homelessness eradication strategies. Their efforts to end unsheltered homelessness are directed toward improving systems, programs, and practices. According to them, what is needed to end unsheltered homelessness in a city is a concerted move toward "a coordinated system of care whereby clients rationally receive the most appropriate services through a shared system of assessment and intake, with a commitment to measuring impact backed up with rigorous evaluations" (2021: 33). Even if we can forgive phrases like "rationally receive the most appropriate services," ending homelessness for these authors will come about by tweaking societal systems that respond to people who are homeless. Like Teixeira, they argue that "the vast majority of public funds devoted to homeless services internationally are spent without any evidence of impact" (2021: 20–21). Accordingly, they recommend that cities need to be guided by evidence that demonstrates which programs and means of collaboration work. With the right knowledge and commitments across the system, progress will be realized because the idealized evidence-informed innovations will enable people who are homeless "to make better choices and achieve better outcomes" (2021: 36). This assertion represents an extreme individualization of the social problem of homelessness, but it underlies a broader commitment within this movement to eradicate homelessness even as the structures that produce homelessness are maintained.

The Vanguard Cities Initiative of the Institute of Global Homelessness is another example of this new movement. In 2017, 13 cities representing six continents signed up to this initiative. They committed "to a specific target on ending or reducing street homelessness by December 2020" (Fitzpatrick et al. 2022: 3). Glasgow and Sydney met their self-defined targets of reducing street homelessness by the end of 2020, and half of the other cities recorded at least some reduction in street homelessness. The Vanguard Cities initiative stresses the importance of a lead agency driving the reduction targets alongside the presence of evidence-based interventions in contributing to their reductions.

What Should We Do about Homelessness? 181

The final example we consider is the Community Solutions organization from the United States and their built-for-zero movement. They have an inspiring mantra: "homelessness is solvable." As with the desire to work with concrete evidence, it is difficult to argue with a mantra that positions homelessness as something that is within our capacity to solve. The Community Solutions organization reports partnering with more than 100 communities across the United States all of which are "measurably and equitably ending homelessness" (Community Solutions 2022b). Moreover, "14 communities have functionally ended homelessness for a population." What is there not to be thrilled about? The MacArthur Foundation was presumably thrilled; in 2021 it granted Community Solutions $100 million to accelerate their strategy to end homelessness in the United States.

The built-for-zero initiative does not contend that ending homelessness in one community means that there are currently no people who are homeless or that no one will be homeless in the future. There is something of a smoke-and-mirrors situation here. The initiative explains that achieving "functional zero" means "that a community has driven that number down toward zero, and is keeping it below the community's capacity to ensure positive exits from homelessness" (Community Solutions 2022a). To determine functional zero, communities provide live data on the number of people who are homeless, very often unsheltered, and on the number of housing allocations. It is a measure of how a community functions to respond to homelessness in real time. Like the examples above, the built-for-zero initiative and the measure of functional zero are empowering, in that they focus on what actors can control within their environment. With data and real-time evidence, those who support and propel these movements are motivated to end homelessness for individuals by doing whatever can be done within the existing system to maximize efficiencies and effectiveness. Referring to built-for-zero, the Community Solutions (2022a) website explains: "Imagine if the homeless system operated like a well-functioning hospital. That hospital will not necessarily prevent people from ever becoming sick. But it will ensure people are triaged appropriately, promptly receive the services they need, and address the illness, preventing further harm."

The above description helps us hone in on the focus of these new movements and their limitations. The analogy to illness and hospitals shows that homelessness is perceived to be an inevitability of life. This is because societal structures that produce homelessness are fixed. The only reasonable place to intervene is after the inevitable has taken place. This includes ensuring that homelessness, once it occurs, is brief. Homelessness, on this reading, is like sickness in a human: over the life course of any human being, sickness is an inevitability, and, as often as not, so too is admission to hospital. Homelessness, as with sickness, just happens, and we need to treat it once it does so. The analogy is problematic because it ignores that sickness, at least many types of sickness, is not actually an inevitability. Society constantly changes – in some ways improves – so that diseases that were taken for granted at some point in history now no longer exist.

There are countless examples of how we have changed society to prevent sickness, including banning lead, asbestos, and other poisonous substances. Similarly, there are far fewer cases of chronic diarrhea because most people now have access to proper sewerage systems and to clean and reliable piped water. But it ought not to be just assumed that everything in our current organization of society is fixed or fine, particularly given that there are still cases of homelessness. We are pleased that health professionals did not dedicate all their efforts to refining better medicines to treat diarrhea but also looked at ways to prevent it by developing infrastructure to provide clean water. In the same way, society can be changed so that homelessness is largely eradicated.

The movements discussed in this section can be summed up as presenting advocacy and work to improve our responses and systems of operation – often based on evidence – even as they say nothing, much less do anything, about the structures within society that produce homelessness and make sustainable exit for the majority impossible. They focus on fixing the system for those people who have already entered homelessness or for at-risk groups on the cusp of homelessness, rather than on fixing the problems in society that lead to their becoming homeless in the first place.

This is not to say that these initiatives have no merit. They do have some value. The reductions reported by the Vanguard Cities, for example, illustrate that some in the homeless population benefited by gaining access to housing. As in Housing First and permanent supportive housing programs – some of which were used by the Vanguard Cities – some people materially benefited in significant ways. These initiatives alone, however, are never going to change society to the extent that the vast majority of people who are

What Should We Do about Homelessness?

homeless receive housing and future generations will not follow them into homelessness. Homelessness will never be eradicated while our current modes of delivering housing and structuring the economy persist. No amount of evidence indicates that improving homelessness programs will be any more effective than a band-aid on a gashing wound. We should be concerned that investing our expertise and cash in these movements, and they do attract massive amounts of both, simply diverts our attention, resources, and momentum away from efforts to prevent homelessness at the structural level.

The call for better evidence – to be rationally informed by what works – ignores two additional problems. First, unlike the evidence-based medicine analogy, homelessness is not a biological problem that can be discretely isolated and treated with pharmaceuticals. Rather, it is a problem that is deeply embedded in ideological ideas about the role of individual versus collective responsibility. The problems that produce homelessness and their solutions (discussed below) have a strong normative gradient. We will challenge some of the proposed solutions that Marybeth Shinn and Jill Khadduri (2020) articulate. Our concern with their proposals notwithstanding, these scholars are cognizant that proposing solutions to homelessness that are incongruent with dominant political norms, even if based on evidence, are likely to be ignored. Writing in the United States, they clearly recognize, for example, that political processes and decisions that Congress is likely to make about distributing resources radically shape what is even thought conceivable as a response to homelessness. As Kathryn Edin and Luke Shaefer (2015) note, concerning welfare reform in the United States, solutions must fit within cultural norms of what is deemed appropriate for the majority of the voting population.

Second, the advocacy for more randomized control trials to produce better evidence for what works to end homelessness ignores the basic reality that the best evidence does not always travel very well. The best evidence about what program works *here* to address a social problem may tell us very little about what program will work effectively *elsewhere*. Nancy Cartwright and Jeremy Hardie (2012) show that it is hopeful at best and naive at worst to think that the best evidence produced from randomized control trials in one area will translate to another area (another city, another state, across international boundaries). This rational idea of evidence-based policy ignores politics in policy-making, ignores the dynamics of

184   What Should We Do about Homelessness?

international policy transfer, and ignores the fact that the recipients of evidence-based programs are themselves diverse. They highlight the failure of evidence-based programs to reduce hunger across borders because, even when effectiveness has been demonstrated in rigorous randomized control trials, the transfer of the program from one country to another does not take account of cultural norms that shape how people will use, or not, programs that have been proven to work elsewhere.

Nothing short of societal transformation

To end and prevent homelessness we need to transform society so that the conditions that produce it are eradicated; we must understand that it is a policy problem, a choice about how we organize society. We can choose differently. The research is clear that homelessness results under conditions where housing is unaffordable due to the inter-action between poverty and a limited supply of affordable housing (Bramley 2017). Where housing prices are high and the availability of subsidized housing minimal, rates of homelessness are excessive (Fargo et al. 2013; Metraux and Culhane 1999; O'Flaherty 2004; Quigley et al. 2001; Shinn et al. 1998). And the same can be said in states where levels of poverty are high, in concert with a low supply of affordable housing (Hanratty 2017). As Byrne and colleagues (2021) show in the United States, income inequality contributes to homelessness indirectly by precluding low-income households from accessing the housing market.

Valesca Lima and colleagues (2022) established that the financiali-zation of private rental housing in Ireland, which includes corporate entities investing in the rental sector, directly increases homelessness by raising rents, promoting housing insecurity through short-term leases, and facilitating evictions.

From a different perspective, it is equally clear that when the state plays an interventionist role by subsidizing or delivering affordable housing, the extent of homelessness in a population is low (Haupert 2021; O'Donnell 2021). Johnson et al. (2019: 1107) concluded that "public housing's strong protective effect is confirmed by model simulations suggesting that approximately 73 percent of cases flowing into homelessness could be avoided if the vulnerable were placed in public housing."

What Should We Do about Homelessness?

The same is true for poverty. When poverty levels are reduced, for example in a universal and comprehensive welfare state (Benjaminsen 2016; Benjaminsen and Andrade 2015; Olsson and Nordfeldt 2008), or even through targeted cash assistance to low-income families in the absence of a universal welfare state (Parolin 2021), the rate of homelessness is also lower. Fitzpatrick, Mackie, and Wood (2021) showed this societal effect with a comparison of Scotland and England. After reporting similar levels of core homelessness in 2010, such as rough sleeping, by 2017 homelessness had increased in England and decreased in Scotland. They point to state policy that had cut welfare and increased housing costs to explain the increase in England, and policy that led to investment in social housing and lower housing market pressures to explain the decrease in Scotland.

The evidence about the structural causes and solutions to homelessness provides a compelling basis to guide what we need to do. Yes, evidence-based programs will be useful, including programs driven by data and collaboratively delivered as part of systems. So too will models of permanent supportive housing. Nor should we discount the value of and, therefore, the need to continue with a range of practices that help to prevent homelessness within existing systems, such as those that put a stop to evictions during Covid-19 (Fitzpatrick, Watts, et al. 2021), specific interventions to support discharge planning for people leaving institutions (Forchuk et al. 2008), or legislative changes that prevent homelessness for people in crisis (Mackie 2015). All of these should continue. However, if we want to measurably reduce homelessness among the masses, prevent it for future generations, and create a more just and productive society, we need transformation. The only way to significantly reduce and prevent homelessness is through reducing poverty and demonstrably increasing forms of housing that are affordable. The short-term ameliorative measures we put in place to deal with structural problems, like shelters to respond to homelessness, have a habit of not actually being so very short term, and even becoming normalized.

Although the recommendation to transform society in order to create more affordable housing and more state assistance is based on analysis of society-wide forces and comparisons across time and place, it will, for many people, be too radical to consider. Extreme transformation is not, however, unfeasible. Examples exist where this is happening at the societal level.

The experiences of Finland represent something of a case study for what transformation might look like. Finland reports several measures of homelessness. Between 2011 and 2017, there was a 31 percent reduction in long-term homelessness and, between 2008 and 2018, a 58 percent reduction in the number of people living in shelters and boarding houses. In the same period, there was a 78 percent reduction in homelessness among people in institutional settings who had no home to exit to and a 12 percent reduction in family homelessness (Allen et al. 2020). The Finish government reports that there were 17,480 people homeless in 1987, whereas in 2021 there were 4,113 (ARA 2022).

Finland achieved such significant reductions that "discussion of the near eradication of homelessness sounds like a viable prospect" (Allen et al. 2020: 100). It was achieved through a systematic commitment to housing, which included building new affordable housing and renovating existing homeless accommodation into permanent housing. "In Finland, individual Housing First services were not, in and of themselves, a tactical response to homelessness, but instead part of a strategy in which housing – living in a home of one's own – was the default goal" (Allen et al. 2020: 106).

In Finland, Housing First is targeted at large-scale homelessness rather than at individuals, with a strong emphasis on new affordable housing stock. In this, the Y-Foundation, whose goal is to end homelessness in Finland, is critical. Established in 1985 with no housing stock, by 2022 this organization had developed and provided 18,000 apartments of social housing. As new social housing was built, they "got rid of shelters." In Helsinki, Finland's capital, there were 600 shelter beds in 2008; by 2016 there were 52 (Y-Foundation 2017).

Scotland is another country that is making measurable progress towards societal transformation to end and prevent homelessness. The results in Scotland in terms of reductions in homelessness are not as profound as those from Finland, in part because Scotland's transformations are more recent and occurred just prior to the outbreak of Covid-19 (Watts et al. 2021). The Scottish government has committed to building 100,000 affordable homes by 2031/32; the goal is to ensure that temporary accommodation is not used for anything other than a crisis. Furthermore, the Scottish government (2021) has committed to an "action plan to ensure we prevent and end homelessness for good." Unlike Finland, where affordable housing has been built and homelessness has been demonstrably reduced, Scotland is more at the aspiration or planning stage. The Scottish example does nevertheless represent optimism for the type of societal transformation that is needed, by focusing, like Finland, on the need for more housing to address homelessness. At the heart of both countries' approaches is the delivery of new state-owned housing. Moreover, both countries have developed welfare systems whereby citizens have access to a range of services including universal healthcare, education, and unemployment benefits.

The effective characteristics of the Finish and Scottish approaches represent something of a bind for international comparisons. We have some broad knowledge about the societal conditions of these countries, but we know much less about how to realize these conditions elsewhere. We are particularly challenged in this respect because they are conditions that many societies do not support. It is too late in this book for me to pull out neoliberalism as a meta-theory to explain homelessness and all the world's problems, but it is the case that, since the 1960s and 1970s, governments across much of the Global North have been reluctant to fund large-scale social housing or engage in wealth distribution to make societies more equal. Progress toward these changes will be, as Fitzpatrick, Mackie, and Wood (2021) note, hard to come by.

The persistence and increasing rates of homelessness in many countries are part of the same processes that are also contributing to widening inequalities globally. Thomas Piketty (2014) shows that growing inequality is embedded within societal structures, citing, for example, the inheritance of wealth from one generation to another. To address these inequalities, a transformation in the tax system, underpinned by new ideas about individual rights and collective responsibilities, is required, yet there is at present little appetite to instigate such a redistributive transformation. Three decades ago, Hopper and Baumohl pointed out people's reluctance to develop the societal transformations required to overcome the systematic failures that manifest in homelessness: "Like an end to racism, the eradication of homelessness in the United States, while universally acclaimed as a goal, is sure to entail much more fundamental change than the nation had bargained for" (1994: 544).

It may be true that, to end and prevent homelessness, we need to transform society so that we have significantly more affordable housing and significantly less poverty. However, given the structures that contribute toward growing inequality, simply stating the need for this transformation is manifestly insufficient. Even though wealthy countries across the globe are now dealing with a major affordable housing problem, which has also become a political problem (Anacker 2019) – one exacerbated by housing costs rising faster than incomes (Wetzstein 2017) – addressing it is a perpetual challenge, not least of all because housing is a commodity. The commodification of housing is not only a wealth-generating machine for property developers and the real estate industry; it also means that many people in society view housing not simply as a place to live, but rather as a resource on which to speculate, or as leverage, or as an investment. Transforming society requires changing how we think about the problem of people being excluded from this resource, and how this resource can be reimagined in a way that brings society together.

Reframing the problem

To facilitate the societal transformation required to end and prevent homelessness, the problem must be reframed. This is critical to how policies are developed to deal with the problem. The requirement to reframe the problem of homelessness as a necessary step toward societal transformation recognizes that social problems do not exist independently in an objective reality. Rather, they are determined through collective decision-making about what to focus on, and importantly, about what and whose voices to ignore (Hervieux and Voltan 2018). The social problem of homelessness, as we show below, can be problematized in myriad different ways that have important implications.

What is true about social problems is also true about social policy. Social policy is not simply a process of politicians and policy-makers responding to objectively defined problems that are in front of them. Rather, social policies work to constitute the nature of the problem. All policy responds to a particular type of problem-framing, and the debates about what the problem is and what should be done about it boil down to competing values about what society should look like. Social policies and the social problems they respond to are thus inherently political. It is because of the values intrinsic to problem-framing that the simple "more evidence is needed" argument falls down (Head 2022). In Carol Bacchi's (2009) terms, policies constitute

What Should We Do about Homelessness?

and structure problems. This critical viewpoint helps us understand how the current problematizations of homelessness inform what we do about it. Such a viewpoint also helps us identify how different problematizations might lead us to something different.

There are two dominant problematizations of homelessness. The first presents the idea that people who are homeless are deficient in some way. We dedicated much of Chapter 5 to examining this through the prism of the homeless identity. The second problematization, a more recent strand, focuses on the problem within our systems of support and intervention. This draws attention to the lack of evidence in how services are delivered. These problematizations lead to different responses, yet they both fail to address what is required. The problem of the homeless individual inspires a range of interventions that seek to change them. Similarly, because people who are homeless are seen as deficient, a range of suboptimal shelter accommodation models seems to be the appropriate response. The problematization of the system, on the other hand, leads to a range of strategies, as exemplified earlier in the chapter, that seek to bring more evidence to the table to inform collaborative responses that overcome limitations in disjointed and ineffective services.

We need to reject these problematizations of homelessness. They represent a barrier to the societal action required to massively increase the supply of affordable housing. It is indeed the case that certain individuals are at a greater risk than others of becoming homeless – as the individual framing may indicate – but this is only under certain conditions. In the presence of affordable housing those individual attributes are far less likely to lead to homelessness (Johnson et al. 2019).

Drawing attention to the structural forces that produce homelessness is critical to garner support for the required societal transformations. To end and prevent homelessness, what we need is not more evidence of programs that work, but, rather, more political will. What is required is sufficient motivation among the public to push elected representatives to change what they prioritize and how they distribute public resources. Writing in the United States, Shinn and Khadduri conclude that "what it takes is the political will to strengthen the income side of safety net and return to the growth in deep rent subsidies last seen in the late 1970s" (2020: 154).

To activate this political will, not only can we frame homelessness as the systematic exclusion of people in multiple ways, we can also

190 What Should We Do about Homelessness?

highlight what their compounded deprivation means for how they live and how this contrasts with our values for society. The voting public can be energized to push elected representatives to act differently when it is clearly highlighted what homelessness amounts to. This includes, for example, how homelessness subverts a person's capacity to participate in society as a citizen, much less be able to exercise their inalienable human rights. In societies where religion is more of a compelling motivator than secular ideals of rights and citizenship, the framing can draw attention to the incongruence of homelessness alongside such concepts "as all people are created in the image of God" or "all people are created in the image of Allah." Framing homelessness as a form of deprivation that subverts people's capacity to comply with widely held values of self-responsibility and caring for kin is another way to capture the public's concern and thus provoke the political will.

If the problem of homelessness is a problem of how we organize society – and I believe that it is – ending and preventing it requires change to fundamental societal structures. The way societies produce, allocate, and operate housing is critical to how homelessness is produced and to what requires changing. Reframing the problem of homelessness to reflect this, and in a way that firmly takes account of what the public is likely to care about, is a necessary step toward this transformation. As Colburn and Aldern (2022) observe, when homelessness is understood in terms of society not producing a sufficient supply of affordable housing, it becomes a problem that we understand how to solve.

De-commodified housing

It is clear that we need more affordable housing and that the problem of homelessness needs to be framed accordingly, yet recent history tells us that producing more affordable housing is unlikely to happen if we continue along the same path. How, then, can this be changed? The answer to this question is probably: "it depends." It depends on where in the world we are. Referring to the United States, Shinn and Khadduri (2020) assert that the most realistic, the most efficient, and the quickest way to increase affordable housing is by increasing the number of federally funded housing vouchers. They propose that 300,000 new housing vouchers are required each year if downward

What Should We Do about Homelessness? 191

pressure on homelessness is to be realized. These vouchers essentially work by the state subsidizing the market to provide affordable housing. This may be a plausible recommendation for the United States, but it is not without critique and its international relevance can be questioned.

Michael Burawoy (2017) points to the massive limitations of housing vouchers to achieve housing justice in the United States. He argues that they can be used by landlords to exploit tenants, and, significantly, they do little toward creating a new supply of housing. Scholars outside the United States regard the use of housing vouchers, or government subsidies to property owners, as a form of reverse welfare (Jacobs 2015). On this analysis, housing vouchers and other forms of private rental subsidy exacerbate inequalities because the state is directly assisting wealthy property-owners to become wealthier as long as people who are poor remain their tenants. Housing vouchers can be criticized for perpetuating the conditions in the market that produce homelessness through the commodification of housing.

In Singapore proposed solutions would look very different from those in the United States. Creating more housing that the vast majority of the population can afford would involve continuing to do what they have been doing for many years. As noted in Chapter 2, roughly 90 percent of Singaporeans are homeowners. This astonishingly high rate of home-ownership, along with the extremely low rates of homelessness, is enabled through a unique model whereby the state plays the fundamental role of owning the land, developing the housing, and creating the active conditions by means of subsidies so that most Singaporeans can be homeowners. This is a heavily interventionist approach to housing affordability, and it operates by enabling individuals to own their own housing. This model is specific to Singapore, as Richard Ronald (2008) points out, and it is hard to imagine it being replicated elsewhere in the world.

Our recommendation for creating significantly more affordable housing must fit within the social, cultural, and political reality of a country. In Finland and Scotland, building large amounts of social housing fits within their context. In most other countries, this is not true, even if they previously valued social housing. Mass building of social housing was associated with post-World War II reconstruction and Keynesian economic and welfare rationales that are no longer seen as palatable. Instead, collaborative forms of housing may represent a positive way forward for many of the countries considered in this book.

Collaborative housing is an umbrella term that captures a multitude of housing forms. These include co-housing, residents' cooperatives, self-help, self-build, community-asset ownership, community land trusts, and more (Czischke et al. 2020; Lang et al. 2020). Collaborative housing forms differ across the globe, including differences in the degrees of collective self-organization and different tenure types. A core characteristic of collaborative housing is, as the name suggests, collaboration. In some forms, collaboration focuses primarily on the internal tenant-to-tenant level; this is particularly the case with co-housing where sharing resources and shared decision-making are emphasized (Czischke et al. 2020). Collaboration here can take place at the design and preconstruction stages, but it is primarily thought of in terms of collaboration among tenants in housing (a community) that has already been constructed. Collaboration can be more widely envisaged, for instance between external stakeholders, including housing providers, municipalities, central governments, and finance sectors. It is these broader forms of collaboration that offer opportunities for this form of housing to be a significant response to homelessness.

Collaborative housing specifically – or, more broadly, direct citizen actions to meet their own needs and the needs of their community – has been imposed top-down from the state and rationalized because of austerity (Czischke 2018). We can see the imposition of these ideas in England when pursuing localism, or similar forces in the United States that promote community solutions to meet local needs aside from what is provided by a distant central authority. This top-down approach to facilitating community responses is motivated by governments' attempts to retreat from welfare provision. As opposed to being part of the solution, Fitzpatrick, Pawson, and Watts (2020) show that localism in England – as part and parcel of austerity – functioned to increase the conditions for homelessness. It is hard to imagine how cutting back on welfare provision is ever going to be a means to create huge swathes of affordable housing.

Collaborative housing need not, however, be an enabler of austerity and governments' refusal to support citizens' needs. There is a growing recognition that collaborative housing can be motivated as a grassroots response to state failure to provide sufficient affordable housing, but with the active support of the state (Lang et al. 2020).

What Should We Do about Homelessness? 193

Although traditionally conceived as a middle-class ideal to realize certain lifestyle and ideological choices (Czischke 2018), collaborative housing can be coordinated action toward a common purpose of creating more de-commodified housing stock. This can be achieved by groups collectively coming together to take land and housing stock off the market to, instead, be managed and delivered affordably by collectives (Thompson 2020).

The groups that constitute collaborative housing must be broadly conceptualized so that they have access to the resources and power required for collaborative housing to produce affordable housing on a large scale. Collaborative housing can be part of creating new supply when collaboration cuts across a diverse section of society. This includes central states for significant funding and legislation; municipalities are critical for planning and, in some jurisdictions, for ensuring that the land is held in public hands in perpetuity. Housing providers and the broader building industry are key stakeholders, for obvious reasons. So too is the finance sector. Fundamental to all of these broad collaborations are local communities. Not only do they need to support the development of large-scale collaborative housing, they will also be key actors in bringing collaborations together and fostering the conditions for collaborative housing to be built and remain sustainable. In this way, collaborative housing models can realize their true potential when they become immediate housing solutions to end homelessness and more long-term contributors as "high-order stewards of land for the benefit of the wider community" (Thompson 2020: 83).

On the one hand, this can be a means to produce more affordable housing, and, on the other, the diverse range of stakeholders involved – central and municipal governments, lending institutions, local communities, and housing providers – represents an opportunity for collaborative housing to be enmeshed within and supported by numerous interest groups in society (Thompson 2020). There are many examples across Europe and the United Kingdom where collaborative housing is producing small-scale affordable housing. Although there is more interest now than at any time in the past half-century (Mullins and Moore 2018), we do not yet know whether collaborative housing can compensate for the state's retreat from welfare provision (Czischke et al. 2020; Lang et al. 2020). Collaborative housing is a worthy model to pursue, particularly as a way of leveraging the current momentum of movements that are

194   What Should We Do about Homelessness?

trying to end homelessness. It can do so in a way that both draws on their strengths (optimism to do something) and overcomes their weakness (leaving the broader housing failure unchanged).

The collaborative housing advocated here is normal housing. We recognize that normality is contested and culturally contingent, but by normal we mean that it must be housing that any citizen could reside in, rather than substandard housing for homeless people. Recall from Chapter 4 that when clothes or beds in carparks are offered up as responses to homelessness, they are predicated on homeless people's distinctiveness and debased status. This means that collaborative housing ought not to be about perpetuating the acceptance of low-quality building or amenities. Housing must meet regular building and design standards. A citizen's right to live in and control their own housing, which is inherent in the collaborative housing idea, means that calls for non-traditional accommodation forms, such as rooming or boarding houses, are not acceptable (Shinn and Khadduri 2020). Collaborative housing is not premised on assumptions of a homeless community or the idea that formerly homeless people want to come together to share resources in communal living spaces based on a collective identity. The diverse sections of society that create collaborative housing are the same people who can also live in it.

Collaborative housing is about communities working together – with the support and resources from stakeholders within and beyond their communities – to build large-scale forms of affordable housing that will result in an exit from homelessness for people and constitute an ongoing form of living that will prevent homelessness for future generations. If this can be achieved at the required scale, collaborative housing must be an outward-looking proposition that sees collaborations across a wide sector of society.

A new way to help

Reframing the problem of homelessness to be one of society rather than of individuals and also proposing that collaborative forms of housing offer a partial solution open up vibrant opportunities for both people who are homeless and those who are trying to help. Recognizing that people who are homeless are not incapable forces us to instantly recognize their agency. Collaborative housing is a

What Should We Do about Homelessness?

resource that fulfils two needs simultaneously: it provides people with the affordable housing they need and offers opportunities for them to exert far greater control over their lives than what was possible when they were homeless.

The central theme illustrated in Chapter 4 was that people who were homeless lamented the accommodation and modes of care that accompany homelessness, viewing them as tantamount to being treated as a child. People constantly describe how their state of homelessness puts them in positions where they are unable to make decisions about their lives. In fact, some people experience homelessness as being subject to control in shelters where they are not even assumed to know what their best interests are. It is this lack of control over day-to-day life that conveys the sense in which homelessness is actually the absence of home (Mallett 2004).

Central to collaborative housing is tenant agency. Czischke and colleagues note that collaborative housing is a means for tenants "to regard themselves, and be regarded, as active agents of their own housing situation" (2020: 7). There is no prescribed or uniform approach to how tenants exert agency in collaborative housing, but collaborative housing is structured so that tenants play some roles in their housing, including lobbying for, designing, building, and contributing to some of the management of their housing. Sabrina Bresson and Anne Labit's (2020) research from France shows that democratic decision-making is necessary to ensure that tenants who come from marginalized backgrounds have a voice in ensuring that collaborative housing is flexibly structured to create the conditions for all people to participate in a way that reflects their interests and capacities. Collaborative housing works best when tenants have the capacity to decide when and how they participate. At its core, it is an approach that represents the antithesis of the subverted autonomy that people who are homeless experience. The tenant engagement underlying the philosophy of collaborative housing means that people who exit homelessness have opportunities to gain the sense of control that was diminished during their homelessness.

The agency that enables control over one's life in collaborative housing is not to be mistaken with changing the conditions of one's life alone. As noted, collaborative housing relies on deep collaborations and partnerships among a diverse sector of society. The role of external stakeholders in collaborative housing proposes new ways for people to help those who are homeless. Throughout this book

196   What Should We Do about Homelessness?

I have illustrated that there is in fact a wide interest among society to help people who are homeless, yet that assistance is often not perceived as particularly helpful by those on the receiving end. In traditional models of helping, where people are supported while they are homeless, there is a mismatch between the aspiration to help and the feeling of being provided for. This reality puts pressure on the idea that all assistance is helpful. People who are homeless want to be helped, but they want that help to enable them to gain power and to achieve a housing outcome.

Collaborative housing can be part of a movement that contributes to the reconceptualizing of supporting fellow citizens. Rather than helping a person who is homeless, citizens can work toward ending homelessness. In this way, the agency that collaborative housing promotes creates conditions for collective autonomy. No longer is there a homeless person subject to help and a non-homeless person helping. In collaborative housing, collective autonomy means people have "the capacity to do this as a group, with others who share a common vision of the housing project" (Czischke et al. 2020: 7).

It is this community engagement that perhaps explains why collaborative housing receives support, not just from those advocating collectivist political philosophies on the left, but also from neoliberal and conservative perspectives. Collaborative housing has a long history in Switzerland, which, as Ivo Balmer and Jean-David Gerber (2018: 361) remark, is noteworthy given that it is a "liberal state par excellence." They point out that recent political intervention is attempting to grow de-commodified forms of collaborative housing across Switzerland at the same time that government is moving toward market-based solutions to social problems. This interest is not unique to Switzerland. As Mayor of London, before he became prime minister, Conservative Boris Johnson wanted to create a network of collaborative housing in London through community land trusts (Thompson 2020).

The appeal of collaborative housing, with its inbuilt assumptions about human agency and communities looking after each other, is worth serious consideration to address homelessness. Many volunteers who provide charitable care to people who are homeless recognize that what they do is limited, but they see the real way forward to address the underlying problems as being out of their hands (Parsell et al. 2021). Collaborative housing can be part of the

What Should We Do about Homelessness? 197

solution to both empower citizens and to produce new affordable and publicly owned housing stock at scale. It is a model that resonates with progressive ideals about justice and rights, on the one hand, and conservative values of looking after one's community and work ethic, on the other.

Improving life and societal cohesion

If we strip it back, this chapter is as much about how we should live in society together as it is about homelessness. Any position we take on what we should do about homelessness is about what we believe should be the proper organization of society. What do people in society deserve for no other reason than because they are human? What responsibility do people have to look after themselves and their families, and how is this individual responsibility collectively enabled? Proposing what we should do about homelessness inevitably means asserting what we think collective responsibility actually means. If we do endorse some level of collective responsibility, and most people do, then we are debating at a different level about what the collective is: a central state, local community, identity-based groups, family.

Because homelessness means, most of the time, an absence of housing, there exists a range of other challenging normative claims that we should bring to mind. It is not just a matter of abstract ideals concerning rights, responsibility, and collectives; it is also about how we distribute expensive assets. In many of the countries considered in these pages, housing is, for all but the wealthiest, one of life's largest financial assets. It is something that we spend big chunks of our working lives paying for. When we advocate de-commodified housing and the provision of housing for people irrespective of anything other than their humanity, we are proposing something that may grate with how we ourselves live. People living in the countries considered in this book value private ownership, and perhaps no more so than when housing is considered. It is for these reasons that simple calls for more affordable and de-commodified forms of housing rarely are widespread or receive broad political support. It is fair to say, as Gertjan Wijburg (2021) observes, that the neoliberal hegemony will be less than thrilled by more de-commodified housing. Pursuing the end and prevention of homelessness will be pursuing a vision for society that is, for many, at odds with their expectations.

If we want to do something significant about homelessness in society, we have to confront the unquestioned marketization of housing and our deeply held values about what housing means and what all people deserve. This is crucial because the changes required to end and prevent homelessness are at the same time changes that will ensure all people live well, and in societies that are more cohesive. It is for this reason that problem-framing is so critical. The framing must not pit one group against another but instead see ending homelessness as something that is unifying. It should therefore be front and center of a more optimistic conversation about how we want to live together. We can articulate this vision as a means of bringing society together rather than splintering it further, based on wealth and identity claims. Young (1986) captures this well when she refers to a community of difference. This means we come together for the collective good, but in a way that recognizes and celebrates our differences.

It is unquestionable that difference matters in terms of homelessness. The number of racial minorities and migrants who experience homelessness (see Chapter 2) means that we have to confront what this difference means for some groups who are systematically excluded from housing. In pursuing the vision for a cohesive society that celebrates a community of difference, we must recognize that ignoring racial disparities will perpetuate them. Reflecting the proposition that ending homelessness improves societal functioning and cohesion, Olivet and colleagues are sage: "Only by explicitly centering racial equity across research, practice, and policy will it be possible to reduce high rates of homelessness among people of color and, ultimately, end homelessness for everyone" (2021: 99).

Homing in specifically on compounding the injustices faced by some groups, and the need for societal intervention explicitly directed toward countering their disadvantage, mean we are equally compelled to confront gender. It is not the case that women are more likely to be homeless than men the world over; it is, rather, that many women become homeless because of violence (criminal assaults) inflicted by men. The transformations required to end and prevent homelessness will involve not only transformations in how we provide affordable housing, but also transformations that address systematic racism and patriarchal norms that routinely disadvantage certain sections of society.

We must transform society to end and prevent homelessness for no other reason than that people who are excluded need housing in order to live as citizens and have their humanity recognized. We need them to have housing for the same reasons.

References

Agrawal, S., and Zoe, C. 2021. Housing and homelessness in Indigenous communities of Canada's north. *Housing Policy Debate*. doi.org/10.1080/10511482.2021.1881986.

Ahmed, S. 1999. Home and away: Narratives of migration and estrangement. *International Journal of Cultural Studies* 2(3): 329–347.

Alaazi, D., Masuda, J., Evans, J., and Distasio, J. 2015. Therapeutic landscapes of home: Exploring Indigenous peoples' experiences of a Housing First intervention in Winnipeg. *Social Science & Medicine* 147: 30–37.

Allen, M., Benjaminsen, L., O'Sullivan, E., and Pleace, N. 2020. *Ending Homelessness: The Contrasting Experiences of Denmark, Finland and Ireland*. Bristol: Policy Press.

Althammer, B. 2014. Transnational expert discourse on vagrancy around 1900. In B. Althammer, A. Gestrich, and J. Grundler (eds.), *The Welfare State and the "Deviant Poor" in Europe, 1870–1933*. London: Palgrave Macmillan, pp. 103–125.

American Civil Liberties Union. 2008. *Domestic Violence and Homelessness*. https://www.aclu.org/sites/default/files/pdfs/dvhomelessness032106.pdf.

Amore, K. 2013. Focusing on conceptual validity: A response. *European Journal of Homelessness* 7(2): 223–236.

Amore, K., Baker, M., and Howden-Chapman, P. 2011. The ETHOS definition and classification of homelessness: An analysis. *European Journal of Homelessness* 5(2): 19–37.

Amore, K., Viggers, H., and Chapman, P. 2021. *Severe Housing Deprivation in Aotearoa New Zealand, 2018*. Department of Public Health, University of Otago, Wellington.

Amster, R. 2003. Patterns of exclusion: Sanitizing space, criminalizing homelessness. *Social Justice* 30(1): 195–221.

Anacker, K. 2019. Introduction: Housing affordability and affordable housing. *International Journal of Housing Policy* 19(1): 1–16.

References 201

Antunes, M., and Ahlin, E. 2017. Youth exposure to violence in the community: Towards a theoretical framework for explaining risk and protective factors. *Aggression and Violent Behavior* 34: 166–177.

Aoki, H. 2006. *Japan's Underclass: Day Laborers and the Homeless*. Melbourne: Trans Pacific Press.

ARA. 2022. *Homelessness in Finland 2021*. Helsinki: The Housing Finance and Development Centre of Finland.

Asad, A. 2020. Struggles obtaining convenient access to showers. *The Borgen Project*. https://borgenproject.org/access–to–showers/.

Asadi, M. 2013. How does it feel to be a problem? The diasporic identity of the homeless. *Qualitative Sociology Review* IX(1): 76–93.

Aubry, T., Bloch, G., Brcic, V., et al. 2020. Effectiveness of permanent supportive housing and income assistance interventions for homeless individuals in high-income countries: A systematic review. *The Lancet Public Health* 5(6): E342–E360.

Aubry, T., Agha, A., Mejia-Lancheros, C., et al. 2021. Housing trajectories, risk factors, and resources among individuals who are homeless or precariously housed. *The Annals of the American Academy* 693: 102–122.

Australian Bureau of Statistics. 2018. *Census of Population and Housing: Estimating Homelessness*. Canberra: Australian Government.

Australian Capital Territory Government. 2016. *Orange Sky Laundry to Service Canberra's Homeless*. https://www.cmtedd.act.gov.au/open_government/inform/act_government_media_releases/barr/2016/orange-sky–laundry–to–serve–canberras–homeless.

Australian Institute of Health and Welfare. 2019. *Specialist Homelessness Services Annual Report 2017–18*. https://www.aihw.gov.au/reports/homelessness–services/specialist–homelessness–services–2017–18/contents/unmet–demand–for–specialist–homelessness–services.

Australian Institute of Health and Welfare. 2021. *Specialist Homelessness Services Annual Report 2020–21*. Canberra: Australian Government.

Bacchi, C. 2009. *Analysing Policy: What's the Problem Represented to Be?* Frenches Forest: Pearson Education.

Backer, T., Howard, E., and Moran, G. 2007. The role of effective discharge planning in preventing homelessness. *The Journal of Primary Prevention* 28: 229–243.

Bahr, H. 1970. Homelessness, disaffiliation, and retreatism. In H. Bahr (ed.), *Disaffiliated Man: Essays and Bibliography on Skid Row, Vagrancy, and Outsiders*. Toronto: University of Toronto Press, pp. 39–50.

Bahr, H. 1973. *Skid Row: An Introduction to Disaffiliation*. New York: Oxford University Press.

Baker, C., Billhardt, K., Warren, J., Rollins, C., and Glass, N. 2010. Domestic violence, housing instability, and homelessness: A review of housing policies and program practices for meeting the needs of survivors. *Aggression and Violent Behavior* 15: 430–439.

Balmer, I., and Gerber, J. 2018. Why are housing cooperatives successful?

References

Insights from Swiss affordable housing policy. *Housing Studies* 33(3): 361–385.

Baptista, I. 2010. Women and homelessness. In E. O'Sullivan, V. Busch-Geertsema, D. Quilgars, and N. Pleace (eds.), *Homelessness Research in Europe*. Brussels: FEANTSA, pp. 163–185.

Baptista, I., and Marlier, E. 2019. *Fighting Homelessness and Housing Exclusion in Europe: A Study of National Polices*. Brussels: European Commission.

Baptista, I., Benaminsen, L., and Pleace, N. 2017. *Family Homelessness in Europe*. Brussels: FEANTSA.

Barile, J., Pruitt, A., and Parker, J. 2020. Identifying and understanding gaps in services for adults experiencing homelessness. *Journal of Community & Applied Psychology* 30(3): 262–277.

Bassuk, E., DeCandia, C., Beach, C., and Berman, F. 2014. *America's Youngest Outcasts: A Report Card on Child Homelessness*. Waltham, MA: The National Center on Family Homelessness at American Institutes for Research.

Batterham, D. 2020. *Public Perceptions of Homelessness: A Literature Review*. Melbourne: Launch Housing.

Bauman, Z. 2004. *Identity: Conversations with Benedetto Vecchi*. Cambridge: Polity.

Baxter, A., Tweed, E., Katikireddi, S., and Thomson, H. 2019. Effects of Housing First approaches on health and well-being of adults who are homeless or at risk of homelessness: Systematic review and meta-analysis of randomised controlled trials. *Journal of Epidemiology and Community Health* 73: 379–387.

Baxter, E., and Hopper, K. 1981. *Private Lives/Public Spaces: Homeless Adults on the Streets of New York City*. New York: Community Services Society.

Beck, E., and Twiss, P. 2018. *The Homelessness Industry: A Critique of US Social Policy*. Boulder, CO: Lynne Rienner Publishers.

Beck, R., Szlapinski, J., Pacheco, N., et al. 2022. Violence and victimisation in the lives of persons experiencing homelessness who use methamphetamine: A scoping review. *Health and Social Care*. doi.org/10.1111/hsc.13716.

Beijer, U., Birath, C., DeMartinis, V., and Klinteberg, B. 2018. Facets of male violence against women with substance abuse problems: Women with a residence and homeless women. *Journal of Interpersonal Violence* 33(9): 1391–1411.

Bence, R., and Udvarhelyi, E. 2013. The growing criminalization of homelessness in Hungary: A brief overview. *European Journal of Homelessness* 7(2): 133–143.

Benjaminsen, L. 2016. Homelessness in a Scandinavian welfare state: The risk of shelter use in the Danish adult population. *Urban Studies* 53(10): 2041–2063.

References

Benjaminsen, L., and Andrade, S. 2015. Testing a typology of homelessness across welfare regimes: Shelter use in Denmark and the USA. *Housing Studies* 30(6): 858–876.

Bimpson, E., Parr, S., and Reeve, K. 2022. Governing homeless mothers: The unmaking of home and family. *Housing Studies* 37(2): 272–291.

Bogue, D. 1963. *Skid Row in American Cities*. Chicago, IL: The University of Chicago Press.

Bowen, E., and Capozziello, N. 2022. Faceless, nameless, invisible: A visual content analysis of photographs in US media coverage about homelessness. *Housing Studies*. doi.org/10.1080/02673037.2022.2084044

Boydell, K., Goering, P., and Morrell-Bellai, T. 2000. Narratives of identity: Re-presentation of self in people who are homeless. *Qualitative Health Research* 10(1): 26–38.

Bramley, G. 2017. *Homelessness Projections: Core Homelessness in Great Britain*. London: Crisis.

Bramley, G., and Fitzpatrick, S. 2018. Homelessness in the UK: Who is most at risk? *Housing Studies* 33(1): 96–116.

Breckenridge, J., Chung, D., Spinney, A., and Zufferey, C. 2015. *National Mapping and Meta-evaluation Outlining Key Features of Effective "Safe At Home" Programs that Enhance Safety and Prevent Homelessness for Women and Their Children Who Have Experienced Domestic and Family Violence*. Sydney: ANROWS.

Brekhus, W. 2003. *Peacocks, Chameleons, Centaurs: Gay Suburbia and the Grammar of Social Identity*. Chicago, IL: The University of Chicago Press.

Brekhus, W. 2020. *The Sociology of Identity*. Cambridge: Polity.

Bresson, S., and Labit, A. 2020. How does collaborative housing address the issues of social inclusion? A French perspective. *Housing, Theory and Society* 37(1): 118–138.

Bretherton, J. 2017. Reconsidering gender in homelessness. *European Journal of Homelessness* 11(1): 1–21.

Broll, R., and Huey, L. 2020. "Every time I try to get out, I get pushed back": The role of violent victimization in women's experience of multiple episodes of homelessness. *Journal of Interpersonal Violence* 35(17–18): 3379–3404.

Burawoy, M. 2017. On Desmond: The limits of spontaneous sociology. *Theory & Society* 46(4): 261–284.

Burns, V., Deslandes-Leduc, J., St-Denis, N., and Walsh, C. 2020. Finding home after homelessness: Older men's experiences in single-site permanent supportive housing. *Housing Studies* 35(2): 290–309.

Busch-Geertsema, V. 2010. Defining and measuring homelessness. In E. O'Sullivan, V. Busch-Geertsema, D. Quilgars, and N. Pleace (eds.), *Homelessness Research in Europe*. Brussels: FEANTSA, pp. 19–39.

Busch-Geertsema, V. 2013. Swimming can better be learned in the water than anywhere else. *European Journal of Homelessness* 7(2): 323–326.

Busch-Geertsema, V. 2014. Housing First in Europe: Results of a European social experimentation project. *European Journal of Homelessness* 8(1): 13–28.

Busch-Geertsema, V., and Fitzpatrick, S. 2008. Effective homelessness prevention? Explaining reductions in homelessness in Germany and England. *European Journal of Homelessness* 2: 69–95.

Busch-Geertsema, V., and Sahlin, I. 2007. The role of hostels and temporary accommodation. *The European Journal of Homelessness* 1: 67–93.

Busch-Geertsema, V., Benjaminsen, L., Filipovič Hrast, M., and Pleace, N. 2014. *The Extent and Profile of Homelessness in European Member States: A Statistical Update*. Brussels: FEANTSA.

Busch-Geertsema, V., Culhane, D., and Fitzpatrick, S. 2016. Developing a global framework for conceptualising and measuring homelessness. *Habitat International* 55: 124–132.

Busch-Geertsema, V., Henke, J., and Steffen, A. 2020. Homelessness in Germany. *European Journal of Homelessness* 14(1): 81–91.

Byrne, T., Henwood, B., and Orlando, A. 2021. A rising tide drowns unstable boats: How inequality creates homelessness. *The Annals of the American Academy* 693: 28–45.

Byrne, T., Munley, E., Fargo, J., et al. 2013. New perspectives on community-level determinants of homelessness. *Journal of Urban Affairs* 35(5): 607–625.

Calvo, F., Watts, B., Panadero, S., et al. 2022. The prevalence and nature of violence against women experiencing homelessness: A quantitative study. *Violence Against Women* 28(6–7): 1464–1482.

Caplow, T. 1970. The sociologist and the homeless man. In H. Bahr (ed.), *Disaffiliated Man: Essays and Bibliography on Skid Row, Vagrancy, and Outsiders*. Toronto: University of Toronto Press, pp. 3–49.

Carr, E. 2011. *Scripting Addiction: The Politics of Therapeutic Talk and American Sobriety*. Princeton, NJ: Princeton University Press.

Cartwright, N., and Hardie, J. 2012. *Evidence-Based Policy: A Practical Guide to Doing it Better*. Oxford: Oxford University Press.

Casey, R., Goudie, R., and Reeve, K. 2008. Homeless women in public spaces: Strategies of resistance. *Housing Studies* 23(6): 899–916.

Centers for Disease Control and Prevention. 2021. *CDC Issues Eviction Moratorium Order in Areas of Substantial and High Transmission*. https://www.cdc.gov/media/releases/2021/s0803–cdc–eviction–order.html.

Chamberlain, C., and Mackenzie, D. 1992. Understanding contemporary homelessness: Issues of definition and meaning. *Australian Journal of Social Issues* 27(4): 274–297.

Chamberlain, C., and Mackenzie, D. 1998. *Youth Homelessness: Early Intervention & Prevention*. Sydney: Australian Centre for Equity through Education.

Chamberlain, C., and Mackenzie, D. 2006. Homeless careers: A framework for intervention. *Australian Social Work* 59(2): 198–212.

Christensen, J. 2013. "Our home, our way of life": Spiritual homelessness

References

and the sociocultural dimensions of Indigenous homelessness in the Northwest Territories (NWT), Canada. *Social & Cultural Geography* 14(7): 804–828.

Christensen, J. 2016. Introduction. In E. Peters and J. Christensen (eds.), *Indigenous Homelessness: Perspectives from Canada, Australia, and New Zealand*. Winnipeg: University of Manitoba Press.

Clarke, A., and Parsell, C. 2019. The potential for urban surveillance to help support people who are homeless: Evidence from Cairns, Australia. *Urban Studies* 56(10): 1951–1967.

Clarke, A., and Wydall, S. 2013. Making safe: A coordinated community response to empowering victims and tackling perpetrators of domestic violence. *Social Policy and Society* 12(3): 393–406.

Clarke, A., Parsell, C., and Vorsina, M. 2020. The role of housing policy in perpetuating conditional forms of homelessness support in the era of Housing First: Evidence from Australia. *Housing Studies* 35(5): 954–975.

Cloke, P., May, J., and Johnsen, S. 2008. Performativity and affect in the homeless city. *Environment and Planning D: Society and Space* 26(2): 241–263.

Cloke, P., May, J., and Johnsen, S. 2010. *Swept Up Lives? Re-Envisioning the Homeless City*. Chichester: Wiley-Blackwell.

Cobb-Clark, D., Herault, N., Scutella, R., and Tseng, Y. 2016. A journey home: What drives how long people are homeless? *Journal of Urban Economics* 91: 57–72.

Cohen, Y., Krumer-Nevo, M., and Avieli, N. 2017. Bread of shame: Mechanisms of othering in soup kitchens. *Social Problems* 64(3): 398–413.

Colburn, G., and Aldern, C. 2022. *Homelessness is a Housing Problem: How Structural Factors Explain US Patterns*. Oakland: University of California Press.

Collins, D., and Stout, M. 2021. Does Housing First policy seek to fulfil the right to housing? The case of Alberta, Canada. *Housing Studies* 36(3): 336–358.

Community Preventive Services Task Force. 2019. *Health Equity: Permanent Supportive Housing with Housing First (Housing First Programs)*. https://www.thecommunityguide.org/findings/health–equity–housing–first–programs.

Community Solutions. 2022a. *Functional Zero*. https://community.solutions/built–for–zero/functional–zero/.

Community Solutions. 2022b. *Homelessness is Solvable*. https://community.solutions/built–for–zero/the–movement/.

Cosgrove, L., and Flynn, C. 2005. Marginalized mothers: Parenting without a home. *Analyses of Social Issues and Public Policy* 5(1): 127–143.

Couloute, L. 2018. *Nowhere to Go: Homelessness among Formerly Incarcerated People*. Prison Policy Initiative. https://www.jstor.org/stable/pdf/resrep27306.pdf?acceptTC=true&coverpage=false&addFooter=false.

206 References

Crane, M., and Warnes, A. 2000. Evictions and prolonged homelessness. *Housing Studies* 15(5): 757–773.

Cresswell, T. 2001. Making up the tramp. In P. Adams, S. Hoelscher and K. Till (eds.), *Textures of Place: Exploring Humanist Geographies*. Minneapolis: University of Minnesota Press, pp. 167–185.

Culhane, D. 2008. The costs of homelessness: A perspective from the United States. *European Journal of Homelessness* 2: 97–114.

Culhane, D., and Metraux, S. 2008. Rearranging the deck chairs or reallocating the lifeboats? Homelessness assistance and its alternatives. *Journal of the American Planning Association* 74(1): 111–121.

Culhane, D., Metraux, S., and Hadley, T. 2002. Public service reductions associated with placement of homeless persons with severe mental illness in supportive housing. *Housing Policy Debate* 13(1): 107–163.

Czischke, D. 2018. Collaborative housing and housing providers: Towards an analytical framework of multi-stakeholder collaboration in housing co-production. *International Journal of Housing Policy* 18(1): 55–81.

Czischke, D., Carriou, C., and Lang, R. 2020. Collaborative housing in Europe: Conceptualizing the field. *Housing, Theory and Society* 37(1): 1–9.

Dej, E., Gaetz, S., and Schwan, K. 2020. Turning off the tap: A typology for homelessness prevention. *The Journal of Primary Prevention* 41: 397–412.

DePaul. 2022. https://depaulfrance.org/services/.

Department of Housing and Urban Development. 2022. *Moving On*. https://www.hudexchange.info/programs/coc/moving-on/.

Desmond, M. 2012. Disposable ties and the urban poor. *American Journal of Sociology* 117(5): 1295–1335.

Despres, C. 1991. The meaning of home: Literature review and directions for future research and theoretical development. *Journal of Architectural and Planning Research* 8(2): 96–114.

DeVerteuil, G. 2014. Does the punitive need the supportive? A sympathetic critique of current grammars of urban injustice. *Antipode* 46(4): 874–893.

Diemer, K., Humphreys, C., and Crinall, K. 2017. Safe at home? Housing decisions for women leaving family violence. *Australian Journal of Social Issues* 52(1): 32–47.

Doran, K., Ragins, K., Iacomacci, A., et al. 2013. The revolving hospital door: Hospital readmissions among patients who are homeless. *Medical Care* 51(9): 767–773.

Dordick, G. 1997. *Something to Lose: Personal Relations and Survival Among New York's Homeless*. Philadelphia, PA: Temple University Press.

Douglas, M. 1991. The idea of a home: A kind of space. *Social Research* 58(1): 287–307.

Dupuis, A., and Thorns, D. 1996. Meaning of home for older home owners. *Housing Studies* 11(4): 485–501.

Dworsky, A., and Courtney, M. 2009. Homelessness and the transition from foster care to adulthood. *Child Welfare* 88(4): 23–56.

References

Dworsky, A., Napolitano, L., and Courtney, M. 2013. Homelessness during the transition from foster care to adulthood. *American Journal of Public Health* 103(S2): S318–S323.

Easthope, H. 2004. A place called home. *Housing Theory and Society* 21(3): 128–138.

Edin, K., and Shaefer, H. 2015. *$2.00 a Day: Living on Almost Nothing in America*. Boston, MA: Houghton Mifflin Harcourt.

Eide, S. 2020. *Housing First and Homelessness: The Rhetoric and the Reality*. New York: Manhattan Institute.

Ellsworth, J. 2019. Street crime victimization among homeless adults: A review of the literature. *Victims & Offenders* 14(1): 96–118.

Ellsworth, J. 2021. Housing and criminality: The effect of housing placement on arrests among chronically homeless adults. *Journal of Social Distress and Homelessness*. doi.org/10.1080/10530789.2021.1897935.

Employment and Social Development Canada. 2019. *Everyone Counts 2018: Highlights. Preliminary Results from the Second Nationally Coordinated Point-in-Time Count of Homelessness in Canadian Communities*. https://www.canada.ca/content/dam/esdc–edsc/documents/programs /homelessness/reports/1981–Reaching_Home–PIT–EN_(3).pdf.

Evans, R., and Forsyth, J. 2004. Risk factors, endurance of victimization and survival strategies: The impact of the structural location of men and women on the experiences within homeless milieus. *Sociological Spectrum* 24(4): 479–505.

Evans, D., and Porter, J. 2015. Criminal history and landlord rental decisions: A New York quasi-experimental study. *Journal of Experimental Criminology* 11: 21–42.

Fahmy, E., Williamson, E., and Pantazis, C. 2016. *Evidence and Policy Review: Domestic Violence and Poverty*. York: Joseph Rowntree Foundation.

Fargo, J., Munley E., Byrne, T., et al. 2013. Community-level characteristics associated with variation in rates of homelessness among families and single adults. *American Journal of Public Health* 103(S2): S340–S347.

Farrell, G., Tilley, N., and Tseloni, A. 2014. Why the crime drop? *Crime and Justice* 43: 421–490.

Farrington, A., and Robinson, W. P. 1999. Homelessness and strategies of identity maintenance: A participant observation study. *Journal of Community & Applied Social Psychology* 9(3): 175–194.

Farrugia, D. 2011. The symbolic burden of homelessness: Towards a theory of youth homelessness as embodied subjectivity. *Journal of Sociology* 47(1): 71–87.

Field, D. 1988. Perspectives on homelessness. In J. Loft and M. Davis (eds.), *Homelessness: An Annotated Bibliography of Australian Research*. Melbourne: Australian Institute of Family Studies, pp. 5–12.

Finch, W. 2022. Homeless man paid £90 by British stag party to have groom's name tattooed on his FOREHEAD in Benidorm is finally getting

it removed after FOUR YEARS of humiliation. *Daily Mail*. https://www
.dailymail.co.uk/news/article–11574003/Homeless–man–paid–stag–party
–grooms–tattooed–FOREHEAD–getting–removed.html.

Fischer, P. 1992. Victimization and homelessness: Cause and effect. *New England Journal of Public Policy* 8(1): 229–245.

Fitzpatrick, K. LaGory, M., and Ritchey, F. 1999. Dangerous places: Exposure to violence and its mental health consequences for the homeless. *American Journal of Orthopsychiatry* 69(4): 438–447.

Fitzpatrick, S. 2005. Explaining homelessness: A critical realist perspective. *Housing, Theory and Society* 22(1): 1–17.

Fitzpatrick, S. 2012. Homelessness: Causation. In Susan J. Smith (ed.), *International Encyclopedia of Housing and Home*. Oxford: Elsevier, pp. 15–24.

Fitzpatrick, S., and Jones, A. 2005. Pursuing social justice or social cohesion? Coercion in street homelessness policies in England. *Journal of Social Policy* 34(3): 389–406

Fitzpatrick, S., and Stephens, M. 2014. Welfare regimes, social values and homelessness: Comparing responses to marginalised groups in six European countries. *Housing Studies*. 29(2): 215–234.

Fitzpatrick, S., Bramley, G., and Johnsen, S. 2013. Pathways into multiple exclusion homelessness in seven UK cities. *Urban Studies* 50(1): 148–168.

Fitzpatrick, S., Busch-Geertsema, V., Watts, B., et al. 2022. *Ending Street Homelessness in Vanguard Cities Across the Globe: An International Comparative Study, Final Report*. https://i–sphere.site.hw.ac.uk /wp–content/uploads/sites/15/2022/03/Final–Report–Ending–Street–Homelessness– in–Vanguard–Cities.pdf.

Fitzpatrick, S., Johnsen, S., and Bramley, G. 2012. Multiple exclusion homelessness amongst migrants in the UK. *European Journal of Homelessness* 6(1): 31–58.

Fitzpatrick, S., Mackie, P., and Wood, J. 2021. Advancing a five-stage typology of homelessness prevention. *International Journal on Homelessness*. 1(1): 79–97.

Fitzpatrick, S., Pawson, H., Bramley, G., and Wilcox, S. 2012. *The Homelessness Monitor: England 2012*. London: Crisis.

Fitzpatrick, S., Pawson, H., and Watts, B. 2020. The limits of localism: A decade of disaster on homelessness in England. *Policy and Politics* 48(4): 541–561.

Fitzpatrick, S., Watts, B., Pawson, H., et al. 2021. *The Homelessness Monitor: England 2021*. Crisis.

Fitzpatrick, S., Watts, B., and Sims, R. 2020. *Homelessness Monitor England 2020: COVID-19 Crisis Response Briefing*. London: Crisis.

Fopp, R. 2002. Increasing the potential for gaze, surveillance and normalisation: The transformation of an Australian policy for people who are homeless. *Surveillance & Society* 1(1): 48–65.

Forchuk, C., Macclure, S., van Beers, M., et al. 2008. Developing and testing

References

209

an intervention to prevent homelessness among individuals discharged from psychiatric wards to shelters and "no fixed address." *Psychiatric and Mental Health Nursing* 15(7): 569–575.

Freeman, M., and Nelson, G. 2008. Editor's introduction. In M. Freeman and G. Nelson (eds.), *Vicarious Vagrants: Incognito Social Explorers and the Homeless in England, 1860–1910*. New Jersey: The True Bill Press.

French Republic. 2021. *When Does the Winter Break Apply?* https://www.service–public.fr/particuliers/vosdroits/F34736.

Gaetz, S. 2013. The criminalization of homelessness: A Canadian perspective. *European Journal of Homelessness* 7(2): 357–362.

Gaetz, S. 2014. *Coming of Age: Reimagining the Response to Youth Homelessness in Canada*. Toronto: Canadian Observatory of Homelessness Press.

Gaetz, S., Barr, C., Friesen, A., et al. 2012 *Canadian Definition of Homelessness*. Toronto: Canadian Observatory of Homelessness Press.

Garcia, I., and Kim, K. 2021. "Many of us have been previously evicted": Exploring the relationship between homelessness and evictions among families participating in the rapid rehousing program in Salt Lake County, Utah. *Housing Policy Debate* 31(3–5): 582–600.

Garratt, E. 2017. "Please sir, I want some more: An explanation of repeat foodbank use." *BMC Public Health* 828.

Gerrard, J., and Farrugia, D. 2015. The "lamentable sight" of homelessness and the society of the spectacle. *Urban Studies* 52(12): 2219–2233.

Gibbs, L., Bainbridge, J., Rosenblatt, M., and Mammo, T. 2021. *How Ten Global Cities Take on Homelessness: Innovations that Work*. Berkley, CA: University of California Press.

Giddens, A. 1984. *The Constitution of Society: Outline of the Theory of Structuration*. Cambridge: Polity.

Giddens, A. 1991. *Modernity and Self-Identity: Self and Society in the Late Modern Age*. Cambridge: Polity.

Glasser, I., and Bridgman, R. 1999. *Braving the Street: The Anthropology and Homelessness*. New York: Berghahn Books.

Glendening, Z., and Shinn, M. 2017. Risk models for returns to housing instability among families experiencing homelessness. *Cityscape: A Journal of Policy Development and Research* 19(3): 309–330.

Goering, P., Veldhuizen, S., Nelson, G., et al. 2016. Further validation of the Pathways Housing First fidelity scale. *Psychiatric Services* 67(1): 111–114.

Gonyea, J., and Melekis, K. 2017. Older homeless women's identity negotiation: Agency, resistance, and the construction of the valued self. *The Sociological Review* 65(1): 67–82.

Gowan, T. 2010. *Hobos, Hustlers and Backsliders: Homeless in San Francisco*. Minneapolis: University of Minnesota Pres.

Greenop, K., and Memmott, P. 2016. "We are good-hearted people, we like to share": Definitional dilemmas of crowding and homelessness in urban Indigenous Australia. In E. Peters and J. Christensen (eds.), *Indigenous*

210 References

Homelessness: Perspectives from Canada, Australia, and New Zealand. Winnipeg: University of Manitoba Press, pp. 270–299.

Grigsby, C., Baumann, D., Gregorich, S., and Roberts-Gray, C. 1990. Disaffiliation to entrenchment: A model for understanding homelessness. *Journal of Social Issues* 46(4): 141–156.

Groot, S., Hodgetts, D., Nikora, L. W., and Rua, M. 2010. Tōku tūrangawaewae: Culture, identity, and belonging for Māori homeless people. In J. Te Rito and S. M. Healy (eds.), *Proceedings of the 4th International Traditional Knowledge Conference.* Auckland: New Zealand's Maori Centre of Research Excellence, pp. 125–133.

Habibis, D. 2011. A framework for reimagining Indigenous mobility and homelessness. *Urban Policy and Research.* 29(4): 401–414.

Hamilton, C. 2010. Consumerism, self-creation and prospects for a new ecological consciousness. *Journal of Cleaner Production* 18(6): 571–575.

Hanratty, M. 2017. Do local economic conditions affect homelessness? Impact of area housing market factors, unemployment, and poverty on community homeless rates. *Housing Policy Debate* 27(4): 640–655.

Hansen, H., Bourgois, P., and Drucker, E. 2014. Pathologizing poverty: New forms of diagnosis, disability, and structural stigma under welfare. *Social Science & Medicine* 103: 76–83.

Harvey, H. 2022. When mothers can't "pay the cost to be the boss": Roles and identity within doubled-up households. *Social Problems* 69(1): 261–281.

Haupert, T. 2021. Do housing and neighborhood characteristics impact an individual's risk of homelessness? Evidence from New York City. *Housing Studies.* doi.org/10.1080/02673037.2021.1982874.

Haven of Hope on Wheels. n.d. https://www.havenofhopeonwheels.org/.

Head, B. 2022. *Wicked Problems in Public Policy: Understanding and Responding to Complex Challenges.* Cham, Switzerland: Palgrave Macmillan.

Heerde, J., and Pallotta-Chiarolli, M. 2020. "I'd rather injure somebody else than get injured": An introduction to the study of exposure to physical violence among young people experiencing homelessness. *Journal of Youth Studies* 23(4): 406–429.

Hennigan, B. 2017. House broken: Homelessness, Housing First, and neoliberal poverty governance. *Urban Geography* 38(9): 1418–1440.

Hennigan, B., and Speer, J. 2019. Compassionate revanchism: The blurry geography of homelessness in the USA. *Urban Studies* 56(5): 906–921.

Henry, M., de Sousa, T., Roddey, C., et al. 2021. *The 2020 Annual Homeless Assessment Report (AHAR) to Congress.* The US Department of Housing and Urban Development. https://www.huduser.gov/portal /sites/default/files/pdf/2020–AHAR–Part–1.pdf.

Henry, M., Watt, R., Rosenthal, L., et al. 2017. *The 2017 Annual Homeless Assessment Report (AHAR) to Congress. Part 1: Point-in-Time Estimates of Homelessness.* https://www.huduser.gov/portal/sites/default/files/pdf /2017–AHAR–Part–1.pdf.

References

Hepburn, P., Louis, R., Fish, J., et al. 2021. US eviction filing patterns in 2020. *Socius: Sociological Research for a Dynamic World* 7: 1–18.

Herbert, C., Morenoff, J., and Harding, D. 2015. Homelessness and housing insecurity among former prisoners. *The Russell Sage Foundation Journal of the Social Sciences* 1(2): 44–79.

Herring, C. 2019. Complaint-oriented policing: Regulating homelessness in public space. *American Sociological Review* 84(5): 769–800.

Herring, C. 2021. Complaint-oriented "services": Shelters as tools for criminalizing homelessness. *The Annals of the American Academy* 693: 264–283.

Herring, C., Yarbrough, D., and Alatorre, L. 2020. Pervasive penalty: How the criminalization of poverty perpetuates homelessness. *Social Problems* 67(1): 131–149.

Hervieux, C., and Voltan, A. 2018. Framing social problems in social entrepreneurship. *Journal of Business Ethics* 151: 279–293.

Hodgetts, D., Cullen, A., and Radley, A. 2005. Television characterizations of homeless people in the United Kingdom. *Analyses of Social Issues and Public Policy* 5(1): 29–48.

Hoffman, L., and Coffey, B. 2008. Dignity and indignation: How people experiencing homelessness view services and providers. *The Social Science Journal* 45(2): 207–222.

Holmes, E., Black, J., Heckelman, A., et al. 2018. "Nothing is going to change three months from now": A mixed methods characterization of food bank use in greater Vancouver. *Social Science & Medicine* 200: 129–136.

Hooghe, M., and Meeusen, C. 2013. Is same-sex marriage legislation related to attitudes toward homosexuality? *Sexuality Research and Social Policy* 10: 258–268.

Hoolachan, J. 2022. Making home? Permitted and prohibited place-making in youth homeless accommodation. *Housing Studies* 37(2): 212–231.

Hopper, K. 2004. Shelters. In D. Levinson (ed.), *Encyclopedia of Homelessness*. Thousand Oaks, CA: Sage, pp. 498–503.

Hopper, K., and Baumohl, J. 1994. Held in abeyance: Rethinking homelessness and advocacy. *American Behavioral Scientist* 37(4): 522–552.

Hrast, M. 2008. Media representations of homelessness and the link to (effective) policies: The case of Slovenia. *European Journal of Homelessness* 2(1): 115–137.

Hudson, A. L., Wright, K., Bhattacharya, D., et al. 2010. Correlates of adult assault among homeless women. *Journal of Health Care for the Poor and Underserved* 21(4): 1250–1262.

Huey, L., and Berndt, E. 2008. "You've gotta learn how to play the game": Homeless women's use of gender performance as a tool for preventing victimization. *The Sociological Review* 56(2): 177–194.

Humphreys, R. 1999. *No Fixed Abode: A History of Responses to the Roofless and the Rootless in Britain*. London: Palgrave Macmillan.

212 References

Irvine, L., Kahl, K., and Smith, J. 2012. Confrontations and donations: Encounters between homeless pet owners and the public. *The Sociological Quarterly* 53(1): 25–43.

Ithaca. 2019. *Ithaca Laundry*. https://ithacalaundry.gr/en/.

Jacob, V., Chattopadhyay, S., Attipoe-Dorcoo, S., et al. 2022. Permanent supportive housing with Housing First: Findings from a community guide systematic economic review. *American Journal of Preventive Medicine* 62(3): e188–e201.

Jacobs, K. 2015. A reverse form of welfarism: Some reflections on Australian housing policy. *Australian Journal of Social Issues* 50(1): 53–68.

Jacobs, K., Kemeny, J., and Manzi, T. 1999. The struggle to define homelessness: A constructivist approach. In S. Hutson and D. Clapham (eds.), *Homelessness: Public Policies and Private Troubles*. London: Cassell, pp. 390–399.

Jasinski, J., Wesely, J., Wright, J., and Mustaine, E. 2010. *Hard Lives, Mean Streets: Violence in the Lives of Homeless Women*. Boston, MA: Northeastern University Press.

Jencks, C. 1995. *The Homeless*. Boston, MA: Harvard University Press.

Joern, R. 2009. Mean streets: Violence against the homeless and the making of a hate crime. *Hastings Race & Poverty Law Journal* 6(2): 305–332.

Johnsen, S., and Fitzpatrick, S. 2010. Revanchist sanitisation or coercive care? The use of enforcement to combat begging, street drinking and rough sleeping in England. *Urban Studies* 47(8): 1703–1723.

Johnsen, S., and Teixeira, L. 2012. "Doing it already?": Stakeholder perceptions of Housing First in the UK. *International Journal of Housing Policy* 12(2): 183–203.

Johnsen, S., Cloke, P., and May, J. 2005. Day centres for homeless people: Spaces of care or fear? *Social & Cultural Geography* 6(6): 787–811.

Johnsen, S., Fitzpatrick, S., and Watts, B. 2018. Homelessness and social control: A typology. *Housing Studies* 33(7): 1106–1126.

Johnson, G., and Tseng, Y. 2014. Health and homelessness. In A. Chigavazira, G. Johnson, J. Moschion, et al. (eds.), *Findings from Waves 1 to 5: Special Topics. Journeys Home Research Report*. Melbourne: Melbourne Institute of Applied Economic and Social Research, pp. 37–52.

Johnson, G., Kuehnle, D., Parkinson, et al. 2014. *Resolving Long-Term Homelessness: A Randomised Controlled Trial Examining the 36-Month Costs, Benefits and Social Outcomes from the Journey to Social Inclusion Pilot Program*. Melbourne: Sacred Heart Mission.

Johnson, G., Parkinson, S., and Parsell, C. 2012. *Policy Shift or Program Drift? Implementing Housing First in Australia*. Melbourne: Australian Housing and Urban Research Institute.

Johnson, G., Scutella, R., Tseng, Y., and Wood, G. 2019. How do housing and labour markets affect individual homelessness? *Housing Studies* 34(7): 1089–1116.

Jones, G. 1997. Youth homelessness and the "underclass." In R. MacDonald (ed.), *Youth, the "Underclass" and Social Exclusion*. London: Routledge, pp. 96–112.

Jones, M. 2016. Does race matter in addressing homelessness? A review of the literature. *World Medical and Health Policy* 8(2): 139–156.

Jordan, A. 1965. Homeless men and the community. *Australian Journal of Social Issues* 2(3): 27–33.

Katz, M. 1986. *In the Shadow of the Poorhouse: A Social History of Welfare in America*. New York: Basic Books.

Kaur, H., Saad, A., Magwood, O., et al. 2021. Understanding the health and housing experiences of refugees and other migrant populations experiencing homelessness or vulnerable housing: a systematic review using GRADE-CERQual. *CMAJ Open* 9(2): E681–E692

Kearns, R. 2006. Places to stand but not necessarily to dwell: The paradox of rural homelessness in New Zealand. In P. Cloke and P. Milbourne (eds.), *International Perspectives on Rural Homelessness*. London: Routledge, Ch. 14.

Kerman, N., Polillo, A., Bardwell, G., et al. 2021. Harm reduction outcomes and practices in Housing First: A mixed-methods systematic review. *Drug and Alcohol Dependence* 228(1).

Kertesz, S., Crouch, K., Milby, J., Cusimano, R., and Schumacher, J. 2009. Housing First for homeless persons with active addiction: Are we overreaching? *The Milbank Quarterly* 87(2): 495–534.

Kirkby, C., and Mettler, K. 2016. *Women First: An Analysis of a trauma-informed, women-centred, harm reduction housing model for women with complex substance use and mental health issues*. Toronto: Canadian Observatory of Homelessness Press.

Kirkman, M., Keys, D., Bodzak, D., and Turner, A. 2010. "Are we moving again this week?" Children's experiences of homelessness in Victoria, Australia. *Social Science & Medicine* 70: 994–1001.

Kostiainen, E. 2015. Pathways through homelessness in Helsinki. *European Journal of Homelessness* 9(2): 63–86.

Kuskoff, E., Parsell, C., Plage, S., et al. 2022. Willing but unable: How resources help low-income mothers care for their children and minimise child protection interventions, *British Journal of Social Work*. doi.org/10.1093/bjsw/bcac027.

Kusmer, K. 2002. *Down and Out, on the Road: The Homeless in American History*. New York: Oxford University Press.

Laliberte, V., Stergiopoulos, V., Jacob, B., and Kurdyak, P. 2020. Homelessness at discharge and its impact on psychiatric readmission and physician follow up: A population-based cohort study. *Epidemiology and Psychiatric Sciences* 29(e21): 1–8.

Lambie-Mumford, H. 2017. *Hungry Britain: The Rise of Food Charity*. Bristol: Policy Press.

Lambie-Mumford, H. 2019. The growth of food banks in Britain and what they mean for social policy. *Critical Social Policy* 39(1): 3–22.

Lambie-Mumford, H., and Silvasti, T. 2020. Introduction: Exploring the growth of food charity across Europe. In H. Lambie-Mumford and T. Silvasto (eds.), *The Rise of Food Charity in Europe*. Bristol: Policy Press, pp. 1–18.

Lancione, M. 2014. Entanglements of faith: Discourses, practices of care and homeless people in an Italian city of saints. *Urban Studies* 51(14): 3062–3078.

Lang, R., Carriou, C., and Czischke, D. 2020. Collaborative housing research (1990–2017): A systematic review and thematic analysis of the field. *Housing, Theory and Society* 37(1): 10–39.

Latimer, E., Rabouin, D., Cao, Z., et al. 2020. Cost-effectiveness of Housing First with assertive community treatment: Results from the Canadian At Home/*Chez Soi* trial. *Psychiatric Services* 71(10): 1020–1030.

Laurenson, P., and Collins, D. 2007. Beyond punitive regulation? New Zealand local governments' responses to homelessness. *Antipode* 39(4): 649–667.

LavaMae[x]. 2022. https://lavamaex.org/.

Lawler, S. 2014. *Identity: Sociological Perspectives*, 2nd edn. Cambridge: Polity.

Lee, B., and Schreck, C. 2005. Danger on the streets: Marginality and victimization among homeless people. *American Behavioral Scientist* 48(8): 1055–1081.

Lee, B., Shinn, M., and Culhane, D. 2021. Homelessness as a moving target. *The Annals of the American Academy* 693: 8–26.

Lee, B., Tyler, K., and Wright, J. 2010. The new homelessness revisited. *Annual Review of Sociology* 36: 501–521.

Leibler, J., Nguyen, D., Leon, C., et al. 2017. Personal hygiene practices among urban homeless persons in Boston, MA. *International Journal of Environmental Research and Public Health* 14(8): 1–9.

Leifheit, K., Linton, S., Raifman, J., et al. 2021. Expiring eviction moratoriums and COVID-19 incidence and mortality. *American Journal of Epidemiology* 190(12): 2503–2510.

Lemke, J. 2008. Identity, development and desire: Critical questions. In C. Caldas-Coulthard and R. Iedema (eds.), *Identity Trouble: Critical Discourse and Contested Identities*. London: Palgrave Macmillan, pp. 17–42.

Lemoine, C., Loubière, S., Boucekine, M., et al. 2021. Cost-effectiveness analysis of housing first intervention with an independent housing and team support for homeless people with severe mental illness: A Markov model informed by a randomized controlled trial. *Social Science & Medicine* 272. https://www.sciencedirect.com/science/article/abs/pii/S0277953621000241.

Lenhard, J. 2022. The economy of hot air: *Habiter*, warmth and security among homeless people at the Gare du Nord in Paris. *Housing Studies* 37(2): 250–271.

References

Liebow, E. 1993. *Tell Them Who I Am: The Lives of Homeless Women*. New York: The Free Press.

Lima, V., Hearne, R., and Murphy, M. 2022. Housing financialisation and the creation of homelessness in Ireland. *Housing Studies*. doi.org/10.1080/02673037.2022.2042493.

Linsell, N. 1962. "Detached": A study of homeless men in the city of Melbourne. *The Australian Journal of Social Work* 15(2): 8–11.

Lister, R. 2021. *Poverty*, 2nd edn. Cambridge: Polity.

Löfstrand, C., and Juhila, K. 2012. The discourse of consumer choice in the Pathways Housing First model. *European Journal of Homelessness* 6(2): 47–68.

Loopstra, R., and Lalor, D. 2017. *Financial Insecurity, Food Insecurity, and Disability: The Profile of People Receiving Emergency Food Assistance from the Trussell Trust Foodbank Network in Britain*. London: The Trussell Trust.

Loubière, S., Lemoine, C., Boucekine, M., et al. 2022. Housing First for homeless people with severe mental illness: Extended 4-year follow-up and analysis of recovery and housing stability from the randomized *Un Chez Soi d'Abord* trial. *Epidemiology and Psychiatric Sciences* 31, e14: 1–9.

MacKenzie, D., and Chamberlain, C. 2003. *Homeless Careers: Pathways In and Out of Homelessness*. Melbourne: Council to the Homeless.

Mackie, P. 2015. Homelessness prevention and the Welsh legal duty: Lessons for international policies. *Housing Studies* 30(1): 40–59.

MacLeod, G. 2002. From urban entrepreneurialism to a "revanchist city"? On the spatial injustices of Glasgow's renaissance. *Antipode* 34(3): 602–624.

Mallett, S. 2004. Understanding home: A critical review of the literature. *The Sociological Review* 52(1): 62–89.

Marcus, A. 2006. *Where Have All the Homeless Gone? The Making and Unmaking of a Crisis*. New York: Berghahn Books.

Margolis, A. 2008. Subversive accommodations: Doing homeless in Tokyo's Ueno Park. In A. Beier and P. Ocobock (eds.), *Cast Out: Vagrancy and Homelessness in Global and Historical Perspectives*. Athens: Ohio University Press, pp. 351–372.

Markowitz, F., and Syverson, J. 2021. Race, gender, and homelessness stigma: Effects of perceived blameworthiness and dangerousness. *Deviant Behavior* 42(7): 919–931.

Marmot, M. 2005. Social determinants of health inequalities. *The Lancet* 365(9464): 1099–1104.

Marr, M. 2012. Pathways out of homelessness in Los Angeles and Tokyo: Multilevel contexts of limited mobility amid advanced urban marginality. *International Journal of Urban and Regional Research* 36(5): 980–1006.

Marvasti, A. 2002. Constructing the service-worthy homeless through narrative editing. *Journal of Contemporary Ethnography* 31(5): 615–651.

216 References

May, J., Cloke, P., and Johnsen, S. 2007. Alternative cartographies of homelessness: Rendering visible British women's experiences of "visible" homelessness. *Gender, Place & Culture* 14(2): 121–140.

Mayock, P., and Sheridan, S. 2012. *Migrant Women and Homelessness: Key Findings from a Biographical Study of Homeless Women in Ireland. Women and Homelessness in Ireland.* Research Paper 2. Dublin: Trinity College Dublin.

Mayock, P., Bretherton, J., and Baptista, I. 2016. Women's homelessness and domestic violence: (In)visible interactions. In P. Mayock and J. Bretherton (eds.), *Women's Homelessness in Europe.* London: Palgrave Macmillan, pp. 127–154.

Mayock, P., Sheridan, S., and Parker, S. 2015. "It's just like we're going around in circles and going back to the same thing ...": The dynamics of women's unresolved homelessness. *Housing Studies* 30(6): 877–900.

McCarthy, L. 2013. Homelessness and identity: A critical review of the literature and theory. *People, Place & Policy Online* 7(1): 46–58.

McKnight, J. 1995. *The Careless Society: Community and its Counterfeits.* New York: Basic Books.

McMordie, L. 2021. Avoidance strategies: Stress, appraisal and coping in hostel accommodation. *Housing Studies* 36(3): 380–396.

McNaughton, C. 2008. *Transitions through Homelessness: Lives on the Edge.* London: Palgrave Macmillan.

Mead, L. 1997. (ed.), *The New Paternalism: Supervisory Approaches to Poverty.* Washington, DC: Brookings Institution Press.

Meinbresse, M., Brinkley-Rubinstein, L., Grassette, A., et al., 2014. Exploring the experiences of violence among individuals who are homeless using a consumer-led approach. *Violence & Victims* 29(1): 122–136.

Mejia-Lancheros C., Lachaud J., Stergiopoulos V., et al. 2020. Effect of Housing First on violence-related traumatic brain injury in adults with experiences of homelessness and mental illness: Findings from the At Home/*Chez Soi* randomised trial, Toronto site. *BMJ Open* 10: e038443.

Memmott, P., Long, S., Chambers, C., and Spring, F. 2003. *Categories of Indigenous "Homeless" People and Good Practice Responses to Their Needs.* Melbourne: Australian Housing and Urban Research Institute.

Menard, A. 2001. Domestic violence and housing. *Violence Against Women* 7(6): 707–720.

Metraux, S., and Culhane, D. 1999. Family dynamics, housing, and recurring homelessness among women in New York City homeless shelters. *Journal of Family Issues* 20(3): 371–396.

Metraux, S., Roman, C., and Cho, R. 2007. *Incarceration and Homelessness.* Washington, DC: National Symposium on Homelessness Research.

Miethe, T., Stafford, M., and Long, J. 1987. Social differentiation in criminal victimization: A test of routine activities/lifestyle theories. *American Sociological Review* 52(2): 184–194.

Milbourne, P., and Cloke, P. 2006. Introduction: The hidden faces of rural homelessness. In P. Cloke and P. Milbourne (eds.), *International Perspectives on Rural Homelessness*. London: Routledge, pp. 1–8.

Miller, D., Creswell, J., and Olander, L. 1998. Writing and retelling multiple tales of a soup kitchen for the homeless. *Qualitative Inquiry* 4(4): 469–491.

Mills, C. W. 2000. *The Sociological Imagination*. New York: Oxford University Press.

Ministry of Social and Family Development. 2019. *State of Homelessness in Singapore*. https://www.msf.gov.sg/media–room/Pages/State–of–homelessness–in–Singapore.aspx.

Mitchell, D. 1997. The annihilation of space by law: The roots and implications of anti-homeless laws in the United States. *Antipode*. 29(3): 303–335.

Mitchell, D., and Heynen, N. 2009. The geography of survival and the right to the city: Speculations on surveillance, legal innovation, and the criminalization of intervention. *Urban Geography* 30(6): 611–632.

Moore, C. 2016. Parliament of Australia. https://parlinfo.aph.gov.au /parlInfo/search/display/display.w3p;db=CHAMBER;id=chamber %2Fhansards%2F6b734b2a–e113–486c–bacc–822e11cbf7e6%2F0248 ;query=Id%3A%22chamber%2Fhansards%2F6b7 34b2a–e113–486c–bacc–822e11cbf7e6%2F0000%22.

Moschion, J., and van Ours, J. 2019. Do childhood experiences of parental separation lead to homelessness? *European Economic Review* 111: 211–236.

Mostowska, M. 2014. "We shouldn't but we do …": Framing the strategies for helping homeless EU migrants in Copenhagen and Dublin. *The British Journal of Social Work* 44(1): i18–i34.

Mostowska, M., and Sheridan, S. 2016. Migrant women and homelessness. In P. Mayock and J. Bretherton (eds.), *Women's Homelessness in Europe*. London: Palgrave Macmillan, pp. 235–263.

Moyo, D. 2010. *Dead Aid: Why Aid Is Not Working and How There Is Another Way for Africa*. London: Penguin.

Mullins, D., and Moore, T. 2018. Self-organised and civil society participation in housing provision. *International Journal of Housing Policy* 18(1): 1–14.

Murran, S., and Brady, E. 2022. How does family homelessness impact on children's development? A critical review of the literature. *Child & Family Social Work*. doi.org/10.1111/cfs.12968.

Murray, C. 1984. *Losing Ground: American Social Policy, 1950–1980*. New York: Basic Books.

Mykyta, L., and Macartney, S. 2012. *Sharing a Household: Household Composition and Economic Well-being: 2007–2010*. Washington, DC: US Census Bureau.

Narayan, A., Kalstabakken, A., Labella, M., et al. 2017. Intergenerational continuity of adverse childhood experiences in homeless families:

218 References

Unpacking exposure to maltreatment versus family dysfunction. *American Journal of Orthopsychiatry* 87(1): 3–14.

National Alliance to End Homelessness. 2021 *State of Homelessness: 2021 Edition*. https://endhomelessness.org/homelessness–in–america/homelessness–statistics/state–of–homelessness–2021/.

National Coalition for the Homeless. 2009. *Hate, Violence, and Death on Main Street USA*. https://nationalhomeless.org/publications/hatecrimes/hate_report_2008.pdf.

National Coalition for the Homeless. 2020. *20 Years of Hate: Reporting on Bias-Motivated Violence against People Experiencing Homelessness in 2018–2019*. https://nationalhomeless.org/wp–content/uploads/2020/12/hate–crimes–2018–2019_web.pdf.

Netto, G., Pawson, H., and Sharp, C. 2009. Preventing homelessness due to domestic violence: Providing a safe space or closing the door to new possibilities. *Social Policy and Administration* 43(7): 719–735.

New South Wales Government. 2017. *NSW will change laws to Remove Tent City*. https://www.nsw.gov.au/media–releases/nsw–will–change–laws–to–remove–tent–city#:~:text=The%20NSW%20Government%20will%20urgently,the%20impasse%20in%20Martin%20Place.

Neuman, W., and Guggenheim, L. 2011. The evolution of media effects theory: A six-stage model of cumulative research. *Communication Theory* 21(2): 169–196.

Newman, A., Rubinstein, D., and Gold, M. 2022. New York City plans to stop homeless people from sheltering in subway. *New York Times*, February 18. https://Www.Nytimes.Com/2022/02/18/Nyregion/Homeless–People–Subway–Trains–Mta.Html.

Nichols, J. 2020. Soup kitchens: The stigma of being poor and the construction of social identity. *International Social Work* 63(5): 584–596.

Nordfeldt, M. 2012. A dynamic perspective on homelessness: Homeless families in Stockholm. *European Journal of Homelessness* 6(1): 105–123.

O'Donnell, J. 2021. Does social housing reduce homelessness? A multistate analysis of housing and homelessness pathways. *Housing Studies* 36(10): 1702–1728.

OECD. 2020. *Policy Brief on Affordable Housing: Better Data and Policies to Fight Homelessness in the OECD*. https://www.oecd.org/housing/data/affordable–housing–database/homelessness–policy–brief–2020.pdf.

OECD. 2021a. *Building for a Better Tomorrow: Policies to Make Housing More Affordable*. https://read.oecd–ilibrary.org/view/?ref=1060_1060075–0ejk3l4uil&title=ENG_OECD–affordable–housing–policies–brief.

OECD. 2021b. *Homeless Population*. https://www.oecd.org/els/family/HC3–1–Homeless–population.pdf.

O'Flaherty, B. 2004. Wrong person and wrong place: For homelessness, the conjunction is what matters. *Journal of Housing Economics* 13(1): 1–15.

O'Flaherty, B. 2010. Homelessness as bad luck: Implications for research

References

219

and policy. In B. O'Flaherty and I. Ellen (eds.), *How to House the Homeless*. New York: Russell Sage Foundation.

O'Grady, B., Kidd, S., and Gaetz, S. 2020. Youth homelessness and self-identity: A view from Canada. *Journal of Youth Studies* 23(4): 499–510.

Okamoto, Y. 2007. A comparative study of homelessness in the United Kingdom and Japan. *Journal of Social Issues* 63(3): 525–542.

Okamura, T., Matoba, Y., Sato, M., et al. 2021. Characteristics of older people who experience homelessness for the first time in later life in Tokyo, Japan: A descriptive study. *Journal of Social Distress and Homelessness*. doi.org/10.1080/10530789.2021.2002632.

Olfson, M., Mechanic, D., Hansell, S., et al. 1999. Prediction of homelessness within three months of discharge among inpatients with schizophrenia. *Psychiatric Services* 50(5): 667–673.

Olivet, J., Wilkey, C., Richard, M., et al. 2021. Racial inequality and homelessness: Findings from the SPARC study. *The Annals of the American Academy* 693: 82–100.

Olsson, L., and Nordfeldt, M. 2008. Homelessness and the tertiary welfare system in Sweden: The role of the welfare state and non-profit sector. *European Journal of Homelessness* 2: 157–173.

Orange Sky Australia. 2020. *Annual Report 2019/20*. https://orangesky.org.au/wp–content/uploads/2020/12/201202_Annual_Report_FINAL_with_Financial_Report.pdf.

Osborne, R. 2002. "I may be homeless, but I'm not helpless": The costs and benefits of identifying with homelessness. *Self and Identity* 1(1): 43–52.

O'Sullivan, E. 2012. Varieties of punitiveness in Europe: Homelessness and urban marginality. *European Journal of Homelessness* 6(2): 69–97.

O'Sullivan, E. 2016. Women's homelessness: A historical perspective. In P. Mayock and J. Bretherton (eds.), *Women's Homelessness in Europe*. London: Palgrave Macmillan, pp. 15–40.

O'Sullivan, E. 2020. *Reimagining Homelessness: From Policy to Practice*. Bristol: Policy Press.

O'Toole, T., Conde-Martel, A., Gibbon, J., and Hanusa, B. 2007. Where do people go when they first become homeless? A survey of homeless adults in the USA. *Health and Social Care* 15(5): 446–453.

Padgett, D. 2007. There's no place like (a) home: Ontological security among persons with serious mental illness in the United States. *Social Science & Medicine* 64: 1925–1936.

Padgett, D., Henwood, B., and Tsemberis, S. 2016. *Housing First: Ending Homelessness, Transforming Systems, and Changing Lives*. New York: Oxford University Press.

Palaszczuk, A. 2016. Outstanding young Queenslanders named Young Australians of the Year. Queensland Government. http://statements.qld.gov.au/Statement/2016/1/25/outstanding–youngqueenslanders–named–young–australians–of–the–year.

Park, G., Kim, S., and Kim, N. 2022. The association between crime victimization and depressive symptoms among homeless people in Korea: A gender stratified analysis. *Journal of Social Distress and Homelessness* 31(1): 65–71.

Parker, J., Reitzes, D., and Ruel, E. 2016. Preserving and protecting well-being among homeless men. *Sociological Perspectives* 59(1): 201–218.

Parkinson, S., and Parsell, C. 2018. Housing First and the reassembling of permanent supportive housing: The limits and opportunities of private rental. *Housing, Theory and Society* 35(1): 36–56.

Parolin, Z. 2021. Income support policies and the rise of student and family homelessness. *The Annals of the American Academy* 693: 46–63.

Parsell, C. 2010. "Homeless is what I am, not who I am." *Urban Policy and Research* 28(2): 181–194.

Parsell, C. 2011. Homeless identities: Enacted and ascribed. *The British Journal of Sociology* 62(3): 442–461.

Parsell, C. 2012. Home is where the house it: The meaning of home for people sleeping rough. *Housing Studies* 27(2): 159–173.

Parsell, C. 2016. Surveillance in supportive housing: Intrusion or autonomy? *Urban Studies* 53(15): 3189–3205.

Parsell, C., and Clarke, A. 2022. Charity and shame: Towards reciprocity. *Social Problems* 69(2): 436–452.

Parsell, C., and Parsell, M. 2012. Homelessness as a choice. *Housing, Theory and Society* 29(4): 420–434.

Parsell, C., and Phillips, R. 2014. Indigenous rough sleeping in Darwin, Australia: "Out of place" in an urban setting. *Urban Studies* 51(1): 185–202.

Parsell, C., and Watts, B. 2017. Charity and justice: Reflections on new forms of homelessness provision in Australia. *European Journal of Homelessness* 11(2): 65–76.

Parsell, C., Clarke, A., and Kuskoff, E. 2023. Understanding responses to homelessness during COVID-19: an examination of Australia. *Housing Studies* 38(1): 8–21.

Parsell, C., Clarke, A., and Perales, F. 2021. *Charity and Poverty in Advanced Welfare States*. Abingdon: Routledge.

Parsell, C., Clarke, A., and Perales, F. 2022. Poverty by design: The role of charity and the cultivated ethical citizen. *Social Policy & Society* 21(4): 525–541.

Parsell, C., Petersen, M., and Culhane, D. 2017. Cost offsets of supportive housing: Evidence for social work. *The British Journal of Social Work* 47(5): 1534–1553.

Parsell, C., Phillips, R., and Tomaszewski, W. 2014. Exiting unsheltered homelessness and sustaining housing: A human agency perspective. *Social Service Review* 88(2): 295–321.

Parsell, C., Stambe, R., and Baxter, J. 2018. Rejecting wraparound support: An ethnographic study of social service provision. *British Journal of Social Work* 48(2): 302–320.

References 221

Parsell, C., ten Have, C., Denton, M., and Walter, Z. 2018. Self-management of health care: Multimethod study of using integrated health care and supportive housing to address systematic barriers for people experiencing homelessness. *Australian Health Review* 42(3): 303–308.

Paul, D., Knight, K., Olsen, P., et al. 2020. Racial discrimination in the life course of older adults experiencing homelessness: Results from the HOPE Home study. *Journal of Social Distress and Homelessness* 29(2): 184–193.

Pawson, H., Parsell, C., Liu, E., et al. 2020. *The Australian Homelessness Monitor: 2020*. Melbourne: Launch Housing.

Pawson, H., Parsell, C., Saunders, P., et al. 2018. *The Australian Homelessness Monitor: 2018*. Melbourne: Launch Housing.

Pearce, J. 2007. *Violence, Power and Participation: Building Citizenship in Contexts of Chronic Violence*. https://opendocs.ids.ac.uk/opendocs/bitstream/handle/20.500.12413/12080/Wp274.pdf?sequence=1&isAllowed=y.

Peled, E., and Muzicant, A. 2008. The meaning of home for runaway girls. *Journal of Community Psychology* 36(4): 434–451.

Perales, F., and Todd, A. 2018. Structural stigma and the health and wellbeing of Australian LGB populations: Exploiting geographic variation in the results of the 2017 same-sex marriage plebiscite. *Social Science & Medicine* 208: 190–199.

Peters, E., and Robillard, V. 2009. "Everything you want is there": The place of the reserve in First Nations' homeless mobility. *Urban Geography* 30(6): 652–80.

Petersen, M., and Parsell, C. 2020. The family relationships of older Australians at risk of homelessness. *The British Journal of Social Work* 50(5): 1440–1456.

Petit, J., Loubiere, S., and Tinland, A., et al. 2019. European public perceptions of homelessness: A knowledge, attitudes and practices survey. *Plos One*. doi.org/10.1371/journal.pone.0221896

Petty, J. 2016. The London spikes controversy: Homelessness, urban securitisation and the question of "hostile architecture." *International Journal for Crime, Justice and Social Democracy* 5(1): 67–81.

Piat, M., Polvere, L., Kirst, M., et al. 2015. Pathways into homelessness: Understanding how both individual and structural factors contribute to and sustain homelessness in Canada. *Urban Studies* 52(13): 2366–2382.

Piketty, T. 2014. *Capital in the Twenty-First Century*. Harvard, MA: The Belknap Press of Harvard University Press.

Pinker, S. 2011. *The Better Angels of our Nature: Why Violence has Declined*. New York: Viking.

Pleace, N. 2000. The new consensus, the old consensus and the provision of services for people sleeping rough. *Housing Studies* 15(4): 581–594.

Pleace, N., and Bretherton, J. 2019. *The Cost Effectiveness of Housing First in England*. London: Homeless Link.

Pleace, N., and Quilgars, D. 2003. Led rather than leading? Research on homelessness in Britain. *Journal of Community & Applied Psychology* 13(2): 187–196.

Poppendieck, J. 1999. *Sweet Charity? Emergency Food and the End of Entitlement*. New York: Penguin.

Preece, J., Garratt, E., and Flaherty, J. 2020. Living through continuous displacement: Resisting homeless identities and remaking precarious lives. *Geoforum* 116: 140–148.

Preston, G., and Reina, V. 2021. Sheltered from eviction? A framework for understanding the relationship between subsidized housing programs and eviction. *Housing Policy Debate* 31(3–5): 785–817.

Purdam, K., Garratt, E., and Esmail, A. 2016. Hungry? Food insecurity, social stigma and embarrassment in the UK. *Sociology* 50(6): 1072–1088.

Quigley, J., and Raphael, S. 2001. The economics of homelessness: The evidence from North America. *European Journal of Housing Policy* 1(3): 323–336.

Quigley, J., Raphael, S., and Smolensky, E. 2001. Homeless in America, homeless in California. *The Review of Economic Statistics* 83(1): 37–51.

Quinn, K., Dickson-Gomez, J., Nowicki, K., et al. 2018. Supportive housing for chronically homeless individuals: Challenges and opportunities for providers in Chicago, USA. *Health and Social Care* 26(1): e31–e38.

Ravenhill, M. 2008. *The Culture of Homelessness*. London: Ashgate.

Reeve, K. 2018. Women and homelessness: Putting gender back on the agenda. *People, Place, and Policy Online* 11(3): 165–174.

Rhee, T., and Rosenheck, R. 2021. Why are black adults over-represented among individuals who have experienced lifetime homelessness? Oaxaca-Blinder decomposition analysis of homelessness among US male adults. *Journal of Epidemiology & Community Health* 75(2): 161–170.

Richard, M., Dworkin, J., Rule, K., et al. 2022. Quantifying doubled-up homelessness: Presenting a new measure using US Census microdata. *Housing Policy Debate*. doi.org/10.1080/10511482.2021.1981976.

Riches, G. 2018. *Food Bank Nations: Poverty, Corporate Charity and the Right to Food*. London: Routledge.

Riley, E., Vittinghoff, E., Kagawa, R., et al. 2020. Violence and emergency department use among community-recruited women who experience homelessness and housing instability. *Journal of Urban Health* 97(1): 78–87.

Robinson, B. 2018. Conditional families and lesbian, gay, bisexual, transgender, and queer youth homelessness: Gender, sexuality, family instability, and rejection. *Journal of Marriage and Family* 80(2): 383–396.

Robinson, T. 2019. No right to rest: Police enforcement patterns and quality of life consequences of the criminalization of homelessness. *Urban Affairs Review* 55(1): 41–73.

Roessler, B. 2021. *Autonomy: An Essay on the Life Well Lived*. Cambridge: Polity.

Rog, D., Marshall, T., Dougherty, R., et al. 2014. Permanent supportive housing: Assessing the evidence. *Psychiatric Services* 65(3): 287–294.

References

223

Ronald, R. 2008. *The Ideology of Home Ownership: Homeowner Societies and the Role of Housing.* London: Palgrave Macmillan.

Roschelle, A., and Kaufman, P. 2004. Fitting in and fighting back: Stigma management strategies among homeless kids. *Symbolic Interaction* 27(1): 23–46.

Rosenberger, R. 2020. On hostile design: Theoretical and empirical prospects. *Urban Studies* 57(4): 883–893.

Rucker, P., and Stein, J. 2019. Trump: Homeless people hurt the "prestige" of Los Angeles, San Francisco. *The Washington Post*, 19 September.

Rutan, D., and Desmond, M. 2021. The concentrated geography of eviction. *The Annals of the American Academy* 693: 64–81.

Sager, R., and Stephens, L. 2005. Client's reactions to religious elements at congregation-run feeding establishment. *Nonprofit and Voluntary Sector Quarterly* 34(3): 297–315.

Sahlin, I. 2005. The staircase of transition: Survival through failure. *Innovation: The European Journal of Social Science Research* 18(2): 115–135.

Sahlin, I. 2020. Moving Targets: On reducing public responsibilities through re-categorising homeless people and refugees. *European Journal of Homelessness* 14(1): 27–54.

Samari, D., and Groot, S. 2021. Potentially exploring homelessness among refugees: A systematic review and meta-analysis. *Journal of Social Distress and Homelessness.* doi.org/10.1080/10530789.2021.1995935.

Sanders, B., and Albanese, F. 2016. *"It's No Life At All": Rough Sleepers' Experiences of Violence and Abuse on the Streets of England and Wales.* London: Crisis.

SBS News. 2018. Camilla finishes her Queensland visit. https://www.sbs .com.au/news/article/camilla–finishes–her–queensland–visit/q0qbb73m0.

Scanlon, K., Whitehead, C., Edge, A., and Udagawa, C. 2019. *The Cost of Homelessness Services in London.* London: London Councils.

Schauz, D. 2014. Convicts in the shadow of the rising German welfare state: Between permanent detention and rehabilitation. In B. Althammer, A. Gestrich and J. Grundler (eds.), *The Welfare State and the "Deviant Poor" in Europe, 1870–1933.* London: Palgrave Macmillan, pp. 191–209.

Schneider, V. 2018. The prison to homelessness pipeline: Criminal record checks, race, and the disparate impact. *Indiana Law Journal* 93(2): 421–456.

Sclar, E. 1990. Homelessness and housing policy: A game of musical chairs. *American Journal of Public Health* 80(9): 1039–1040.

Scottish Government. 2021. *Housing to 2040.* https://www.gov.scot/binaries /content/documents/govscot/publications/strategy–plan/2021/03/housing –2040–2/documents/housing–2040/housing–2040/govscot%3Adocument /housing–2040.pdf.

Sharam, A., and Hulse, K. 2014. Understanding the nexus between poverty and homelessness: Relational poverty analysis of families experiencing homelessness in Australia. *Housing Theory and Society* 31(3): 294–309.

224 References

Sharkey, P., Torrats-Espinosa, G., and Takyar, D. 2017. Community and the crime decline: The causal effect of local nonprofits on violent crime. *American Sociological Review* 82(6): 1214–1240.

Sharone, O. 2013. Why do unemployed Americans blame themselves while Israelis blame the system? *Social Forces* 91(4): 1429–1450.

Shildrick, T., and MacDonald, R. 2013. Poverty talk: How people experiencing poverty deny their poverty and why they blame "the poor." *The Sociological Review* 61(2): 285–303.

Shinn, M., and Khadduri, J. 2020. *In the Midst of Plenty: Homelessness and What To Do About It*. Hoboken, NJ: Wiley Blackwell.

Shinn, M., Weitzman, B.C., Stojanovic, D., et al. 1998. Predictors of homelessness among families in New York City: From Shelter request to housing stability. *American Journal of Public Health* 88(11): 1651–1657.

Silvasti, T. 2015. Food aid: Normalising the abnormal in Finland. *Social Policy & Society* 14(3): 471–482.

Simpson Reeves, L., Clarke, A., Kuskoff, E., and Parsell, C. 2022. Fulfilling and desperately needed: An Australian media representation of responses to homelessness. *Australian Journal of Social Issues* 57(4): 783–797.

Sisson, L., and Lown, D. 2011. Do soup kitchen meals contribute to suboptimal nutrient intake & obesity in the homeless population? *Journal of Hunger & Environmental Nutrition* 6(3): 312–323.

Smith, N. 1996. *The New Urban Frontier: Gentrification and the Revanchist City*. London: Routledge.

Smith, S. and Lipsky, M. 1993. *Nonprofits for Hire: The Welfare State in the Age of Contracting*. Harvard, MA: Harvard University Press.

Snow, D., and Anderson, L. 1993. *Down on Their Luck: A Study of Homeless Street People*. Berkeley: University of California Press.

Snow, D., and Mulcahy, M. 2001. Space, politics, and the survival strategies of the homeless. *American Behavioral Scientist* 45(1): 149–169.

Snyder, E. 2014. The Bodelschwingh initiative: A transcontinental examination of German Protestant welfare, 1880–1933. In B. Althammer, A. Gestrich and J. Grundler (eds.), *The Welfare State and the "Deviant Poor" in Europe, 1870–1933*. London: Palgrave Macmillan, pp. 150–171.

Somerville, P. 1997. The social construction of home. *Journal of Architectural and Planning Research* 14(3): 226–245.

Stadler, S., and Collins, D. 2021. Assessing Housing First programs from a right to housing perspective. *Housing Studies*. doi.org/10.1080/02673037 .2021.1982873.

Stefancic, A., and Tsemberis, S. 2007. Housing First for long-term shelter dwellers with psychiatric disabilities in a suburban county: A four-year study of housing access and retention. *Journal of Primary Prevention* 28(3–4): 265–279.

Stergiopoulos, V., Mejia-Lancheros, C., Nisenbaum, R. 2019. Long-term effects of rent supplements and mental health support services on housing and health outcomes of homeless adults with mental illness: Extension

References

225

study of the At Home/*Chez Soi* randomised controlled trial. *The Lancet Psychiatry* 6(11): 915–925.

Stone, M. 2017. Helping the homeless: A soup kitchen in London. In S. Cohen, C. Fuhr, and J. Bock (eds.), *Austerity, Community Action, and the Future of Citizenship in Europe*. Bristol: Policy Press, pp. 157–168.

Stuart, F. 2016. *Down, Out, and Under Arrest: Policing and Everyday Life in Skid Row*. Chicago, IL: The University of Chicago Press.

Szeintuch, S. 2022. Homeless without benefits: The non-take-up problem. *Housing Studies*. doi.org/10.1080/02673037.2020.1823330.

Takahashi, L., McElroy, J., and Rowe, S. 2002. The sociospatial stigmatization of homeless women with children. *Urban Geography* 23(4): 301–322.

Tan, H., and Forbes-Mewett, H. 2018. Whose "fault" is it? Becoming homeless in Singapore. *Urban Studies* 55(16): 3579–3595.

Tapim, F. 2013. Man charged with attempted murder over Brisbane arrow shooting of homeless man. ABC News. https://www.abc.net.au/news/2013-06-14/man-charged-with-attempted-murder-over-brisbane-arrow-shooting/4753154.

Teixeira, L. 2020. The impact manifesto: Doing the right things to end homelessness for good. In L. Teixeira and J. Cartwright (eds.), *Using Evidence to End Homelessness*. Bristol: Policy Press, pp. 1–20.

Temesvary, Z. 2019. Hungarian homeless people in Basel: Homelessness and social exclusion from a lifeworld-oriented social work perspective. *European Journal of Homelessness* 13(2): 29–51.

Teo, P., and Chiu, M. 2016. An ecological study of families in transitional housing: "Housed but not homed." *Housing Studies* 31(5): 560–577.

Thiery, N. 2008. Accommodation for women accompanied by children in CHRS: What impact on parental identity? *Sociétés et Jeunesses en Difficulté* 5. http://sejed.revues.org/index2992.html.

Thompson, M. 2020. From co-ops to community land trusts: Tracing the historical evolution and policy mobilities of collaborative housing movements. *Housing, Theory and Society* 37(1): 82–100.

Tiderington, E., Goodwin, J., and Noonan, E. 2022. Leaving permanent supportive housing: A scoping review of Moving On Initiative participant outcomes. *Housing Studies*. doi.org/10.1080/02673037.2022.2045006.

Tipple, G., and Speak, S. 2009. *The Hidden Millions: Homelessness in Developing Countries*. London: Routledge.

Titmuss, R. 2019. *The Gift Relationship: From Human Blood to Social Policy*. Bristol: Policy Press.

Tomas, A., and Dittmar, H. 1995. The experience of homeless women: An exploration of housing histories and the meaning of home. *Housing Studies* 10(4): 493–515.

Tomaszewski, W., Smith, J., Parsell, C., et al. 2017. Young, anchored and free? Examining the dynamics of early housing pathways in Australia. *Journal of Youth Studies*. 20(7): 904–926.

Toolis, E., and Hammack, P. 2015. The lived experience of homeless youth: A narrative approach. *Qualitative Psychology* 2(1): 50–68.

Tronto, J. 1993. *Moral Boundaries: A Political Argument for an Ethics of Care.* London: Routledge.

Tronto, J. 2015. *Who Cares? How to Reshape a Democratic Politics.* Ithaca, NY: Cornell University Press.

Tsai, J., Lee, C., Byrne, T., et al. 2017. Changes in public attitudes and perceptions about homelessness between 1990 and 2016. *American Journal of Community Psychology* 60(3–4): 599–606.

Tsai, J., Lee, C., Shen, J., et al. 2019. Public exposure and attitudes about homelessness. *Journal of Community Psychology* 47(1): 76–92.

Tsai, J., Pietrzak, R., and Szymkowiak, D. 2021. The problem of veteran homelessness: An update for the new decade. *American Journal of Preventive Medicine* 60(6): 774–780.

Tsemberis. S. 2010. Housing First: Ending homelessness, promoting recovery, and reducing costs. In B. O'Flaherty and I. Ellen (eds.), *How to House the Homeless.* New York: Russell Sage Foundation, pp. 37–56.

Tsemberis, S., and Eisenberg, R. 2000. Pathways to housing: Supported housing for street-dwelling homeless individuals with psychiatric disabilities. *Psychiatric Services* 51(4): 487–493.

Tsemberis, S., Gulcur, L., and Nakae, M. 2004. Housing First, consumer choice, and harm reduction for homeless individuals with a dual diagnosis. *American Journal of Public Health* 94(4): 651–656.

Turnbull, M. 2016. Remarks at AskIzzy launch, Melbourne. https://www.malcolmturnbull.com.au/media/remarks–at–askizzy–launch–melbourne.

Udvarhelyi, H. 2014. "If we don't push homeless people out, we will end up being pushed out by them": The criminalization of homelessness as state strategy in Hungary. *Antipode* 46(3): 816–834.

United Kingdom. 2018. *Homelessness Data: Notes and Definitions.* https://www.gov.uk/guidance/homelessness–data–notes–and–definitions#:~:text=their%20current%20accommodation.–,Statutory%20homelessness,statutory%20duty%20to%20provide%20assistance.&text=Such%20statutorily%20homeless%20households%20are%20referred%20to%20as%20'acceptances'.

United States Interagency Council on Homelessness. 2010. *Opening Doors: Federal Strategic Plan to Prevent and End Homelessness.* https://www.usich.gov/resources/uploads/asset_library/Opening%20Doors%202010%20FINAL%20FSP%20Prevent%20End%20Homeless.pdf.

United States Interagency Council on Homelessness. 2012. *Searching Out Solutions: Constructive Alternatives to the Criminalization of Homelessness.* https://www.usich.gov/tools–for–action/searching–out–solutions/.

United States Interagency Council on Homelessness. 2020. *Expanding the Toolbox: The Whole-of-Government Response to Homelessness.* https://www.usich.gov/resources/uploads/asset_library/USICH–Expanding–the–Toolbox.pdf.

References 227

van Laere, I., de Wit, M., and Klazinga, N. 2009. Pathways into homelessness: Recently homeless adults problems and service use before and after becoming homeless in Amsterdam. *BMC Public Health* 9(3): 1–9.

Veness, A. 1993. Neither homed nor homeless: Contested definitions and the personal world of the poor. *Political Geography* 12(4): 319–340.

Viggers, H., Keall, M., Wickens, K., Howden-Chapman, P. 2017. Increased house size can cancel out the effect of improved insulation on overall heating energy requirements. *Energy Policy* 107: 248–257.

Walby, S., Towers, J., and Francis, B. 2016. Is violent crime increasing or decreasing? A new methodology to measure repeat attacks making visible the significance of gender and domestic relations. *The British Journal of Criminology* 56(6): 1203–1234.

Waldron, J. 1991. Homelessness and the issue of freedom. *UCLA Law Review* 39(1): 295–324.

Wallace, S. 1965. *Skid Row as a Way of Life*. Totowa, NJ: The Bedminster Press.

Walsh, T. 2005. Won't pay or can't pay? Exploring the use of fines as a sentencing alternative for public nuisance type offences in Queensland. *Current Issues in Criminal Justice* 17(2): 217–238.

Walter, Z., Jetten, J., Parsell, C., and Dingle, G. 2015. The impact of self-categorizing as "homeless" on well-being and service use. *Analyses of Social Issues and Public Policy* 15(1): 333–356.

Wardhaugh, J. 1999. The unaccommodated women: Home, homelessness and identity. *The Sociological Review* 47(1): 91–109.

Watson, J. 2018. *Youth Homelessness and Survival Sex: Intimate Relationships and Gendered Subjectivities*. Abingdon: Routledge.

Watson, S. (with Austerberry, H.) 1986. *Housing and Homelessness: A Feminist Perspective*. London: Routledge & Kegan Paul.

Watts, B., and Blenkinsopp, J. 2022. Valuing control over one's immediate living environment: How homelessness responses corrode capabilities. *Housing Theory and Society* 39(1): 98–115.

Watts, B., and Fitzpatrick, S. 2018. *Welfare Conditionality*. Abingdon: Routledge.

Watts, B., Bramley, G., Fitzpatrick, S., et al. 2021. *The Homelessness Monitor: Scotland 2021*. London: Crisis.

Watts, B., Bramley, G., Pawson, H., et al. 2022. *The Homelessness Monitor: England 2020*. London: Crisis.

Watts, B., Fitzpatrick, S., and Johnsen, S. 2018. Controlling homeless people? Power, interventionism and legitimacy. *Journal of Social Policy* 47(2): 235–252.

Watts, B., Littlewood, M., Blenkinsopp, J., and Jackson, F. 2018. *Temporary Accommodation in Scotland: Final Report*. https://pure.hw.ac.uk/ws/portalfiles/portal/23430074/SB_TempAccom%20mReport_FinalReport.pdf.

Westbrook, M., and Robinson, T. 2021. Unhealthy by design: Health and safety consequences of the criminalization of homelessness. *Journal of Social Distress and Homelessness* 30(2): 107–115.

Wetzstein, S. 2017. The global urban housing affordability crisis. *Urban Studies* 54(14): 3159–3177.

Whitbeck, L., Hoyt, D., Yoder, K., et al. 2001. Deviant behavior and victimization among homeless and runaway adolescents. *Journal of Interpersonal Violence* 16(11): 1175–1204.

Whiteford, M. 2010. Hot tea, dry toast and the responsibilisation of homeless people. *Social Policy & Society* 9(2): 193–205.

Wijburg, G. 2021. The de-financialization of housing: Towards a research agenda. *Housing Studies* 36(8): 1276–1293.

Wilder Research. 2007. *Overview of Homelessness in Minnesota 2006*. https://www.wilder.org/sites/default/files/imports/Homelessoverview2006 _3–07.pdf.

Wilkinson, R., and Pickett, K. 2009. *The Spirit Level: Why More Equal Societies Almost Always Do Better*. London: Allen Lane.

Willse, C. 2015. *The Value of Homelessness: Managing Surplus Life in the United States*. Minneapolis: University of Minnesota Press.

Wilson, C. 1956. *The Outsider*. Boston, MA: Houghton Mifflin.

Winetrobe, H., Rhoades, H., Rice, E., et al. 2017. "I'm not homeless, I'm houseless": Identifying as homeless and associations with service utilization among Los Angeles homeless young people. *Journal of Social Distress and the Homeless* 26(1): 16–24.

Wolch, J., and Dear, M. 1993. *Malign Neglect: Homelessness in an American City*. San Francisco, CA: Jossey-Bass.

Wolch, J., Dear, M., and Akita, A. 1988. Explaining homelessness. *Journal of the American Planning Association* 54(4): 443–453.

Wright, S. 2021. A year after launching a mobile shower and laundry services for the homeless, Hope Vibes looks to expand. *City Metro*. https:// qcitymetro.com/2021/10/11/a–year–after–launching–a–mobile–shower –and–laundry–services–for–the–homeless–hope–vibes–looks–to–expand/.

Yeoh, S. 2017. The world class city, the homeless and soup kitchens in Kuala Lumpur. *Current Sociology* 65(4): 571–586.

Y-Foundation. 2017. *A Home of Your Own*. https://ysaatio.fi/assets/files /2018/01/A_Home_of_Your_Own_lowres_spreads.pdf.

Young, I. 1986. The ideal community and the politics of difference. *Social Theory and Practice* 12(1): 1–26.

Young, I. 2011. *Responsibility for Justice*. Oxford: Oxford University Press.

Zufferey, C. 2014. Questioning representations of homelessness in the Australian print media. *Australian Social Work* 67(4): 525–536.

Index

*Pages in **bold** refer to boxes in the text.*

abolition/elimination of homelessness
    see ending homelessness
addresses, fixed 8
African Americans *see* Black people
age of homeless people 5–6
agency, human 26–30, 194–6
  and identity 110, 127, 129
Agrawal, Sandeep 52, 55
Ahlin, Eileen 72
Ahmed, Sara 12
airports 77
Alaazi, Dominic 19
Alberta, Canada 174
alcohol misuse *see* substance abuse
Aldern, Clayton 26–30, 32, 190
Allen, Mike 54, 150–1
Althammer, Beate 113
Amore, Kate 12, 13, 15, 21
Amster, Randall 138
Anderson, Leon 96, 115–16, 124
Antunes, Maria 72
Aoki, Hideo 34
architecture 139–41
Asad, Ayesha 90
Asadi, Muhammed 119
Asian people 50, 51
Assertive Community Outreach teams
    161
Aubry, Tim 33, 163, 164, 165, 169
austerity measures 86, 192

Australia 2
  and affordable housing 33, 155
  and charity 87, 88, 89–90, 91
  and criminalization of homelessness
    142, 143, 148–9
  and family relationships 39–41,
    124–5
  and homelessness services 89–90,
    97, 106, 130
    and charity 87, 88, 91
    laundries 86, 87
    showers 87, 90
  and identity 112–13, 130
    self-identity 123, 124–5, **127–8**
  and Indigenous people 18, 52, 143
  and social problems 33, 38, 41,
    45, 46
  and social/public housing 33, 87
  and supportive housing models
    169, 174
  and unsheltered homelessness 124,
    148–9
  and violence 64, 65, 68–9, 73–4
    and domestic and family violence
      38, 45
Australian Institute of Health and
    Welfare 155
autonomy
  and affordable housing 195, 196
  and charity 89, 91–5, 106

230 Index

autonomy (*cont.*)
  and family relationships 103, 129, 130
  and home 105, 106
  and homelessness services 83–4, 85, **102**, 104–6
    and charity 89, 91–5, 106
    and infantilization 98–9, 195
    and judgment 93–4, 95, 96–7
    and personal independence 91, 92–5, 99
    shelters 95, 96–7, 98–9, 103, 149
    and stigma 92, 104
  and identity 129, 130
    and judgment 114, 120, 135
    and labeling 22, 109, 114–15, 121–2, 131
    and sense of self 119, 120, 123, 125, 126, 130, 134
  and otherness 92, 111–12, 118–21
  and privacy 17–18, 84, 96, 105
  and respect 93, 98, 136
  and self-determination 99, 105, 162
  and self-sufficiency 101, 116, 174
  and sense of self 107, 168
    and identity 119, 120, 123, 125, 126, 130, 134
  and social change 195, 196
  and supportive housing models 162, **167–8**
  and women 98, 103, 129–30

Bacchi, Carol 188–9
Bahr, Howard 114, 132, 133
Baker, Charlene 39
Balmer, Ivo 196
Baptista, Isabel 153
Barile, John 87
Bauman, Zygmunt 122
Baumohl, Jim 155–6, 187
Baxter, Ellen 63, 165
Beck, Elizabeth 10, 56
Beck, Rozelen 61
beds 72, 150, 186
behavior, homeless 95, 115, 117, 120, 124
  see also deviancy
Belfast, Northern Ireland 63

Belgium 141
belongings, personal 139, 143, **146**
benches, anti-sleep 140
Benjaminsen, Lars 44
Berlin 51
Black people 49–50, 51, 52–3
Blenkinsopp, Janice 63, 98, 100
Bogue, Donald 112
Boston, United States 32
Bowen, Elizabeth 25–6
Boydell, Katherine 123
Bramley, Glen 36
Brekhus, Wayne 111, 122
Bresson, Sabrina 195
Bridgman, Rae 77
Bristol, UK 74–5
Broll, Ryan 78
Budapest, Hungary 139
building industry 193
built-for-zero movement 181
Burawoy, Michael 191
Busch-Geertsema, Volker 13, 21, 50, 51, 154, 156, 160, 169
buses 75, 87
Byrne, Thomas 32, 184

cafés **127–8**
California **68**, 138
Calvo, Fran 59, 70
Canada 14–15, 105, 123
  and affordable housing 33, 142
  and Indigenous people 18–20, 52, 55
  and supportive housing models 161, 169, 174–5
Canadian Observatory of Homelessness 14–15
capitalism 7, 173
Caplow, Theodore 112
Cappozziello, Nicole 25–6
car parks 87, 132
care, institutional 42–3, 47–8
  see also shelters
Carr, E. Summerson **101–2**
Cartwright, Nancy 182
Casey, Rionach 71, 77
causal mechanisms of homelessness 28–30
  see also housing, affordable; poverty

Index

CCTV 73, 148–9
Central Eastern European people 51
Centre for Homelessness Impact, UK
178, 179–80
Chamberlain, Chris 117
change, social 10, **68**, 165–6, 177–9,
189–96
and affordable housing 189, 190–5
and autonomy 195, 196
and inequality 8, 191
and citizenship rights 190, 194
evidence-led 179–80, 182–3, 185
and inequality 8, 9, 191
and rental housing 189, 191
United Kingdom 9, 191, 192, 196
United States 181, 189, 190–1, 192
see also ending homelessness
charities as role models 89
charity 85–95
and Australia 87, 88, 89–90, 91
and autonomy 89, 91–5, 106
charitable care 8–9, 83, 196–7
and deprivation 88, 90
and ethics 82, 86, 88
and government/state
responsibilities/actions 85–6,
89–90
and identity 92, 132
and Italy 87, 92
and religious organizations 87, 93
and resource provision 86–90
and day centers 86, 89
and shelters 87, 156
and soup kitchens 86, 87, 88,
89, 92
and social problems 25, 26
United Kingdom 85, 86–7, 94
United States 85, 87, 88, 90, 93
and volunteers 85, 89–90, 91, 92,
93
see also homelessness services
child protection system **40–1**, 43, 79
childhood poverty 36
children 5, 47–8, 103–4
families with children 35, 50, 79,
100–3, 132
and family relationships **40–1**, 129
and violence 78, 79
choice, personal
and deviancy 7, 24–5, 26

homelessness as a choice 7–8, 25,
55–6, 133–4
and supportive housing models
162, 165, **168**
Christensen, Julia 18, 19, 55
churches 87
citizen action 192
citizenship/citizenship rights 8, 54–5,
172
and ending homelessness 140, 161
and government/state
responsibilities/actions 81, 86,
140, 144
and social change 190, 194
Clarke, Andrew 149
Cloke, Paul 3, 63, 64, 77, 86, 88,
107
clothing, women's 76
clothing donations 87
Cobb-Clark, Deborah 34–5
coercion of rough sleepers 144–57
coercive behavior 39
Coffey, Brian 93, 98
Cohen, Yael 91–2
co-housing 192
Colburn, Gregg 26–30, 32, 190
Collins, Damian 147, 174
colonization 19, 55
commodification of housing 188,
190–4, 198
communities, local 193, 194
community identity 115, 116–17
community organizations 4, 80, 143
Community Preventive Services Task
Force, US 168–9
Community Solutions organization,
US 181
comparison, social 123–4
conditionality 93, 153–4, 157, 162
consequences of homelessness 103–4,
125
conservatism 196
continuum of care model *see* staircase
model
Continuum of Care program,
Housing and Urban
Development, Department of
(HUD) 14
control, social 107, **167–8**, 195
see also autonomy

Index

control trials 179, 183–4
Cornwall, Duchess of 90
Cosgrove, Lisa 103
cost benefits 166–75
  see also housing models, supportive
countries, wealthy 10, 17, 188
Courtney, Mark 47–8
Covid-19 2–3, 46, 54
Crane, Maureen 47
criminal behavior 53, 117, 143–4
criminal history 48
criminal justice system 45, 53, 141–4, 166, 169
criminalization of homelessness 137–9, 141–2, 144–9, 157
Culhane, Dennis 27, 155, 166, 170, 171
culture
  cultural norms 17–19, 44, 182, 183
  and identity change 115–16, 117, 118
  subculture 115–16, 117
culture, Japanese 118
Czischke, Darinka 195

dangerous places 61, 71, 74, 144, **145–6**
day centers 74–5, 86, 89
degradation 92–5
dehumanization 26, **145**
  and identity 124, 128, 131
  and violence **67–8**, 71
democracy 1, 195
Denmark 44, 50
Department of Housing and Urban Development (HUD), US 14, 32, 48, 49, 174
dependency *see* autonomy
dependent relationships 107
deprivation 20–2, 172, 190
  and charity 88, 90
  forced 21–2, 104
  and identity 112, 120, 124
design features 131, 139–41
Desmond, Matthew 36
destigmatization 6–7
Destitute Persons Act, Singapore 17
Detroit 32
devaluation 118–19

DeVerteuil, Geoff 142, 144
deviancy
  as a choice 7, 24–5, 26, 133
  and identity 113, 117, 118, 120, 125, 151, 189
  Skid Row 111, 112, 115
Dickens, Charles 92
dignity 88, 89, 92, **168**
disabled people 14, 26
disaffiliation 114–15
disasters, natural 109
discharge planning 5, 42–3, 47–8, 185
Dittmar, Helga 77
domestic and family violence (DFV) 37–41, 78–9, 80, 198
Dordick, Gwendolyn 62–3, 72, 77
dormitories 63, 131, 134
Dublin 51
Dworsky, Amy 47–8

Eastern European people 50, 51
economic development and growth 138
economic downturns 29, 53
Edin, Kathryn 79, 182
education 8, 41, 164
Eide, Stephen 162–3
elder abuse 41
Elizabeth, homeless woman **40–1**
Ellsworth, Joshua 59–60, 61, 62
embarrassment 99
emergency accommodation 15
  see also shelters
employment/unemployment 8, 29, 34, 36, 164
  and identity 117, 118, 125
ending homelessness 137–41, 177–99
  and affordable housing 171, 177, 185, 186, 189
  and citizenship/citizenship rights 140, 161
  and cost benefits 168, 169, 170–4
  and cultural norms 182, 183
  and good intentions 91, 179
  and government/state responsibilities/actions 171–3, 179, 181, 186–7
    United Kingdom 2, 139, 140, 186

Index

United States 137–9, 181, 182, 187
  and neoliberalism 172, 197
  and permanent supportive housing 160, 163–4, 168, 170–1, 173–5, 185, 186
  and poverty 172, 177, 185
  and targets 178, 180
  and welfare state 142, 182, 187
  see also change, social
England 51, 185, 192
  and government/state responsibilities/actions 46, 144–7
  and supportive housing models 160, 169
  and violence 63, 64, 75, 76
  and women 45, 71, 76
ethics 82, 86, 88, 140–1
Eurocentrism 18
Europe 15, 85–6
  and government/state responsibilities/actions 33, 141–2, 150
  and race/racism 50–1, 53–4
  and rehabilitation 132, 153
  and shelters 150, 153
  and social problems 25, 38
  and supportive housing models 169, 174
European Typology on Homelessness and Housing Exclusion (ETHOS) 15–16, 21
European Union (EU) 53–4, 141–2
eviction 48, 185
  Finland 42, 47
  and social problems 42, 46–7, 153
exclusion, social 8, 11, 118–21, 126, 142, 153, 189–90
  see also autonomy
exploitation 79, 191

failings, individual 24–5, 27–8
failure, societal 1–2, 5–6, 20–1, 182
  and shelters 151–2, 156
  and social problems 49, 55–6
families with children 35, 50, 79, 100–3, 132
  and informal housing 79, 103
family dissolution 39–41

family relationships 47–8
  and Australia 39–41, 124–5
  and autonomy 103, 129, 130
  and children **40–1**, 129
  and gender issues 42, 45–6
  and identity 124–5, 130–1, 135
  and social problems 28, 29, 36, 39–41, 45, 55
  and young people 41, 42, 43, 44, 45, 130–1
Fargo, Jamison 32
Farrington, Alice 123
Farrugia, David 119
filth 113, 119, 120, 138
finance sector 193
fines 137, **146**, 147
Finland 39, 50, 186
  and eviction 42, 47
  and social/public housing 186, 191
Fischer, Pamela 60
Fitzpatrick, Kevin 58
Fitzpatrick, Suzanne 27–8, 29–30, 36, 44, 46, 39, 51, 146–7, 185, 187, 192
Florida 71
Flynn, Cheryl 103
food aid/foodbanks 85
Fopp, Rodney 97, 154–5
Forbes-Mewett, Helen 28–9
foster care 43, 48, 49
France 46–7, 87, 103, 139–40, 169, 195
  and migrants 50, 51
free will 91
friendships 77–8, 124

Gaetz, Stephen 142
gender issues 6, 126–30, 198
  and family relationships 42, 45–6
  and identity 123, 126–30
  and stigma 42, 45–6
  United Kingdom 69, 71
  United States 42, 70–1, 73, 128
  and violence 69–74, 76–7, 80
    and safety/security 73–4, 76–7
  see also domestic and family violence (DFV); violence, sexual; women
Gerber, Jean-David 196
Germany 44, 51, 132

234 Index

Gerrard, Jessica 119
Gibbs, Linda 11, 180
Giddens, Anthony 27, 121
Glasgow 141, 180
Glasser, Irene 77
Glendening, Zachary 33
Gonyea, Judith 129, 131, 134
government/state responsibilities/
actions 2–3, 42–7, 136–58
and affordable housing 33–5, 142,
190–5, 196
and public subsidies 33, 34,
190–1
and welfare state 192, 193
and charity 85–6, 89–90
and citizenship/citizenship rights
81, 86, 140, 144
and criminalization of homelessness
137–9, 141–2, 144–9
Australia 142, 148–9
and dangerous places 144,
145–6
and fines 137, **146**, 147
and punitivity 141–2, 144, 145,
147, 148
United States **145–6**, 147, 148,
157
and discharge planning 5, 42–3,
47–8, 185
and ending homelessness 171–3,
179, 181, 186–7
United Kingdom 2, 139, 140,
186
United States 137–9, 181, 182,
187
Europe 33, 141–2, 150
and healthcare/health and social
care 160–1, 165–6, 169,
171–3, 175
and homelessness services 85–6,
89–90, **101**
and legislation 17, 137–9, 185
United States 75, **145–6**
and violence **68**, 69, 75
and neoliberalism 142, 172, 187,
196
and police involvement 142–3, 144
and poverty 36–7, 85, **145–6**
and ending homelessness 172,
177, 185

and welfare state 37, 85, 185
and public spaces 139–41, 142–3,
144–6
and San Francisco 142–3, **145**
and Scotland 2, 150, 185, 186
and sick people **145**, 171–3
and supportive housing models
160–1, 165–6, 169, 171–3,
175
and trigger events 43, 45–6
and violence 45, 143–4
legislation **68**, 69, 75
voucher schemes 33, 161, 190–1
see also Australia; Canada;
homelessness services; New
Zealand; United Kingdom;
United States; welfare state
Gowan, Teresa 24, 64, 99
Greece 87
Greenop, Kelly 18, 19
Grigsby, Charles 117
Groot, Shiloh 124

Hanratty, Maria 36
Hansen, Helena 172
harassment, police 143, 144
Hardie, Jeremy 182
harm-reduction 162
Harvey, Hope 103
hate crime 66–9, 73
Haupert, Tyler 33
healthcare/health and social care
160–1, 165–6
and cost benefits 169, 171–3, 175
Heerde, Jessica 62, 65
help 90, **102**, 107–8, 194–7
Helsinki 186
Hennigan, Brian 148, 173
Henry, Meghan 5
Hepburn, Peter 46
Herring, Chris 138–9, 142–3, **145–6**
history and identity 111–14
Hoffman, Lisa 93, 98
home, meaning of 11–12, 18–19, 20,
58, **167–8**
as a place of safety 73, 105,
109–10
home ownership 34, 191, 197
homeless experiences 57–81, 109–35
see also autonomy; domestic

Index

and family violence (DFV);
 family relationships; rough
 sleeping; shelters; violence,
 homeless people as victims and
 perpetrators of
homelessness, chronic 61
 and identity 117, 135
 and supportive housing models
 155, 160, 161, 163
 and cost benefits 166–8, 170,
 172, 174, 175
 United States 14, 26
homelessness, concealed 3–4, 15,
 78–9, 80, 144
homelessness, overt 3, 78
 see also homelessness, unsheltered;
 rough sleeping
homelessness, revolving door 42–3
homelessness, rural 3
homelessness, statutory 15, 16
homelessness, unsheltered 3, 17, 71,
 180
 Australia 124, 148–9
 and criminalization of homelessness
 141, 142, 146, 148–9
 and identity 124, 125
 see also rough sleeping
homelessness, urban 3
homelessness as a choice 7–8, 25,
 55–6, 133–4
homelessness as a form of freedom
 7–8
homelessness definitions 3, 11–16,
 17, 20–2
homelessness industries 10
homelessness policy 16–20, 132,
 136–58
homelessness services 11, 82–108,
 149–57
 and affordable housing 89, 97,
 101, 154–5
 Australia 89–90, 97, 106, 130
 and charity 87, 88, 91
 laundries 86, 87
 showers 87, 90
 and autonomy 83–4, 85, **102**,
 104–6
 and charity 89, 91–5, 106
 and infantilization 98–9, 195
 and judgment 93–4, 95, 96–7

and personal independence 91,
 92–5, 99
 shelters 98–9, 103, 149
 and stigma 92, 104
 and identity 116, 118, 130, 131,
 133–4
 laundries 86, 87
 and paternalism 97, 99, 107
 and privacy 84, 96
 and rehabilitation **101**, 132–3
 shelters 99, 100, 133, 152–5,
 157–8
 United States 132, 133
 and religious organizations 87, 93
 shelters 87, 95–104, 149–57, 189
 and autonomy 95, 96–7, 98–9,
 103, 149
 and paternalism 97, 99
 and rehabilitation 99, 100, 133
 and surveillance 95–6, 97–104
 United States 96–7, 98, 99
 showers 87–8, 90
 soup kitchens 86, 87
 and staff 62–3, 95–6, 105–6
 and substance abuse 99–100,
 101–2, 133
 United Kingdom 86–7, 94, 99, 131
 and Scotland 95, 98, 150
 shelters 63, 96, 98, 99, 150
 and soup kitchens 88, 89
 United States 87, 90, **101–2**, 133
 and charity 87, 90, 93
 and identity 130, 131, 132
 shelters 87, 95, 96–7, 98, 99,
 103
 and welfare state 85–6, **101**
 and women 98, 100–3, 131
 and shelters **40–1**, 78, 98
 see also charity
homelessness solutions/ending
 homelessness 177–99
Hoolachan, Jennifer 95, 96
Hopper, Kim 63, 155–6, 165, 187
hostels see shelters
housing, adequate 17, 18, 20–1,
 38–9, 155
housing, affordable 30–5, 48, 190–5
 Australia 33, 155
 and autonomy 195, 196
 and Canada 33, 142

236 Index

housing, affordable (*cont.*)
  and ending homelessness 171, 177, 185, 186, 189
  and government/state responsibilities/actions 33–5, 142, 190–5, 196
    and public subsidies 33, 34, 190–1
    and welfare state 192, 193
  and homelessness services 89, 97, **101**, 154–5
    shelters 97, 154, 155
  and housing, rented 30–1, 33
  and housing market 28, 30–1, 32, 35–7, 48, 135
  and labor market 24, 37
  and OECD 31, 34
  and poverty 28, 36, 184
  and Singapore 34–5, 191
  and social change 189, 190–5, 196
    and autonomy 195, 196
    and inequality 8, 191
  and social problems 23, 26, 27, 30–5, 43, 56
  and social/public housing 33, 184
  and supportive housing models 160, 163, 165, **168**
  United Kingdom 35, 191, 192, 196
  United States 33, 34, 155, 184
    and social change 189, 190–1, 192
    social problems 31, 32
  and violence **68**, 69, 73
  and voucher schemes 33, 161, 190–1
  and welfare state 192, 193
housing, collaborative 191–7
housing, definition 11–12
housing, doubled-up 78–9, 103
housing, importance of 1
housing, informal 78–9, 103
housing, normal 194
housing, permanent supportive 160, 163–4, 168, 170–1, 173–5, 185, 186
  see also housing models, supportive
housing, rental
  and affordable housing 30–1, 33
  private sector 33, 161, 184, 191
  rental charges 31, 32, 33, 44, 184

  and social change 189, 191
  and supportive housing models 161, 170
housing, social/public 161, 187
  and affordable housing 33, 184
  Australia 33, 87
  Finland 186, 191
  and social problems **40–1**, 44
  United Kingdom 34, 185, 191
housing, temporary *see* shelters
housing advisors 47
Housing First 159, 160–6, **167–8**, 173, 186
housing market
  and affordable housing 28, 30–1, 32, 35–7, 48, 135
  and poverty 35–7, 55, 56
housing models, supportive 159–76
  and affordable housing 160, 163, 165, **168**
  and autonomy 162, **167–8**
  and Canada 161, 169, 174–5
  and chronic homelessness 155, 160, 161, 163
    and cost benefits 166–8, 170, 172, 174, 175
  and cost benefits 166–75
    and Australia 169, 174
    and Canada 169, 174–5
    and chronic homelessness 166–8, 170, 172, 174, 175
    and ending homelessness 168, 170–4
    and healthcare/health and social care 169, 171–3, 175
    and taxpayers 166, 170, 171, 172, 174
    United States 170, 173, 174–5
  and Europe 169, 174
  and healthcare/health and social care 160–1, 165–6
    and cost benefits 169, 171–3, 175
  Housing First 159, 160–6, **167–8**, 173, 186
  housing-led approach 162, 165
  housing-ready approach 153, 154, 155, 156, 162, 165
  and human rights 162, 174
  and personal choice 162, 165, **168**

Index

and rental housing 161, 170
and sick people
  and cost benefits 174, 175
  and mental health 161, 163,
    164, 165
  and stability 163–4, 169
  and staircase model 152–4, 162,
    164, 165, 166
  and substance abuse 164, 165
  United Kingdom 160, 161, 169,
    170
  United States 161, 166, 170, 173,
    174–5
housing providers 42, 46, 193
Huey, Laura 76, 78
Hulse, Kath 79
human rights 162, 174, 190
humanitarian aid 156
Hungarian people 87
Hungary 139

identities, multiple 121, 126, **127–8,**
  134
identity 18–19, 109–35, 137, 148
  and Australia 112–13, 130
    self-identity 123, 124–5, **127–8**
  and autonomy 129, 130
    and judgment 114, 120, 135
    and labelling 22, 109, 114–15,
      121–2, 131
  and charity 92, 132
  and chronic homelessness 117, 135
  and culture 115–16, 117, 118
  and dehumanization 124, 128, 131
  and deprivation 112, 120, 124
  and deviancy 113, 117, 118, 120,
    125, 151, 189
    Skid Row 111, 112, 115
  and employment/unemployment
    117, 118, 125
  and family relationships 124–5,
    130–1, 135
  and gender issues 123, 126–30
  and homeless behavior 115, 117,
    120, 124
  and homelessness services 116,
    118, 130, 131, 133–4
    United States 130, 131, 132
  and human agency 110, 127, 129
  and marginalization 121, 122

  and normality 111, 112, 121,
    123–4, 125
  and older people 129, 131
  and otherness 111–12, 118–21
  and poverty 21, 22, 118, 121–2
  and power 110, 122, 129
  and sense of self 119, 120, 123,
    125, 126, 130, 134
  and shelters 118, 123, 126, 130,
    131
  and stereotyping 111–14, 120, **127**
  and stigma 113, 118–21, 124, 129
  and substance abuse 112, 115, 117
  United Kingdom 113, 121, 124,
    131
  United States 111–12, 113,
    118–19, 123, 128
    and homelessness services 130,
      131, 132
    self-identity 123, 124, 125
  and unsheltered housing 124, 125
  and women 123, 126–30, 131
  and young people 119, 124, 126,
    130–1
identity, community 115, 116–17
identity, self- 92, 117, 122–6, **127–8**
identity change 114–22
identity hierarchy 123
inclusion, social 140, 142, 144
income support 37
independence, personal 91, 92–5, 99
Indigenous people 18–19, 124, 143
  and Australia 18, 52, 143
  and Canada 18–20, 52, 55
  and colonization 19, 55
  and New Zealand 19, 52
  and race/racism 51–2, 55
inequality 6–7, 8–9, 187, 191
infantilization 98–9, 195
Institute of Global Homelessness
  180
institutionalization 23, 113, 119
intentions, good 91, 179
interdependency 2–3, 84
intimate partner violence (IPV) *see*
  domestic and family violence
  (DFV)
Ireland 46, 98, 113, 184
irrigation systems 140
Irvine, Leslie 125

238 Index

Israel 92
Italy 50, 87, 92

Jacobs, Keith 17, 21
Japan 15, 34, 51, 118
Jasinski, Jana 71, 78, 118–19
Jencks, Christopher 150
Joern, Raegan 69
Johnsen, Sarah 86, 89, 146–7
Johnson, Boris 196
Johnson, Guy 33
Jones, Gill 41
Jones, Marian 49
judgment
    and homelessness services 93–4,
        95, 96–7
    and identity 114, 120, 135
Juhila, Kirsi 173

Katz, Michael 170
Kaufman, Peter 124
Kearns, Robin 19
Keynesianism 191
Khadduri, Jill 182, 189, 190
Khan, Sadiq 35
Kirkman, Maggie 104
Kostiainen, Eeva 39
Kuala Lumpur 89
Kuhn, Thomas 159

labeling 22, 109, 114–15, 121–2, 131
Labit, Anne 195
labor market 1, 6, 113
    and affordable housing 24, 37
    labor market policies 34, 37, 54
    and race/racism 53, 54
Lancione, Michele 87, 92
land ownership 19, 34, 35, 191
language, use of 22, **102**, 134
Latimer, Eric 169
Latino/Hispanic people 50
laundries 86, 87
Laurenson, Penelope 147
LavaMae^x charity 87–8
Lawler, Steph 121–2
Lee, Barrett 29, 37, 53, 58, 61, 65,
    70, 178
legislation 17, 47, 137–9, 185
    United States 14, 75, **145–6**
    and violence **68**, 69, 75

Lemoine, Coralie 169
Lenhard, Johannes 139–40
Liebow, Elliot 128
life experience 7, 20, 53
lifestyle exposure framework 61
lifestyle theory 72
Lima, Valesca 184
Lister, Ruth 21, 106–7, 122
living conditions 20, 21, 39, 151
    and shelters 152, 156–7
lobby groups 5
Local Government Board, UK 113
localism 192
Löfstrand, Cecilia 173
London 51, 89, 170
    and affordable housing 35, 196
    and ending homelessness 139, 140
London School of Economics 170
loneliness 75, 77
Los Angeles 32, 147
    and homelessness services 96–7,
        99, 133, 156
    see also Skid Row
Loubiére, Sandrine 164
lumberjacks 111

MacArthur Foundation 181
MacKenzie, David 117
Mackie, Peter 185, 187
MacLeod, Gordon 141
Malaysia 89
Mallett, Shelley 11–12, 105
Malmö, Sweden 54
Marcus, Anthony 96, 99
marginalization 60, 61, 72, 121, 122
Margolis, Abby 118
market leverage 34
Marlier, Eric 153
Marr, Matthew 34
Marvasti, Amir 95
Marx, Karl 177
masculine behavior 76
May, Jon 63, 75, 76
Mayock, Paula 38, 78, 98
McKinney-Vento Homeless Assistance
    Act (later Homeless Emergency
    Assistance and Rapid
    Transition to Housing Act),
    US 14
McMordie, Lynne 63, 99

Index

239

McNaughton, Carol 131
meaning-making 12
media coverage 25–6
mega-shelters 97, 99, 133, 147
Meinbresse, Molly 58, 70, 71
Melekis, Kelly 129, 131, 134
Memmott, Paul 18, 19
men, homeless 132
mental health 23, 130, **145**, 153,
  166–8
  and supportive housing models
    161, 163, 164, 165
  and violence 61, 75
mental health services 47–8
methamphetamines 61–2
Metraux, Steve 27, 155, 166, 170,
  171
migrants 50–1, 54
Milbourne, Paul 3
Miller, Dana 88
Mills, C. Wright 27, 31–2
Minnesota 38
Miscellaneous Offences Act,
  Singapore 17
Mitchell, Don 120, 137–8
money, public 9, 179
morality 129, 171
mortality 1
Moschion, Julie 39–41
motherhood 79, 129–30
  see also families with children;
    parenting
Moving On initiative 174
Moyo, Dambisa 156
Mulcahy, Michael 60, 61

National Coalition for the Homeless
  66, **67–8**
neoliberalism 8, 86
  and ending homelessness 172, 197
  and government/state
    responsibilities/actions 142,
    172, 187, 196
Netherlands 42
networks, social 28, 36, 103, 117
New York
  and home 96, 105
  and supportive housing models
    161, 166
  and violence 62–3, 75

New York Times 23
New Zealand 15, 124
  and government/state
    responsibilities/actions 45, 147
  and Indigenous people 19, 52
Nichols, Joe 92
non-homeless public 66–9, 120, 122
non-metropolitan areas, US 32
normality 111, 112, 121, 123–4, 125
Northern Ireland 63, 99

O'Donnell, James 32–3
OECD (Organization for
  Economic Cooperation and
  Development) 1, 31, 34
offenders/prisoners 5
O'Grady, Bill 123, 126, 130
Okamoto, Yoshihiro 51
older people 47, 65
  and identity 129, 131
  Singapore 24, 29
  and social problems 29, 41
  and women 6, 129, 131
Olivet, Jeffrey 52, 198
Orange Sky Australia charity 88, 90
Osborne, Randall 117
O'Sullivan, Eoin 113, 141, 150, 156
otherness 92, 111–12, 118–21
O'Toole, Thomas 87
Ours, Jan van 39–41
outsiders 116
overcrowding 18

Padgett, Deborah 105, 159–60,
  167–8, 171–2
Pallotta-Chiarolli, Maria 62, 65
parenting 79, 100, 103, 129
Paris 50, 51, 139–40
Park, Gum-Ryeong 59
Parker, Josie 130
Parolin, Zachary 37
Parsell, Cameron 41, 94, 124–5, 131,
  149
passivity 94, **127**
paternalism 26, 147, 162
  and homelessness services 97, 99,
    107
Pathways to Housing program 160–1
patriarchy 6, 56, 69
Paul, Dereck 53

Pawson, Hall 51, 192
perpetrators of violence 64–5, **67–8**, 69
personal relationships 77–9, 100, 116, 124
pet ownership 125
Petersen, Maree 41
Petty, James 140
Philadelphia 53, 132
Pickett, Kate 9
Piketty, Thomas 187
Pleace, Nicholas 27, 160
police involvement 142–3, 144
political will 5, 189–90
population, homeless 13, 16
Portland, Oregon 93, 98
poverty 35–7, 39, 53
    and affordable housing 28, 36, 184
    and government/state responsibilities/actions 36–7, 85, **145–6**
    and ending homelessness 172, 177, 185
    and welfare state 37, 85, 185
    and housing market 35–7, 55, 56
    and identity 21, 22, 118, 121–2
    United Kingdom 36, 85, 185
    United States 36, 37, **145–6**, 184
poverty, childhood 36
power 110, 122, 129
predictors of homelessness 36, 78
Preece, Jenny 124, 126
Preston, Gregory 44, 53
pride **167–8**
prisoner discharge 5, 42–3, 47–8, 185
privacy 17–18, 84, 96, 105
private sector 33, 35, 161, 184, 191
problem framing 188–90, 198
problematization 4–8, 135, 188–9
property law 47
public spaces 139–41, 142–3, 144–6
public transport 75
punitivity 26, 141–2, 144, 145, 147, 148
Purdam, Kingsley 85

queuing 92, 106
Quigley, John 30–1

race/racism 49–55, 56, 198
    and Europe 50–1, 53–4
    and Indigenous people 18, 51–2, 55
    and labor market 53, 54
    migrants 50–1, 54
    and trauma/persecution 53, 55
    United Kingdom 50, 51, 53, 54
    United States 49–50, 51–3
rape 70, 71
Raphael, Steven 30–1
rates of homelessness 32, 34, 49–50, 186
rates of sexual violence 70
Ravenhill, Megan 38, 58, 64
reality, social/realism 28
recidivism 5
rehabilitation 113–15, 147–9
    and conditionality 93, 97, 99, 153–4, 157, 162
    and Europe 132, 153
    and homelessness services **101**, 132–3
    shelters 97, 99, 100, 133, 152–5, 157–8
    United States 132, 133
    and substance abuse 133, 153
    United States 133, 147, 148, 152–3
    and Skid Row 97, 99
Reina, Vincent 44, 53
relationships *see* family relationships; personal relationships; social relationships
religious organizations 87, 93, 132
removal, coercive 144–57
rental charges 31, 32, 33, 44, 184
Republican party, US 162
residence, nighttime 14
resource allocation/provision 16, 21, 88–90
respect 93, 98, 136
responsibility, collective 183, 187, 197–9
Rhee, Taeho 53
Richard, Molly 78–9
Riley, Elise 59, 70
Rob, homeless person 77
Robinson, Brandon 42, 45
Robinson, W. Peter 123
Roessler, Beate 84, 106

role models 89
Ronald, Richard 191
room checks 95–6
Roschelle, Anne 124
Rosenheck, Robert 53
rough sleeping 3, 64, 144–9, 151,
    180
  and violence 63–4, 75
rules 72, 96, 99–100, 103

safe at home programs 45
safety/security 73–4, 75, 76–7,
    79–80
safety/security features 131
Sager, Rebecca 93
Sahlin, Ingrid 54, 156
St. Louis, United States 32
San Francisco 32, 59, 99, 124
  and government/state
    responsibilities/actions 142–3,
    145
Sanders, Ben and Albanese, Francesca
    59, 66–8, 75
sanitation practices **146**
Santa Clara Country 32
Scandinavia 44, 50, 173
Schauz, Desiree 132
Schneider, Valerie 48
Schreck, Christopher 58, 61, 65, 70
Sclar, Elliott 23
Scotland 41, 63
  and government/state
    responsibilities/actions 2, 150,
    185, 186
  and homelessness services 95, 98,
    150
  and social/public housing 185, 191
self, sense of 107, 168
  and identity 119, 120, 123, 125,
    126, 130, 134
self-blame 119
self-determination 99, 105, 162
self-harm 63
self-identity 92, 117, 122–6, **127–8**
self-protection 74–9, 80
self-sufficiency 101, 116, 174
service users, homeless 82–108
  see also homelessness services
sexuality 44, 45, 76
Shaefer, Luke 79, 182

Sharam, Andrea 79
shelterization theory 118
shelters 87, 95–104, 149–57, 186,
    189
  and affordable housing 97, 154,
    155
  and autonomy 95, 96–7, 98–9,
    149
  and charity 87, 156
  design of shelters 131
  and Europe 150, 153
  and government/state
    responsibilities/actions **145**,
    149–57
    United States **145**, 147, 150
  and identity 118, 123, 126, 130,
    131
  and living conditions 152, 156–7
  mega-shelters 97, 99, 133, 147
  and paternalism 97, 99
  and rehabilitation 99, 100, 133,
    152–5, 157–8
  and conditionality 97, 99, 153,
    154, 157
  and resource provision 87, 156
  and rules 72, 96, 99–100, 103
  and societal failure 151–2, 156
  and staff 62–3, 95–6
  and substance abuse 95, 99–100,
    153
  and surveillance 95–6, 97–104
  United Kingdom 63, 96, 98, 99,
    150
  United States 62–3, 78, 87, 95,
    155, 156
    and autonomy 95, 96–7, 98,
    103
    government/state responsibilities/
      actions **145**, 147, 150
    and rehabilitation 99, 152–3
    and Skid Row 96–7, 147
  value of 151, 155–6
  and violence **40–1**, 62–3, 75
    and sexual violence 71, 72, 78
  and women **40–1**, 78, 98
Shinn, Marybeth 33, 182, 189, 190
showers 87–8, 90
sick people 24, 26, 170, 171–3, 174,
    175
sickness analogy 181–2

242 Index

Singapore 17, 148
  and affordable housing 34–5, 191
  home ownership 34, 191
  land 34, 35, 191
  older people 24, 29
Skid Row
  and identity 111–12, 114–15, 133
  and rehabilitation 97, 99
  and shelters 96–7, 147
Snow, David 96, 115–16, 124
Snow, David 60, 61
Snyder, Edward 132
social class 89, 121, 138
social norms 65, 111, 113
social policy 7, 135, 188
social problems 4–5, 23–56, 188
  and individual failings 24–5, 27–8
  and societal failure 49, 55–6
  see also domestic and family
      violence (DFV); family
      relationships; gender issues;
      poverty; race/racism; substance
      abuse; violence, homeless
      people as victims and
      perpetrators of
social processes 5, 7, 8, 117
social relationships 28, 84, 88, 89,
    124
social skills 89
society 6–7, 8–9, 17–19, 136–58
  see also criminalization of
      homelessness; ending
      homelessness; rehabilitation
Somerville, Peter 12
soup kitchens 86, 87, 88–9, 92
South Korea 59, 70
Spain 59, **67**, 69
Speak, Suzanne 13
spikes 139, 140
squatting 64
stability 33, 36, 163–4, 169
Stadler, Sophie 174
staff of homelessness services 62–3,
    95–6, 105–6
staircase model 152–4, 162, 164,
    165, 166
Stephens, Mark 44
Stephens, Susan 93
stereotyping 49, 111–14, 120, **127**
stigma 6–7, 92–5

and gender issues 42, 45–6
and homelessness services 92, 104
and identity 113, 118–21, 124,
    129
Stockholm 51
Stone, Martin 89
structure, societal 26–30, 31–2
Stuart, Forrest 96–7, 99, 133, 147,
    156, 157
subculture 115–16, 117
subsidies, public 34, 44, 190–1
substance abuse 44
  alcohol misuse 29, 38, **40–1**, 62,
    112, 115
  and domestic and family violence
    38, **40–1**
  drug abuse 61–2, 63
  and homelessness services 99–100,
    101–2, 133
  and identity 112, 115, 117
  and rehabilitation 133, 153
  and shelters 95, 99–100, 153
  and supportive housing models
    164, 165
  and violence 61–2, 63, 64
support 159
surveillance 73–4, 148–9
  CCTV 73, 148–9
  and homelessness services 95–6,
    97–104
survival 65–6, 86–8, 116
Sweden 51, 54
Switzerland 87, 141, 196
Sydney, Australia 24, 180

Takahashi, Lois 130
Tan, Harry 28–9
targets 178, 180
taxation 187
taxpayers 166, 170, 171, 172, 174
Teixeira, Lígia 178–9
Temesvary, Zsolt 87
temporary accommodation 15
  see also shelters
Temporary Assistance to Needy
    Families (TANF) 37
Terresa, Mother 82
territory 64
Thiery, Nathalie 103
Thompson, Matthew 193

Index

243

Tiderington, Emmy 174
Tipple, Graham 13
Titmuss, Richard 82
Tomas, Annabel 77
Tomaszewski, Wojtek 43
Toolis, E. and Hammack, P. 125
top-down approach to affordable
housing 192
tramps 7, 113, 116
trauma/persecution 53, 73
and race/racism 53, 55
and women 40, 78
trigger events 37–49, 53
see also discharge planning;
domestic and family violence
(DFV); eviction; family
relationships; migrants; race/
racism
Tronto, Joan 83
Trump, Donald 138
Tsemberis, Sam 160, 161, 165
Twiss, Pamela 10, 56
Twist, Oliver 92

United Kingdom 15
and affordable housing 35, 191,
192, 196
and charity 85, 86–7, 94
and gender issues 45, 69, 71, 76
and government/state
responsibilities/actions 45, 46,
85, 150
and ending homelessness 2, 139,
140, 186
England 46, 144–7
Scotland 2, 150, 185, 186
and homelessness services 86–7,
94, 99, 131
and Scotland 95, 98, 150
shelters 63, 96, 98, 99, 150
soup kitchens 88, 89
and identity 113, 121, 124, 131
and poverty 36, 85, 185
and social change 9, 191, 192, 196
and social problems 42, 44
and domestic and family violence
38, 45
and race/racism 50, 51, 53, 54
and social/public housing 34, 185,
191

and statutory homelessness 15, 16
and supportive housing models
160, 161, 169, 170
and violence 38, 45, 59, 64, 66–8,
69
England 63, 64, 75, 76
and welfare state 85, 185
and women 45, 71, 76
see also England; Northern Ireland;
Scotland
United States
and affordable housing 33, 34,
155, 184
and social change 189, 190–1,
192
and social problems 31, 32
voucher schemes 33, 161,
190–1
and charity 85, 87, 88, 90, 93
and chronic homelessness 14, 26
and disabled people 14, 26
and gender issues 42, 70–1, 73,
128
and government/state
responsibilities/actions 2, 5,
46, 48
and criminalization of
homelessness 142–3, **145–6**,
147, 148, 157
and ending homelessness 137–9,
181, 183, 187
legislation 14, 75, **145–6**
and poverty 37, **145–6**
and rehabilitation 147, 148
San Francisco 142–3, **145**
shelters **145**, 147, 150
and welfare state 37, 85, 147,
182
and home/homelessness definitions
14, 19
and homelessness services 90
and charity 87, 90, 93
and identity 130, 131, 132
Los Angeles 96–7, 99, 133, 156
and rehabilitation 132, 133
shelters 87, 95, 96–7, 98, 99,
103, 156
soup kitchens 87, 88
and substance abuse **101–2**, 133
and housing, rented 32, 33

244 Index

United States (*cont.*)
  and identity 111–12, 113, 118–19, 123, 128
    and homelessness services 130, 131, 132
    self-identity 123, 124, 125
    Skid Row 111–12, 114–15, 133
  and legislation 14, 75, **145–6**
  and rehabilitation 147, 148, 152–3
    homelessness services 132, 133
    and Skid Row 97, 99
  shelters 62–3, 78, 87, 155, 156
    and autonomy 95, 96–7, 98, 103
    government/state responsibilities/actions 145, 147, 150
    and rehabilitation 99, 152–3
    and Skid Row 96–7, 147
  and social change 181, 189, 190–1, 192
  and social problems 24–5, 38, 42, 56
    and affordable housing 31, 32
    and poverty 36, 37, **145–6**, 184
    and race/racism 49–50, 51–3
  and supportive housing models 161
    and cost benefits 166, 168–9, 170, 173, 174–5
  and violence 62–3, 65, 75
    domestic and family violence 38
    and homeless experiences 58, 59
    and non-homeless people 66, 67–8, 69
    and self-protection 78, 79
    and sexual violence 70–1, 73, 78
    and women 78, **101–2**, 103

vacancy rate 30, 31
vagrancy legislation, Singapore 17
vagrants *see* tramps
validation, social 21, 110
Vanguard Cities Initiative, Institute of Global Homelessness 180, 182
Veness, April 19
vents, hot air 139–40
veterans 5
violence, homeless people as victims and perpetrators of 58–81
  and affordable housing 68, 69, 73
  and Australia 64, 65, 68–9, 73–4

  and domestic and family violence 38, 45
  and children 78, 79
  and concealed homelessness 78–9, 80
  and dangerous places 61, 74
  and dehumanization 67–8, 71
  and gender issues 69–74, 76–7, 80
  and government/state responsibilities/actions 45, 143–4
    legislation 68, 69, 75
  and hate crime 66–9, 73
  and marginalization 60, 61, 72
  and mental health 61, 75
  and non-homeless people 66–8, 69
  and perpetrators of violence 64–5, 67–8, 69
  and rough sleeping 63–4, 75
  and self-protection 74–9, 80
  and shelters 40–1, 62–3, 75
    and sexual violence 71, 72, 78
  and Spain 59, 67, 69
  and substance abuse 61–2, 63, 64
  United Kingdom 59, 64, 66–8, 69
    England 63, 64, 75, 76
  United States 58, 59, 65, 75, 79
    New York 62–3, 75
    and non-homeless people 66, 67–8, 69
    and self-protection 78, 79
  and women 78–9, 80
    and domestic and family violence 38, 39, 56, 198
    and self-protection 76–7, 79
    and sexual violence 69–71, 78
  see also domestic and family violence (DFV); violence, sexual
violence, sexual 62, 69–74
  rape 70, 71
  and safety/security 73–4, 76–7
  and shelters 71, 72, 78
  and women 69–71, 78
violence rates 66
volunteers 26, 107, **127**, 196
  and charity 85, 89–90, 91, 92, 93
voucher schemes 33, 161, 190–1

Waldron, Jeremy 104

Index

Wallace, Samuel 111, 115
Walsh, Tamara 142
Walter, Zoe 123, 130, 131
Wardhaugh, Julia 128
Warnes, Anthony 47
Washington, DC 32, 69
Watts, Beth 46, 63, 98, 100, 141
wealth, distribution of 187, 197
weapon carrying 65
welfare state 43, 55
  and affordable housing 192, 193
  and criminalization of homelessness
    142, 144–9
  and ending homelessness 142, 182,
    187
  and homelessness services 85–6,
    101
  and poverty 37, 85, 185
  United Kingdom 85, 185
  United States 37, 85, 147, 182
wellbeing 100, 130–1, 165
Whitbeck, Les B. 59, 70
Whiteford, Martin 94
Wijburg, Gertjan 197
Wilkinson, Richard 9
Willse, Craig 17, 172
Winetrobe, Hailey 123, 130
winter break policy 46–7
Wolch, Jennifer 117
women 54

  and autonomy 98, 103, 129–30
  and homelessness services 98,
    100–3, 131
    and shelters **40–1**, 78, 98
  and identity 123, 126–30, 131
  and motherhood 79, 129–30
  and older people 6, 129, 131
  and patriarchy 6, 56, 69
  and trauma/persecution 40, 78
  United Kingdom 45, 71, 76
  United States 78, **101–2**, 103
  and violence 78–9, 80
    and domestic and family violence
      38, 39, 56, 198
    and self-protection 76–7, 79
    and sexual violence 69–71, 78
  Wood, Jenny 185, 187
working classes 121

Yellowknife, Canada 52
Yeoh, Seng-Guam 88–9
Y-Foundation, Finland 186
Young, Iris Marion 84, 198
young people 5, 41–2, 65
  and family relationships 41, 42,
    43, 44, 45, 130–1
  and identity 119, 124, 126, 130–1

zero, functional 181
Zoe, Celine 52, 55